THE EARLIEST CHRISTIAN HERETICS

D1248408

THE EARLIEST CHRISTIAN HERETICS

Readings from Their Opponents

Edited by
ARLAND J. HULTGREN
and
STEVEN A. HAGGMARK

FORTRESS PRESS
MINNEAPOLIS

THE EARLIEST CHRISTIAN HERETICS
Readings from Their Opponents

Fortress ex libris publication 2008

Copyright © 1996 Fortress Press, an imprint of Augsburg Fortress. All rights reserved. Except for brief quotations in critical articles or reviews, no part of this book may be reproduced in any manner without prior written permission from the publisher. Visit http://www.augsburgfortress.org copyrights/contact.asp or write to Permissions, Augsburg Fortress, Box 1209, Minneapolis, MN 55440.

Where not otherwise indicated Scripture quotations are from the New Revised Standard Version of the Bible, copyright © 1989 by the Division of Christian Education of the National Council of the Churches of Christ in the USA. Used by permission. All rights reserved.

Cover design: David Meyer
Cover image: *Basilisk*, from *Signs and Symbols in Christian Art*. Used by permission of the Samuel H. Kress Foundation
Interior design: The HK Scriptorium

Library of Congress Cataloging-in-Publication Data
The earliest Christian heretics : readings from their opponents /
edited by Arland J. Hultgren and Steven A. Haggmark.
p. cm.
Includes bibliographical references and indexes.
ISBN 978-0-8006-2963-2 (alk. Paper)
1. Heresies, Christian—Early works to 180. 2. Heretics, Christian—Early works to 180.
3. Christian literature, Early.
I. Hultgren, Arland J., 1939-   II. Haggmark, Steven A., 1948-
BT1313.E37 1996
273'.1—dc20   96-24928

The paper used in this publication meets the minimum requirements of American National Standard for Information Sciences—Permanence of Paper for Printed Library Materials, ANSI Z329.48-1984
Manufactured in the U.S.A.

To the Memory of Our Fathers
Living Still
Arnold E. Hultgren
and
Astor Haggmark

Contents

PART III: OTHER TEACHERS AND SECTS OF THE SECOND CENTURY

Preface

While preparing for class instruction in a course on orthodoxy and heresy in the first two centuries, the editors of this volume discovered what seemed at the time to be incredible. Surely, one would think, there must be an anthology of ancient texts concerning the earliest Christian heretics and heresies. Such an anthology would have brief introductions to the various texts; it would be useful for students and teachers; and it would serve as a quick and handy reference for students, teachers, scholars, and other interested persons. But to the surprise of the editors, such a volume could not be found. The only way they could proceed was to place several large, complicated volumes on library reserve and, where legally possible, to photocopy pages for classroom use.

The present volume arose from that situation and has been prepared to meet a need that must be shared by many others. It contains texts that have been used in actual course work with students, plus additional texts to make it useful for a wider audience.

The task of selecting texts and writing introductions to them has been a collaborative effort. Although each of the introductions was drafted first by one of the editors, it was submitted to the other for possible revisions. The selection of texts was made on the basis of proposals of one editor to the other, followed by counterproposals and eventual consensus. The result is that a high degree of consistency has been achieved throughout the work—at least in the estimation of the editors.

The editors thank the various publishers of works drawn upon for permission to reprint portions included. The publishers and the works used are listed in the Acknowledgments. Finally, thanks are rendered too to the ever-competent staff of the library of Luther Seminary, St. Paul, Minnesota, and the editors at Fortress Press, who have made this work possible.

Arland J. Hultgren
Steven A. Haggmark

Sources of Quotations and Bibliographical Information

SOURCE AS CITED IN TEXT

The Ante-Nicene Fathers, ed.
  A. Roberts and J. Donaldson.

Early Christian Fathers, ed.
  C. Richardson.

Eusebius, *History of the Church*,
  trans. G. Williamson.

Gnosis, ed. W. Foerster.

FULL INFORMATION

The Ante-Nicene Fathers, ed.
  Alexander Roberts and James Donaldson, 10 vols. (Buffalo: The Christian Literature Company, 1885–97;
  reprinted, Peabody, Mass.: Hendrickson Publishers, 1994).

Early Christian Fathers, ed. Cyril C.
  Richardson, Library of Christian
  Classics 1 (Philadelphia: Westmin-
  ster Press, 1953).

Eusebius, *The History of the Church
  from Christ to Constantine*, trans.
  G.A. Williamson (Minneapolis:
  Augsburg Publishing House, 1975).

Gnosis: A Selection of Gnostic Texts, ed.
  Werner Foerster, 2 vols. (Oxford:
  Clarendon Press, 1972–74).

Gnosticism, ed. R. M. Grant.	*Gnosticism: A Source Book of Heretical Writings from the Early Christian Period*, ed. Robert M. Grant (New York: Harper & Brothers, 1961).
Irenaeus, *Against the Heresies*, trans. D. Unger.	Irenaeus, *Against the Heresies*, trans. Dominic J. Unger, rev. John J. Dillon, Ancient Christian Writers 55 (New York: Paulist Press, 1992).
New Testament Apocrypha, ed. W. Schneemelcher	*New Testament Apocrypha*, ed. Wilhelm Schneemelcher, 2 vols. (Philadelphia: Westminster Press, 1963–65).
Panarion, trans. P. R. Amidon	*The* Panarion *of St. Epiphanius, Bishop of Salamis: Selected Passages*, trans. Philip R. Amidon (New York: Oxford University Press, 1990).
Saint Justin Martyr, trans. T. B. Falls.	*Saint Justin Martyr*, trans. Thomas B. Falls; vol. 6 of *The Fathers of the Church* (New York: Christian Heritage, 1949).
Tertullian Adversus Marcionem, trans. E. Evans.	*Tertullian Adversus Marcionem*, trans. Ernest Evans, 2 vols. (Oxford: Clarendon Press, 1972).

Acknowledgments

The readings from ancient authors contained in this volume are from English translations provided in previously published works, as listed below. In each case the excerpts are used by permission of the publishers.

The editors have made slight alterations where necessary for the sake of readability. Footnotes, some unnecessary brackets, and occasional numerals marking the text in the originals have often been omitted. The exception is that editorial emendations, conjectures, scriptural references, and additions for ease of reading that exist in the originals continue to be marked with brackets, regardless of their form in the originals (whether brackets, parentheses, or other signs). In addition, since the texts from the *Panarion* of Epiphanius are frequently marked by section numbers, these have been enclosed in brackets for ease of reading. Other additions made by the editors of this volume have been marked with double brackets. The person who must do a close reading of the texts with the help of editorial matters in the originals may want to consult the latter.

Alexandrian Christianity, ed. John E. L. Oulton and Henry Chadwick, Library of Christian Classics 2 (Philadelphia: Westminster Press, 1954) 42, 45.

The Ante-Nicene Fathers, ed. Alexander Roberts and James Donaldson, 10 vols. (Buffalo: The Christian Literature Company, 1885–97; reprinted, Peabody, Mass.: Hendrickson Publishers, 1994) 4.59; 5.47–49, 51, 58, 75–77, 79–82, 85–90, 109–10, 112–16, 123–24, 127–28, 144, 146–48, 223–28, 230.

Early Christian Fathers, ed. Cyril C. Richardson, Library of Christian Classics 1 (Philadelphia: Westminster Press, 1953) 258–59, 279.

Eusebius, *The History of the Church from Christ to Constantine*, trans. G. A. Williamson (Minneapolis: Augsburg Publishing House, 1975) 136–39, 158–60, 163–65, 217–26, 229–36, 256–57, 315–19.

Gnosis: A Selection of Gnostic Texts, ed. Werner Foerster, 2 vols. (Oxford: Clarendon Press, 1972–74) 1.32–33, 35–38, 40–41, 59–61, 64–74.

Gnosticism: A Source Book of Heretical Writings from the Early Christian Period, ed. Robert M. Grant (New York: Harper & Brothers, 1961) 23–27, 42–47.

Irenaeus, *Against the Heresies*, trans. Dominic J. Unger, rev. John J. Dillon, Ancient Christian Writers 55 (New York: Paulist Press, 1992) 23–24, 33–34, 39–40, 51–52.

New Testament Apocrypha, ed. Wilhelm Schneemelcher, 2 vols. (Philadelphia: Westminster Press, 1963–65) 2.686–87.

The Panarion *of St. Epiphanius, Bishop of Salamis: Selected Passages*, trans. Philip R. Amidon (New York: Oxford University Press, 1990) 66, 70, 84, 94–95, 103, 106–9, 113, 143–46, 148–49, 156–57, 162–63, 166, 168, 175–76, 209–10, 218–19.

Saint Justin Martyr, trans. Thomas B. Falls (New York: Christian Heritage, 1949) 200–202, 218–19, 347–49.

Tertullian Adversus Marcionem, trans. Ernest Evans, 2 vols. (Oxford: Clarendon Press, 1972) 1.5, 7, 49–51, 67, 73–75, 81, 193–95; 2.261–65, 275.

Introduction

THE NATURE, PURPOSE, AND SCOPE
OF THIS COLLECTION

The first and second centuries of the Christian church were the most formative of all for their theological and organizational developments. That era witnessed the rise of the writings of the New Testament, the Apostolic Fathers, and some of the Apologists. It saw also the development of liturgies and church orders, the shaping of doctrine in controversies, the facing of persecution, the proliferation of sects, and much more. And yet the person who looks for written sources on a particular topic from that era runs into difficulty. The ancient texts, except for the New Testament, are accessible only to those who have an excellent theological library at their disposal, and even then the sources are scattered about in formidable collections.

What is needed in this situation is a series of volumes that contain excerpts from the ancient writers about various issues of their times and that provide brief introductions to the texts being quoted. As obvious as this is, such a series does not exist.

This volume contains excerpts from ancient writers about the so-called "heresies" and "heretics" of the first and second centuries, along with necessary introductions to them. These writings are exceedingly important for the study of early Christianity and theology. Yet they are difficult to track down, and the process is often more time-consuming than many would consider worthwhile. Prior to this volume, no anthology has existed to enable the nonspecialist to experience reading what the ancient authors actually had to say concerning the heresies and heretics.

Another important reason for having the texts readily available is that we now have a new body of literature that sheds light on some ancient heretical movements, particularly Gnosticism. In 1945 an amazing discovery was made at Nag Hammadi in Egypt. Some fifty-two tractates of ancient texts were found, many of which were written by gnostic Christians and preserved in earthen jars. These have been published in English translation.[1] The introduction to that volume by its editor tells of the details of discovery and the significance of the find. The aftermath of that discovery has caused students of the New Testament and early Christian history and theology to reassess what the ancients said about the Gnostics. Now that the Nag Hammadi texts are available, there is reason to have the other texts available in one place to make comparisons and connections. Some have claimed that the ancient "orthodox" writers presented a one-sided view of the heretics. Others have maintained that a comparison with the Nag Hammadi texts shows how fair the orthodox were. The advantage of having an anthology of the ancient writings about the heretics is that the reader of these and of the Nag Hammadi texts can make judgments on matters case by case.

This volume focuses on persons and movements of the first and second centuries, mostly the second. There is nothing particularly urgent in making the year A.D. 200 a hard and fast marker of epochs of history. Yet a terminus for such a book as this must be decided upon. The editors have made a decision to hold the flow of history in check at A.D. 200 partly for manageability but also because it is a rough marker of a significant change. Thereafter, during the third and fourth centuries, the major theological issues have to do primarily with trinitarian and christological definitions leading up to the great ecumenical councils. The first two centuries had to do with the more urgent and fundamental tasks of defining the scope and limits of what Christianity itself was to become. Although the Christian writers of the first two centuries had to address basic questions of trinitarian and christological importance, they had to do so in a time of testing from external forces that the later church, more confident of its continued existence, did not have to face.

What were some of those forces? In the spring of 1981 a new journal appeared, called simply *The Second Century* (which has continued since 1993 under the new title, *Journal of Early Christian Studies*). It is published by Johns Hopkins University Press. The persons who launched that journal faced some of the same questions the editors of this volume have had to

---

1. *The Nag Hammadi Library in English*, ed. James M. Robinson, 3rd ed. (San Francisco: HarperCollins, 1988).

face. Why is the second century so important, and why can it be considered a rather discrete era? In an editorial in the first issue of that journal Everett Ferguson argued that the second century is important because it is a border at which so many interests meet. It is of interest to biblical scholars, historians of the early church, specialists in Judaism, scholars in Greco-Roman studies, historians of philosophy, art historians, and others.[2] We would add to this list persons interested specifically in Gnosticism and in major figures who, though they were considered heretics, made lasting contributions to Christian thought, such as Marcion, Valentinus, Basilides, Montanus, and their followers.

It has been a truism, and remains so, that heretical scriptures, thinkers, and ideas have been mediated to us by those who successfully fought against them. We have always, and rightfully so, been cautious about lending the full weight of truth to the assessment of apologists and heresiologists as they reported the views of their opponents. We cannot be certain of our footing when we depend only upon the assessment of the victors in a struggle. Yet we are able to gain access to greater understanding of what is at stake in a struggle by reading the accounts of the victors in conjunction with the newly discovered material of their opponents.

Our hope, as editors, is that a single-volume collection of apologetic and antiheretical writings that can be read and studied along with newly discovered or newly translated extrabiblical and nonorthodox material will aid in understanding the basis of first- and second-century struggles.

We have resisted the temptation to provide excessively involved introductions to the material that follows. A straightforward collection of primary material, with minimal commentary, will serve readers well, especially when the purpose is to gain an introduction to the period, its players, and their ideas. This collection, then, is designed for college or seminary use in introductory courses. It would be read in conjunction with New Testament courses that seek to understand the use of Scripture in the earliest periods of the church. The book's relevance to church history courses is also clear since it collects and arranges material from extensive sources. We also envision the collection as a useful tool in history courses that seek to understand the intellectual history of the Mediterranean basin in the first centuries of the Common Era. Finally, an anthology of this type is useful as an introduction to theological argumentation prior to the Council of Nicea and the particular nature of the theological problems of the preconciliar period.

2. Everett Ferguson, "A New Journal," *The Second Century* 1/1 (Spring 1981): 4.

We see a purely practical use for a collection such as this because we realize that a library with a collection of ante-Nicene writings cannot be assumed at every college or institution whose faculty or students might desire to explore them.

There is a strict limit to technical argument in this volume. We have, however, sought to provide bibliographic sources for the student and scholar interested in pursuing ideas or personalities further.

The principles of selection are as follows:

1. To provide examples of types of argument used in apologetic and antiheretical writings. This includes examples of attacks on the personal lifestyles of opponents as well as on their ideas.

2. To include material that is our sole source of the heresies involved, such as material concerning the Quartodecimans.

3. To make material more accessible by eliminating, as much as possible, the repetition of arguments and material that the reader would encounter in reading the full-scale original writings.

4. To select descriptive material that can be compared to recently available collections of primary material.

The choice of writings has been determined by judgments that may be contested by others. It may be that any future editions of this or similar volumes should contain more, or express an alternative vantage point. Some rather passionate presentations have ended up on the editors' floor in consideration of space and audience. In some ways, any selected material is an affront to the body of work from which it is taken. But the editors are of the opinion that such a volume should not contain less than what is here for most purposes. The specialist and researcher will naturally want to go beyond what is provided.

CONTEXTS FOR THIS COLLECTION

There is a broader justification for a collection of this kind. That justification has to do with the prevailing (and often unspoken) presuppositions of biblical and patristic scholars, systematic theologians, and historians. Those presuppositions are stated bluntly by Albert C. Outler in an essay contained in the first issue of the journal *The Second Century*:

> "New Testament" scholars seem not to be as interested as one might think they should be in the aftermath of the production of the New Testament or in its complex functions in the development of faith and

order in the church of later ages. Sometimes they seem to pass from the New Testament to the present without the intervention of the "time of the church." ... From this it is natural to regard patristic theology as more or less retrograde ("Greek," "static," "ecclesiastical"—"patristic"!). Patrologists, for their part, return the compliment by regarding the New Testament and the first century as theologically underdeveloped. ... Even when taken as prototype, the New Testament requires the fourth–sixth century developments as climax.[3]

These predilections must be addressed and overcome. Can a better appreciation for the issues and debates during the first and second centuries help overcome these prejudices? What were some of these issues, and how are they important to the various theological disciplines? Two considerations are important for this discussion—one from a biblical studies perspective, the other from a historical/systematic perspective.

The Context within Biblical Studies

Traditionally it has been taken for granted that heresy was a departure from "the faith once delivered to the saints" (Jude 3). One finds warrant for that view in various early Christian writers. Clement of Rome, for example, wrote near the end of the first century (ca. A.D. 96) that the gospel was given by Jesus to the apostles, who appointed bishops and deacons after testing them—presumably in order to guard the gospel in its purity.[4] A few years later Hegesippus (ca. A.D. 100–180) wrote that heresy came about by the deceitfulness of false teachers after the death of the apostles,[5] and at the close of the second century Tertullian (ca. A.D. 160–225) wrote that truth came before falsehood and that all heresy is a recent (or late) innovation.[6]

In 1934, however, a book by Walter Bauer was published in Germany that called for a reassessment of the traditional view.[7] Bauer argued that in many geographical areas of antiquity—including Asia Minor, Greece, Syria, and Alexandria—"heresy" preceded "orthodoxy." "Orthodoxy," he

3. Albert C. Outler, "Methods and Aims in the Study of the Development of Catholic Christianity," *The Second Century* 1/1 (Spring 1981): 13.

4. *1 Clement* 42.1-4.

5. Quoted by Eusebius, *Ecclesiastical History* 3.32.8.

6. Tertullian, *Against Marcion* 4.7; 5.19.

7. The English version of the book is: Walter Bauer, *Orthodoxy and Heresy in Earliest Christianity* (Philadelphia: Fortress Press, 1971).

said, "represented the form of Christianity supported by the majority in Rome"[8] that became ascendant in the second century and victorious in other areas to the east around A.D. 200.[9] The church at Rome, according to Bauer, was regarded as the church of Peter and Paul, and it was not influenced by heretical teachers. By means of its superior organizational powers the church at Rome was able to extend its influence elsewhere. The heretical groups in those places, even though they were often in the majority, were not united and were no match to counter the power of the leaders of the church at Rome. Other forms of Christianity, considered heretical in retrospect, gave way to Roman Christianity (orthodoxy).[10] According to Bauer's view, then, one should not espouse the traditional view of heresy as a departure from orthodoxy. Orthodoxy was an achievement, a triumph over earlier forms of Christianity that must be regarded as heretical.

Bauer's book has received criticisms at several points, which cannot be reviewed here.[11] What is important to point out, however, is the enormous influence the book has had on the study not only of early Christianity of the second century and later, but even of the New Testament and first century Christianity. Essentially that influence can be stated as follows. If it is the case that heresy preceded orthodoxy in many areas, it follows that so-called heretical views may well go back to the very beginning, the earliest interpretations of Jesus and his message. And if that is the case, then the so-called heretical views (as in Gnosticism) may be regarded as alternative, rather than incorrect (and "heretical"), interpretations.

This view has been strengthened by the discovery of the Nag Hammadi documents. Those writings illustrate the existence of traditions about Jesus and his message, and interpretations of them, that can be regarded as heretical by the standards of orthodoxy. Moreover, they have been taken as evidence to support the view that there were indeed diverse interpretations of Jesus and his message during the first two centuries. What one reads in the New Testament, the Apostolic Fathers, and the early Apologists is only one slice of the whole.

Reading the ancient authors who opposed heretical teachers and movements of the first and second century can thus be helpful even in the study of the New Testament. One can see lines of continuity, for example, from

8. Ibid., 229.

9. Ibid., 21, 53, 229.

10. Ibid., 102, 230–31, 240.

11. For a survey of criticisms, see Arland J. Hultgren, *The Rise of Normative Christianity* (Minneapolis: Fortress Press, 1994), 9–13.

a New Testament writer, such as Paul, to a figure near the close of our era, such as Irenaeus. In each case we hear the "orthodox" voice (if we can use that term so early) being raised against its opponents. Our own grasp of the views of the latter depends primarily on what the orthodox voice provides. But one can also see lines of continuity not only among the orthodox, but also among their opponents. Gnosticism, for example, developed over time, and one cannot attribute the views of later gnostic leaders to persons in the apostolic era. Yet the study of gnostic teachings of the second century does illumine its antecedents in the first, the era when most of the New Testament was written. The net result is that our understanding of the New Testament and other early Christian literature is enriched by a reading of those sources which speak of the heretical teachers and movements of the first two centuries.

The Context within Historical and Systematic Theology

The significance of the trinitarian, christological, and anthropological issues leading up to the councils at Nicea and Chalcedon has long been considered of foundational importance for later dogmatic and systematic theological history. In general, the historical period covered in this collection is regarded as "preconciliar" in more than a chronological sense. The theological development of the first two centuries has been perceived as formative at best. The terminology is often regarded as imprecise, and the issues and concerns are considered unfocused in comparison to those of later periods and controversies. If we view the history of theological development as the process of focused conflict over increasingly well-defined issues, this assessment is obviously true.

There is, however, another aspect of theological development that must be taken into consideration. Was there a tendency on the part of post-conciliar writers to retroject later issues into the first two centuries?

Frequently the writings of antiheretical writers composed after the Council of Nicea are included here along with writings contemporaneous with writings and thinkers ultimately viewed as heretical or dangerous to the faith. One of the advantages of this procedure is that it enables the reader to observe how earlier, more contemporaneous writings were appropriated in later works affected by arguments put forth in a post-Nicean environment. Clearly, the later heresiologists used the material of their predecessors as a foundation for their own. Whatever changes of perspective or expansions occur in the writings of the later heresiologists, however, there is continuity in particular themes with the earlier works that can be investigated apart from the specifics of the conciliar struggles. The continuity is an interesting phenomenon in itself. As one moves from early to late writings, one can observe the continuities and disjunctions of theological development during the period between the death of Christ and the Council of Nicea.

Understanding the first- and second-century debates has become increasingly important in our times. The sheer abundance of competing religious systems of the second century bears a marked resemblance to the plurality of modern and postmodern worldviews. In many ways we have more in common with the currents of pluralism of the second century than with the theological conflicts of the fourth and fifth centuries, when Christianity was on the ascendancy. Insofar as that is the case, it is fruitful to analyze and understand just how second-century Christian thinking regarding the person of Jesus related to its own complex and pluralistic environment.

What kinds of thought-worlds did Christian apologists face? This question can be approached in many ways. For example, could it be that the theological issue most important in the first two centuries of the church's existence was not the trinitarian issue *per se*, nor the christological issue as defined later at Chalcedon, but the scandalous notion (to both Greek and Hebrew ears) of the incarnation itself?[12] Or, could it be that the issue of martyrdom, and attitudes toward martyrdom as the highest possible proclamation of Jesus Christ, were the primary drivers of the writings of the antiheresiologists?[13]

Often, either the humanity or the divinity of Jesus Christ is the issue at hand among the Ebionite, gnostic, Marcionite, adoptionist, and the two monarchian viewpoints. The issue of the divine/human person was joined primarily in terms of the meaning of incarnation.

It is the divinity of Christ that is scandalous to the Jewish Christian who has been steeped in the expectation of the anointed, human Jewish Messiah. That view is upheld by Trypho in his dialogue with Justin Martyr:

> And Trypho said, "Those who affirm Him to have been a man, and to have been anointed by election, and then to have become Christ, appear to me to speak more plausibly than you who hold those opin-

12. Cf. Oskar Skarsaune, *Incarnation: Myth or Fact?*, Concordia Scholarship Today Series (St. Louis: Concordia Publishing House, 1991).

13. Cf. Elaine H. Pagels, "Christology in Dialogue with Gnosticism," in *Christology in Dialogue*, ed. Robert F. Berkey and Sarah A. Edwards (Cleveland: Pilgrim Press, 1993), 79.

ions which you express. For we all expect that Christ will be a man [born] of men, and that Elijah when he comes will anoint Him. But if this man appear to be Christ, He must certainly be known as man [born] of men.[14]

From the viewpoint of Jewish expectation, the scandal of the New Testament figure of Christ Jesus is the breakdown of the separation between Creator and creature. Trypho found no problem in Justin's appeal to Scripture for an "implied plurality or structure within the essence of God," but he found Justin's Christology to be, "from a Jewish perspective, the overstepping of the boundary between God and humanity which the incarnation implied."[15] In terms of Trypho's presuppositions and expectations, the gospel as proclaimed by Justin Martyr is scandalous.

Likewise, the scandal arises from the Greek perspective in view of the philosophical impossibility of God becoming a human being. This is a scandal because of the particular view of God in Greek thought. Witness Celsus' remarks to Christians and Jews:

God is good, and beautiful, and blessed, and that in the best and most beautiful degree. But if he come down among men, he must undergo a change, and a change from good to evil, from virtue to vice, from happiness to misery, and from best to worst. Who, then, would make choice of such a change? It is the nature of a mortal, indeed, to undergo change and remoulding, but of an immortal to remain the same and unaltered. God, then, could not admit of such a change.[16]

God either really changes himself, as these assert, into a mortal body, and the impossibility of that has been already declared; or else he does *not* undergo a change, but only causes the beholders to imagine so, and thus deceives them, and is guilty of falsehood.[17]

O Jews and Christians, no God or son of a God either came or will come down (to earth).[18]

---

14. Justin Martyr, *Dialogue with Trypho*, 49.1, in *The Ante-Nicene Fathers: Translations of the Writings of the Fathers Down to A.D. 325*, ed. Alexander Roberts and James Donaldson, 10 vols. (Buffalo: Christian Literature Publishing Co., 1885–97), 1:219. The *Ante-Nicene Fathers* is hereafter cited as *ANF*, followed by a page number. This quotation was cited in the same context by O. Skarsaune, *Incarnation—Myth or Fact?*, 14.

15. O. Skarsaune, *Incarnation—Myth or Fact?*, 47.

16. Origen, *Against Celsus* 4.14, *ANF* 4:502. Cited in this context by O. Skarsaune, *Incarnation—Myth or Fact?*, 18.

17. *Against Celsus* 4.18, *ANF* 4:504. Note that it is a deception that the divine Christ pulls off, in many gnostic Christologies, in relation to the crucifixion.

18. *Against Celsus* 5.2, *ANF* 4:543.

To the Greek mind, the alteration in divine being necessary to account for the incarnation is unthinkable. Despite the Greek mythology that would seem to countenance a divine morphology, the distinctive critique of a Celsus against Christian views of incarnation is a profound demythologizing of that form of Greek thought, making the incarnation a scandal.

Observing the debates of the first centuries of the church leads one to see two things clearly. First, both Greek and Jew, albeit from opposite perspectives and expectations, viewed the distinction between God and the human as violated in the Christian insistence on incarnation. For the Jewish thinker, the rejection of the incarnation arises from the expectation of the Messiah as a human, earthly figure. For the Greek thinker, the rejection of the incarnation arises from the notion of the absolute impassibility of God. The point of early church apologists and antiheretical writers was, in part, against adoptionist Christologies (such as the Ebionites) on the one hand, and against Docetists (such as the Gnostics) on the other. Both tendencies, from different perspectives, sought to show the foolishness and scandal of the gospel of the incarnation. Even if not all gnostic systems were loath to ascribe suffering to Jesus as the Christ,[19] the nature of the incarnation as it relates to Christ's suffering is vital to the use of Scripture and later trinitarian and christological debates.

The interaction of Christians with Jewish and Greek thinkers, such as Trypho and Celsus, was not primarily a debate within well-defined parameters of Christian discourse. Rather, the debate was carried on among different religious systems about the one called Jesus the Christ. Later debates surrounding the Councils of Nicea and Chalcedon would be intra-Christian debates. They would become debates, for the most part, among those who spoke from within a self-reflective system of thought that is self-consciously normative.

So much of current theological discussion is among traditions and worldviews that are not rooted in a self-conscious Christian worldview. These discussions do not follow internally recognized rules for Christian theological discourse. In spite of the strongly polemical and personal nature of the first-century debates, is it not possible that we share an arena for debate more like theirs than that of the fourth, the fifth, the twelfth, or even the sixteenth century? Is not, for example, the debate over the moral rigidity of the Ebionites or the Montanists (including Tertullian) relevant to the debates over the place of moral values in our own societies?

19. E. Pagels, "Christology in Dialogue with Gnosticism," 73.

While the Nicean and post-Nicean councils are rightfully normative for Christian doctrine, the first two centuries surely have an integrity and value of their own. If we can remove the lenses of the great councils for a while, we can begin to see that some of the issues confronted prior to A.D. 200 are current for us as well. The internal integrity of the period demands our attention.

While the selection of writings in this collection contains much more than early christological discussions and debates, it is our hope that the pieces selected will assist in investigating the contours of the early church's Christology as well as other issues that might be of aid to teachers and students of the Western biblical and theological traditions.

Part I

The Apostolic and Sub-Apostolic Era

Simon Magus and the Simonians

Simon Magus (first century A.D.) or Simon "the Magician," as the word "magus" means, was a native of Gitta in Samaria and the exponent of an early form of Gnosticism. The earliest account of his activities is recorded in the Acts of the Apostles 8:9-24, written by Luke the Evangelist in the last two decades of the first century. His encounter with Philip and his subsequent baptism would have occurred in the early thirties, after he had already gained some fame in the practice of magic. Later he settled in Rome during the time of the Emperor Claudius (A.D. 41–54). Irenaeus speaks of Simon as the one "from whom all heresies originated" (*Against Heresies* 1.23.2), which must be considered an exaggerated claim, but his comment is typical of the contempt that the heresiologists had for Simon and his followers. Not all the teachings of the Simonians, named after Simon, can be traced back to the historical Simon. By the time that Origen (A.D. 185–254) wrote his *Against Celsus* (*Contra Celsum*, ca. A.D. 250), the Simonians had virtually ceased to exist (1.57). Simon himself probably died around A.D. 70.

1.1. Acts 8:9-24. Written by Luke the Evangelist, ca. A.D. 80–90.
New Revised Standard Version translation.

According to Luke, Simon was a magician in Samaria prior to becoming a Christian. He tried to purchase spiritual powers and was rebuked by the apostle Peter.

Now a certain man named Simon had previously practiced magic in the city and amazed the people of Samaria, saying that he himself was some-

15

one great. All of them, from the least to the greatest, listened to him eagerly, saying, "This man is the power of God that is called Great." And they listened eagerly to him because for a long time he had amazed them with his magic. But when they believed Philip, who was proclaiming the good news about the kingdom of God and the name of Jesus Christ, they were baptized, both men and women. Even Simon himself believed. After being baptized, he stayed constantly with Philip and was amazed when he saw the signs and great miracles that took place.

Now when the apostles at Jerusalem heard that Samaria had accepted the word of God, they sent Peter and John to them. The two went down and prayed for them that they might receive the Holy Spirit (for as yet the Spirit had not come upon any of them; they had only been baptized in the name of the Lord Jesus). Then Peter and John laid their hands on them, and they received the Holy Spirit. Now when Simon saw that the Spirit was given through the laying on of the apostles' hands, he offered them money, saying, "Give me also this power so that anyone on whom I lay my hands may receive the Holy Spirit." But Peter said to him, "May your silver perish with you, because you thought you could obtain God's gift with money! You have no part or share in this, for your heart is not right before God. Repent therefore of this wickedness of yours, and pray to the Lord that, if possible, the intent of your heart may be forgiven you. For I see that you are in the gall of bitterness and the chains of wickedness." Simon answered, "Pray for me to the Lord, that nothing of what you have said may happen to me."

1.2. Justin, *Apology* 1.26. Rome, ca. A.D. 155.

Source: *Early Christian Fathers*, ed. C. Richardson, 258–59.

Justin addresses Emperor Antonius Pius (emperor A.D. 138–61), his sons, the senate, and the people concerning Simon, Menander, and Marcion. According to Justin, both Simon and Menander were from Samaria. Simon was active as a miracle worker and teacher in Rome. Menander was his pupil and performed magic and taught in Syria. Marcion came from Pontus in Asia Minor and taught in Rome. Followers of all these teachers considered themselves Christians. Justin records that stories of their immorality were common. He implies that since these persons were not persecuted, they were not faithful Christians.

After Christ's ascent into heaven the demons put forward various men who said that they were gods, and you not only did not persecute them, but thought them worthy of honors. One was a certain Simon, a Samaritan from the village of Gitta, who in the time of Claudius Caesar [[A.D. 41–54]], through the arts of the demons who worked in him, did mighty works of magic in your imperial city of Rome and was thought to be a god. He has been honored among you as a god by a statue, which was set up on the River Tiber, between the two bridges, with this inscription in Latin, SIMONI DEO SANCTO [[To Simon the Holy God]]. Almost all the Samaritans, and a few in other nations, confess this man as their first god and worship him as such, and a woman named Helena, who traveled around with him in those days, and had formerly been a public prostitute, they say was the first Concept produced from him. Then we know of a certain Menander, who was also a Samaritan, from the village of Capparetaea, who had been a disciple of Simon's, and was also possessed by the demons. He deceived many at Antioch by magic arts, and even persuaded his followers that he would never die; there are still some who believe this [as they learned] from him. Then there is a certain Marcion of Pontus, who is still teaching his converts that there is another God greater than the Fashioner. By the help of the demons he has made many in every race of men to blaspheme and to deny God the Maker of the universe, professing that there is another who is greater and has done greater things than he. As we said, all who derive [their opinions] from these men are called Christians, just as men who do not share the same teachings with the philosophers still have in common with them the name of philosophy, thus brought into disrepute. Whether they commit the shameful deeds about which stories are told—the upsetting of the lamp, promiscuous intercourse, and the meals of human flesh, we do not know; but we are sure that they are neither persecuted nor killed by you, on account of their teachings anyway.

1.3. Justin, *Apology* 1.56. Rome, ca. A.D. 155.

Source: *Early Christian Fathers*, ed. C. Richardson, 279.

Justin continues his address to the emperor, the senate, and the people of Rome. He indicates that he and others are bearing a petition to the emperor, the senate, and the people which denounces Simon and his followers. Simon

*must have impressed the Romans earlier, since they had dedicated a statue to
him as a god.*

Simon lived in your own imperial city of Rome under Claudius Caesar
[[A.D. 41–54]], and so impressed the Sacred Senate and the Roman people
that he was thought to be a god and was honored with a statue like the
other gods whom you honor. We ask you therefore to join the Sacred Senate and your people as joint judges of this petition of ours, so that if any are
ensnared by his teachings they may be able to learn the truth and flee from
this error. And, if you will, destroy the statue.

1.4. Irenaeus, *Against Heresies* 1.23.1-4. Lyons, ca. A.D. 190.

Source: *Gnosticism*, ed. R. M. Grant, 23–25.

*According to Irenaeus, Simon had a wife named Helen, a former prostitute.
Moreover, Simon taught a "docetic" Christology, in which Christ simply
appeared to be a human being, but was not, and to suffer, but did not. Irenaeus
refers also to the existence of Simonian clergy (priests) at his own time and
testifies to the term "Simonians" as a sect.*

1. Simon the Samaritan was a magician.... He eagerly proceeded to
contend against the apostles, so that he himself might seem to be famous,
and he investigated all magic still more carefully so that he could compel
the multitude to marvel—since he lived under Claudius Caesar [[A.D. 41–
54]], by whom, it is said, he was honoured with a statue because of his
magic.

He was glorified as a god by many, and he taught that he himself was the
one who was to appear among the Jews as Son, would descend in Samaria
as Father, and would come among the other nations as Holy Spirit. He said
that he was the Absolute Sovereignty, i.e., the Father above all, and was
willing to be called whatever men call him.

2. Simon the Samaritan, from whom all heresies originated, provided
his sect with subject matter of this kind. He led about with him a certain
Helen, after he had redeemed her from a life of prostitution in Tyre, a city
of Phoenicia. He said she was the first conception of his mind, the Mother
of all, through whom in the beginning he had the idea of making angels
and archangels. This Thought, leaping forth from him and knowing what

her father willed, descended to the lower regions and generated angels and powers, by whom this world was made. But after she generated them, she was held captive by them because of envy, for they did not want to be considered the offspring of anyone else. For Simon was entirely unknown to them; his Thought was held captive by the powers and angels emitted by her. She suffered all kinds of humiliation from them, so that she did not run back upwards to her Father but was even enclosed in a human body, and through the ages transmigrated as from one vessel to another, into other female bodies.

She was in that Helen because of whom the Trojan war was undertaken. Therefore when Stesichorus vilified her in his poems he was deprived of eyesight; later, when he repented and wrote the *Palinodes*, in which he praised her, his sight was restored.

Transmigrating from body to body, and always enduring humiliation from the body, she finally became a prostitute; she was the "lost sheep" [Luke 15:6].   3. For this reason he [[=Christ]] came, in order to rescue her first and free her from her bonds, then to offer men salvation through his "knowledge."

For when the angels misgoverned the world, since each of them desired the primacy, he came for the reformation of affairs; he descended, transformed and made like the powers and authorities and angels, so that among men he appeared as a man, though he was not a man, and he seemed to suffer in Judaea, though he did not suffer.

The prophets spoke their prophecies under the inspiration of the angels who made the world. Therefore those who have set their hope on Simon and Helen pay no further attention to them and do what they wish as free agents. For "by his grace men are saved, not by just works" [Eph. 2:8]. For actions are just not by nature but by convention, in accordance with the decrees of the angels who made the world and intended to lead men into slavery [cf. Gal. 4:9] through precepts of this kind. Therefore he announced that the world would be destroyed and that those who were his would be freed from the rule of those who made the world.

4. Therefore the priests and their mysteries live promiscuously and perform magic, in so far as each is able to do so. They employ exorcisms and incantations and are constantly occupied with love-philtres, love-magic, familiar spirits, dream-inducers, and other abstruse matters. They have an image of Simon made in the likeness of Zeus and one of Helen in the likeness of Athena, and they worship these. They also bear a name derived from Simon, the founder of their impious doctrine, and are called Simoni-

ans, since from them the knowledge of the false name took its beginnings, as one can learn from their own statements.

1.5. Origen, *Against Celsus* 1.57. Alexandria, ca. A.D. 250.

Source: *Gnosis*, ed. W. Foerster, 1:32.

According to Origen, the Simonian sect was nearly extinct by the time he wrote the following lines.

The magician Simon also, the Samaritan, wanted to win some through magic, and he deceived them at that time. But now one cannot find thirty all told in the world, and perhaps this number is too high. Even in Palestine they are very few, and nowhere in the rest of the world is his name to be found.

1.6. Hippolytus, *Refutation of All Heresies* 6.4, 7, 9, 13-15.
      Rome, ca. A.D. 230.

Source: *The Ante-Nicene Fathers*, ed. A. Roberts and J. Donaldson, 5:75– 77, 79–81.

Hippolytus attacks Simon's interpretations of Scripture and accuses him of plagiarizing from the philosopher Heraclitus. He also tells of Simon's view of the "principle of the universe" and of humanity's relationship to it. How much of this can actually be attributed to Simon is questionable. Hippolytus attributes to Simon what is known of the Simonians of his own day.

4. Now Simon, both foolishly and knavishly paraphrasing the law of Moses, makes his statements [in the manner following]: For when Moses asserts that "God is a burning and consuming fire" [Deut. 4:24], taking what is said by Moses not in its correct sense, he affirms that fire is the originating principle of the universe. [But Simon] does not consider what the statement is which is made, namely, that it is not that God is a fire, but a burning and consuming fire, [thereby] not only putting a violent sense upon the actual law of Moses, but even plagiarizing from Heraclitus the Obscure. And Simon denominates the originating principle of the uni-

verse an indefinite power, expressing himself thus: "This is the treatise of a revelation of [the] voice and name [recognisable] by means of intellectual apprehension of the Great Indefinite Power. Wherefore it will be sealed, [and] kept secret, [and] hid, [and] will repose in the habitation, at the foundation of which lies the root of all things." And he asserts that this man who is born of blood is [the aforesaid] habitation, and that in him resides an indefinite power, which he affirms to be the root of the universe.

Hippolytus describes the doctrine of creation taught in the Simonian system.

7. For, [[Simon]] says, he is in the habit of considering that all these portions of the fire, both visible and invisible, are possessed of perception and a share of intelligence. The world, therefore, that which is generated, was produced from the unbegotten fire. It began, however, to exist, he says, according to the following manner. He who was begotten from the principle of that fire took six roots, and those primary ones, of the originating principle of generation. And, he says, that the roots were made from the fire in pairs, which roots he terms "Mind" and "Intelligence," "Voice" and "Name," "Ratiocination" and "Reflection." And that in these six roots resides simultaneously the entire indefinite power potentially, [however] not actually. And this indefinite power, he says, is he who stood, stands, and will stand. Wherefore, whensoever he may be made into an image, inasmuch as he exists in the six powers, he will exist [there] substantially, potentially, quantitively, [and] completely. [And he will be a power] one and the same with the unbegotten and indefinite power. If, however, he may continue only potentially in the six powers, and has not been formed into an image, he vanishes, he says, and is destroyed in such a way as the grammatical or geometrical capacity in man's soul. For when the capacity takes unto itself an art, a light of existent things is produced; but when [the capacity] does not take unto itself [an art], unskilfulness and ignorance are the results; and just as when [the power] was nonexistent, it perishes along with the expiring man.

Here Hippolytus describes the six days of creation in the Simonian interpretation of Genesis.

9. When, therefore, Moses has spoken of "the six days in which God made heaven and earth, and rested on the seventh from all His works" [Gen. 2:2], Simon, in a manner already specified, giving [these and other

passages of Scripture] a different application [from the one intended by the holy writers], deifies himself. When, therefore, [the followers of Simon] affirm that there are three days begotten before sun and moon, they speak enigmatically of Mind and Intelligence, that is, Heaven and Earth, and of the seventh power, [I mean] the indefinite one. For these three powers are produced antecedent to all the rest. But when they say, "He begot me prior to all the Ages" [Prov. 8:22-23], such statements, he says, are alleged to hold good concerning the seventh power. Now this seventh power, which was a power existing in the indefinite power, which was produced prior to all the Ages, this is, he says, the seventh power, respecting which Moses utters the following words: "And the Spirit of God was wafted over the water" [Gen. 1:2]; that is, says [the Simonian], the Spirit which contains all things in itself, and is an image of the indefinite power about which Simon speaks, —"an image from an incorruptible form, that alone reduces all things into order." For this power that is wafted over the water, being begotten, he says, from an incorruptible form alone, reduces all things into order. When, therefore, according to these [heretics], there ensued some such arrangement, and [one] similar [to it] of the world, the Deity, he says, proceeded to form man, taking clay from the earth. And he formed him not uncompounded, but twofold, according to [his own] image and likeness. Now the image is the Spirit that is wafted over the water; and whosoever is not fashioned into a figure of this, will perish with the world, inasmuch as he continues only potentially, and does exist actually. This, he says, is what has been spoken, "that we should not be condemned with the world" [1 Cor. 11:32]. If one, however, be made into the figure of [the Spirit], and be generated from an indivisible point, ... [such a one, albeit] small, will become great. But what is great will continue unto infinite and unalterable duration, as being that which no longer is subject to the conditions of a generated entity.

Hippolytus describes here an elaborate system of emanations in the system of the Simonians.

13. Therefore, according to this reasoning, Simon became confessedly a god to his silly followers, as that Libyan, namely, Apsethus—begotten, no doubt, and subject to passions, when he may exist potentially, but devoid of propensions. [And this too, though born from one having propensions, and uncreated though born] from one that is begotten, when He may be fashioned into a figure, and, becoming perfect, may come forth from two

of the primary powers, that is, Heaven and Earth. For Simon expressly speaks of this in the "Revelation" after this manner: "To you, then, I address the things which I speak, and [to you] I write what I write. The writing is this: there are two offshoots from all the Æons, having neither beginning nor end, from one root. And this is a power, viz., Sige, [who is] invisible [and] incomprehensible. And one of these [offshoots] appears from above, which constitutes a great power, [the creative] Mind of the universe, which manages all things, [and is] a male. The other [offshoot], however, is from below [and constitutes] a great Intelligence, and is a female which produces all things. From whence, ranged in pairs opposite each other, they undergo conjugal union, and manifest an intermediate interval, namely, an incomprehensible air, which has neither beginning nor end. But in this is a father who sustains all things, and nourishes things that have beginning and end. This is he who stood, stands, and will stand, being an hermaphrodite power according to the pre-existent indefinite power, which has neither beginning nor end. Now this [power] exists in isolation. For Intelligence, [that subsists] in unity, proceeded forth from this [power], [and] became two. And that [father] was one, for having in himself this [power] he was isolated, and, however, he was not primal though pre-existent; but being rendered manifest to himself from himself, he passed into a state of duality. But neither was he denominated father before this [power] would style him father. As, therefore, he himself, bringing forward himself by means of himself, manifested unto himself his own peculiar intelligence, so also the intelligence, when it was manifested, did not exercise the function of creation. But beholding him, she concealed the Father within herself, that is, the power; and it is an hermaphrodite power, and an intelligence. And hence it is that they are ranged in pairs, one opposite the other; for power is in no wise different from intelligence, inasmuch as they are one. For from those things that are above is discovered power; and from those below, intelligence. So it is, therefore, that likewise what is manifested from these, being unity, is discovered [to be] duality, an hermaphrodite having the female in itself. This, [therefore,] is Mind [subsisting] in Intelligence; and these are separable one from the other, [though both taken together] are one, [and] are discovered in a state of duality."

14. Simon then, after inventing these [tenets], not only by evil devices interpreted the writings of Moses in whatever way he wished, but even the [works] of the poets. For also he fastens an allegorical meaning on [the story of] the wooden horse and Helen with the torch, and on very many

other [accounts], which he transfers to what relates to himself and to Intelligence, and [thus] furnishes a fictitious explanation of them. He said,
however, that this [Helen] was the lost sheep. And she, always abiding
among women, confounded the powers in the world by reason of her surpassing beauty.... But, again, those who become followers of this impos-
tor—I mean Simon the sorcerer—indulge in similar practices, and
irrationally allege the necessity of promiscuous intercourse. They express
themselves in the manner following: "All earth is earth, and there is no dif-
ference where any one sows, provided he does sow." But even they con-
gratulate themselves on account of this indiscriminate intercourse,
asserting that this is perfect love, and employing the expressions, "holy of
holies," and "sanctify one another." For [they would have us believe} that
they are not overcome by the supposed vice, for that they have been
redeemed. "And [Jesus], by having redeemed Helen in this way," [Simon
says,] "has afforded salvation to men through his own peculiar intelligence. For inasmuch as the angels, by reason of their lust for pre-eminence,
improperly managed the world, [Jesus Christ] being transformed, and
being assimilated to the rulers and powers and angels, came for the restoration [of things]. And so [it was that Jesus] appeared as man, when in reality he was not a man. And [so it was] that likewise he suffered—though
not actually undergoing suffering, but appearing to the Jews to do so—in
Judea as 'Son,' and in Samaria as 'Father' and among the rest of the Gentiles as 'Holy Spirit.'" And [Simon alleges] that Jesus tolerated being styled
by whichever name [of the three just mentioned] men might wish to call
him. "And that the prophets, deriving their inspiration from the world-
making angels, uttered predictions [concerning him]." Wherefore, [Simon
said,] that towards these [prophets] those felt no concern up to the present,
who believe on Simon and Helen, and that they do whatsoever they please,
as persons free; for they allege that they are saved by grace. For that there is
no reason for punishment, even though one shall act wickedly; for such a
one is not wicked by nature, but by enactment. "For the angels who
created the world made," he says, "whatever enactments they pleased,"
thinking by such [legislative] words to enslave those who listened to them.
But, again, they speak of a dissolution of the world, for the redemption of
his own particular adherents.

15. This Simon, deceiving many in Samaria by his sorceries, was
reproved by the Apostles, and was laid under a curse, as it has been written
in Acts. But he afterwards abjured the faith, and attempted these [aforesaid
practices]. And journeying as far as Rome, he fell in with the Apostles; and

to him, deceiving many by his sorceries, Peter offered repeated opposition. This man, ultimately repairing to … [and] sitting under a plane tree, continued to give instruction [in his doctrines]. And in truth at last, when conviction was imminent, in case he delayed longer, he stated that, if he were buried alive, he would rise the third day. And accordingly, having ordered a trench to be dug by his disciples, he directed himself to be interred there. They, then, executed the injunction given; whereas he remained [in that grave] until this day, for he was not the Christ. This constitutes the legendary system advanced by Simon, and from this Valentinus derived a starting-point [for his own doctrine. This doctrine, in point of fact, was the same with the Simonian, though Valentinus] denominated it under different titles: for "Nous," and "Aletheia," and "Logos," and "Zoe," and "Anthropos," and "Ecclesia," and Æons of Valentinus, are confessedly the six roots of Simon, viz., "Mind" and "Intelligence," "Voice" and "Name," "Ratiocination" and "Reflection."

1.7. *Clementine Homilies* 2.22-25. Syria, third century A.D.

Source: *Gnosticism*, ed. R. M. Grant, 25–27.

Although a relatively late source, this passage sums up traditions concerning Simon and the Simonians. Some of its claims concerning Simon go beyond previous sources, however, such as those about his having lived in Egypt and his relationship to John the Baptist, which are not likely to have a basis in history. The passage shows an elaboration of traditions about Simon in the third century.

22. This Simon's father was Antonius, his mother Rachel. By race he is a Samaritan, from the village of Gitthae, six *schoeni* [about 30 miles] from the city [of Samaria]. He was very active in Alexandria, Egypt … and after gaining great skill in magic and becoming elated, he wished to be regarded as a certain Highest Power, above even the God who made the universe. Sometimes he intimates that he is Christ by calling himself the Standing One. He used this title to indicate that he would always "stand," since there was no cause of corruption which would make his body fail. He says that the God who made the universe is not the highest, and he does not believe that the dead will be raised. He rejects Jerusalem and substitutes Mount Gerezim. Instead of our real Christ he proclaims himself. He alle-

gorises the content of the law in accordance with his own presuppositions and, though he says there will be a judgment, he does not expect one. For if he were convinced that he would be judged by God he would not venture to be impious towards God himself. For this reason some persons—who do not know that, using religion as a cloak, he steals away the essence of the truth, and who faithfully believe the hope and the judgment which he says will somehow take place—go to destruction.

23. His infiltration of [Christian] religious teaching took place in this way. There was a certain John who baptized every day. In accordance with the doctrine of Pairs he was the forerunner of our Lord Jesus. And as the Lord had twelve apostles, corresponding to the twelve solar months, so also John had thirty leaders totalling up to the monthly reckoning of the moon. In this number was a woman named Helen, so that not even this might lack a special significance. Since a woman is half a man, she made the number of the Thirty incomplete, just as in the case of the moon, whose cycle does not take a complete month. And though Simon was the first and most highly approved of the Thirty in John's view, he did not succeed John after his death for this reason:

24. Simon was absent in Egypt for the practice of magic when John was killed, and a certain Dositheus, desiring John's Office, falsely announced that Simon was dead and succeeded to rule over the sect. Not long after, Simon returned and strongly laid claim to the place as his own, though when he met Dositheus he did not demand it back, since he knew that whoever attains power irregularly is not removed. Therefore with assumed friendship he gives himself for a while to the second place under Dositheus. After a few days, however, he took his place among the thirty fellow-disciples and began to slander Dositheus as not having delivered the doctrines correctly. He said that Dositheus did so not because of jealous refusal but because of ignorance. One time Dositheus, who perceived that this artful accusation of Simon was destroying his reputation in the eyes of the majority, so that they did not think he was the Standing One, came in a rage to the usual assembly and, finding Simon, struck him with a staff. The staff seemed to pass through Simon's body as if he were smoke. In amazement Dositheus thereupon says to him, "If you are the Standing One, I too will worship you." When Simon said, "I am," Dositheus, who knew that he himself was not the Standing One, fell down and worshipped; and, associating himself with the twenty-nine leaders, he set Simon in his own place of reputation. Thus, not long afterwards, Dositheus himself, while Simon stood, fell down and died.

25. Simon goes about in company with Helen and, even until now, as you see, stirs up the crowds. He says that he has brought down this Helen from the highest heavens to the world; she is Queen [*kyria*], since she is all-maternal Being and Wisdom [Sophia]. For her sake, he says, the Greeks and the barbarians fought, imagining an image of the truth; for she who really existed was then with the very First God. But by allegorising certain matters of this sort, fictitiously combined with Greek myths, he deceives many, especially by his performance of many marvellous wonders, so that—if we did not know that he does these things by magic—we ourselves would also have been deceived.

Nicolaus and the Nicolaitans

Nicolaus (mid-first century A.D.) was appointed a deacon in Jerusalem by the Twelve in the early thirties, according to the Acts of the Apostles (6:5). As such, he belonged to the first generation of Christianity. He is identified in the same verse in Acts as "a proselyte of Antioch." Other than these items of information, however, nothing more is related concerning him in Acts or the rest of the New Testament.

The Nicolaitans are mentioned for the first time in the Book of Revelation (2:1-7, 12-17) near the end of the first century A.D. and then in other early Christian literature. In the writings of Irenaeus (*Against Heresies* 1.26.3), Hippolytus (*Refutation* 7.24), and Eusebius (*Ecclesiastical History* 3.29) they are said to have been followers of Nicolaus of Antioch and his teaching, but that claim may be incorrect. In any case, the sect appears to have gone out of existence by the year A.D. 200. Eusebius (*Ecclesiastical History* 3.29) calls the Nicolaitans a "very short-lived sect."

2.1. Revelation 2:1-7, 12-17. Patmos, ca. A.D. 95.
New Revised Standard Version translation.

In chapters two and three of Revelation the writer records a series of letters to seven churches in Asia Minor. According to the author, these letters were dictated to him by Christ and were to be addressed to the "angel" [= bishop] of each church. The letter to Ephesus attests the existence of the Nicolaitans in Asia Minor at the end of the first century A.D. and the opposition of the Ephesian church against them. On the other hand, the congregation at Pergamum has some members associated with the sect.

2:1-7. "To the angel of the church in Ephesus write: These are the words of him who holds the seven stars in his right hand, who walks among the seven golden lampstands:

"I know your works, your toil and your patient endurance. I know that you cannot tolerate evildoers; you have tested those who claim to be apostles but are not, and have found them to be false. I also know you are enduring patiently and bearing up for the sake of my name, and that you have not grown weary. But I have this against you, that you have abandoned the love you had at first. Remember then from what you have fallen; repent, and do the works you did at first. If not, I will come to you and remove your lampstand from its place, unless you repent. Yet this is to your credit: you hate the works of the Nicolaitans, which I also hate. Let anyone who has an ear listen to what the Spirit is saying to the churches. To everyone who conquers, I will give permission to eat of the tree of life that is in the paradise of God."

2:12-17. "And to the angel of the church in Pergamum write: These are the words of him who has the sharp two-edged sword:

"I know where you are living, where Satan's throne is. Yet you are holding fast to my name, and you did not deny your faith in me even in the days of Antipas my witness, my faithful one, who was killed among you, where Satan lives. But I have a few things against you: you have some there who hold to the teaching of Balaam, who taught Balak to put a stumbling block before the people of Israel, so that they would eat food sacrificed to idols and practice fornication. So you also have some who hold to the teaching of the Nicolaitans. Repent then. If not, I will come to you soon and make war against them with the sword of my mouth. Let anyone who has an ear listen to what the Spirit is saying to the churches. To everyone who conquers I will give some of the hidden manna, and I will give a white stone, and on the white stone is written a new name that no one knows except the one who receives it."

2.2. Irenaeus, *Against Heresies* 1.26.3. Lyons, ca. A.D. 190.

Source: *Gnosticism*, ed. R. M. Grant, 43.

Irenaeus claims that the Nicolaitans originated from the Nicolaus of Acts 6:5, which is actually questionable, and he accuses them of sexual immorality and eating meat offered to idols, which he could have derived from Revelation 2:14. It is not clear that he had information from any additional sources.

The Nicolaitans have as their master Nicolaus, one of the seven who were first ordained to the diaconate by the apostles [Acts 6:5]; they live promiscuously. Who they are is most fully revealed in the Revelation of John [2:6,15]; they teach that fornication is a matter of indifference and that one should eat meats sacrificed to idols. Therefore the Word has spoken of them thus: "But you have this, that you hate the works of the Nicolaitans, which I also hate" [[Rev. 2:6]].

2.3. Hippolytus, *Refutation of All Heresies* 7.24. Rome, ca. A.D. 230.

Source: *The Ante-Nicene Fathers*, ed. A. Roberts and J. Donaldson, 5:115.

Already at the time of Hippolytus it is said that the Gnostics are divided into a variety of sects, and it appears in the following passage that Hippolytus considered the Nicolaitans to be one of them. (On the other hand, Epiphanius does not classify them as Gnostics in Panarion *25.2.1, although at 25.7.1-2 and 26.1.1 he says that the gnostic sects have derived some of their teachings from Nicolaus and the Nicolaitans.) Hippolytus has derived the actual information given about them below from the Book of Revelation; and it does not appear that he had additional information.*

There are, however, among the Gnostics diversities of opinion; but we have decided that it would not be worthwhile to enumerate the silly doctrines of these [heretics], inasmuch as they are [too] numerous and devoid of reason, and full of blasphemy. Now, even those [of the heretics] who are of a more serious turn in regard of the Divinity, and have derived their systems of speculation from the Greeks, must stand convicted [of these charges]. But Nicolaus departed from correct doctrine, and was in the habit of inculcating indifferency of both life and food. And when the disciples [of Nicolaus] continued to offer insult to the Holy Spirit, John reproved them in the Apocalypse as fornicators and eaters of things offered unto idols.

2.4. Eusebius, *Ecclesiastical History* 3.29. Caesarea, ca. A.D. 325.

Source: Eusebius, *History of the Church*, trans. G. Williamson, 139.

Eusebius draws upon the Revelation of John, Acts 6:5, and the writings of Clement of Alexandria for his account of Nicolaus and the Nicolaitans. According to him, the sect had ceased to exist. Although he accepts the view that the sect was known for its sexual immorality, he goes against Clement in claiming that Nicolaus himself, as well as his son and daughters, could not be accused of it.

In their day, too, the very short-lived sect of the Nicolaitans came into existence. It is mentioned in the Revelation of John. These sectaries laid claim to Nicolaus, who like Stephen was one of the deacons appointed by the apostles to assist those in want. Clement of Alexandria in Book III of his *Miscellanies* gives this account of him:

This man, we are told, had an attractive young wife. After the Savior's Ascension the apostles accused him of jealousy, so he brought his wife forward and said that anyone who wished might have her. This action, we are told, followed from the injunction "the flesh must be treated with contempt"; and by following example and precept crudely and unquestioningly the members of the sect do in fact practise utter promiscuity. But my own information is that Nicolaus had no relations with any woman but his wife; and that, of his children, his daughters remained unmarried till the end of their days and his son's chastity was never in doubt. Such being the case, his bringing the wife whom he loved so jealously into the midst of the apostles was the renunciation of desire, and it was mastery of the pleasures so eagerly sought that taught him the rule "treat the flesh with contempt." For in obedience to the Savior's command, I imagine, he had no wish to serve two masters, pleasure and Lord. It is believed that Matthias also taught this, that we must fight against the flesh and treat it with contempt, never yielding to it for pleasure's sake, but must nourish the soul through faith and knowledge.

Chapter 3

Menander

Menander (first century and early second century A.D.) was a Samaritan by origin, a pupil of Simon Magus, and a proponent of an early form of Gnosticism in Syria. According to Irenaeus, Menander claimed to be the redeemer sent by the invisible god for the salvation of humanity. He was the teacher of Satorninus (Syrian Gnostic) and Basilides (Alexandrian Gnostic). According to Epiphanius (*Panarion* 22.2.1-4), the sect of Menander was virtually extinct by the end of the fourth century A.D.

3.1. Justin, *Apology* 1.26. Rome, ca. A.D. 155.

See reading 1.2 above.

3.2. Justin, *Apology* 1.56. Rome, ca. A.D. 155.

See reading 1.3 above.

3.3. Irenaeus, *Against Heresies* 1.23.5. Lyons, ca. A.D. 190.

Source: *Gnosis*, ed. W. Foerster, 1:33.

Irenaeus describes the basic theological teachings of Menander, including the doctrine of a higher, unknown god, the creation of the world by angels, and salvation through knowledge (gnosis). Distinctive to this sect is a form of baptism into its founder.

[Simon's] successor was Menander, a Samaritan by race, who himself attained to the highest point of magic. He said that the first Power was unknown to all, but that he himself was the one who was sent by the invisible as a saviour for the salvation of men. The world was made by angels, whom he too—like Simon—said had been brought forth by Ennoia. He added that he brought it about through the magic knowledge that was taught by him that he conquered the angels who created the world. His disciples received resurrection through baptism into him, and they can no longer die, but remain without growing old and immortal.

Cerinthus

Cerinthus (late first century and early second century A.D.) was an early gnostic teacher in Asia Minor. Little is known about his background. Hippolytus says that he was schooled in the "teaching of the Egyptians" (*Refutation* 7.21), which could imply that he was educated at Alexandria, although not necessarily. With Cerinthus there is for the first time the explicit teaching that Christ (as a spiritual power) descended upon Jesus at his baptism and departed from him prior to his crucifixion. A similar teaching is also expressed by Basilides (cf. Irenaeus, *Against Heresies* 1.24.4), the famous gnostic teacher of Alexandria some fifty years later.

4.1. Irenaeus, *Against Heresies* 1.26.1. Lyons, ca. A.D. 190.

Source: *Gnosis*, ed. W. Foerster, 1:35–36.

In this earliest extant text concerning Cerinthus, Irenaeus sets forth some of the major teachings of this early Gnostic. According to Irenaeus, Cerinthus taught that the world was created by an inferior god (a demiurge), that Jesus was the son of both Joseph and Mary (thus denying the virginal conception), and that Christ resided temporarily in Jesus for the purpose of revelation, but did not share in the death of the human figure Jesus.

A certain Cerinthus in Asia taught that the world was not made by the first God, but by a power which was widely separated and remote from that supreme power which is above the all, and did not know the God who is over all things. Jesus, he suggested, was not born of a virgin, for that seemed to him impossible, but was the son of Joseph and Mary, just like all the rest of men but far beyond them in justice and prudence and wisdom. After his baptism Christ descended upon him in the form of a dove, from the power that is over all things, and then he proclaimed the unknown Father and accomplished miracles. But at the end Christ separated again from Jesus, and Jesus suffered and was raised again, but Christ remained impassible, since he was pneumatic.

4.2. Hippolytus, *Refutation of All Heresies* 7.21. Rome, ca. A.D. 230.

Source: *The Ante-Nicene Fathers*, ed. A. Roberts and J. Donaldson, 5:114.

Hippolytus essentially repeats what has been said already by Irenaeus, except that he adds how Christ came upon Jesus, namely, in the form of a dove at his baptism, and that the human Jesus did in fact rise again after his death. Christ, however, did not suffer.

But a certain Cerinthus, himself being disciplined in the teaching of the Egyptians, asserted that the world was not made by the primal Deity, but by some virtue which was an offshoot from that Power which is above all things, and which [yet] is ignorant of the God that is above all. And he supposed that Jesus was not generated from a virgin, but that he was born son of Joseph and Mary, just in a manner similar with the rest of men, and that [Jesus] was more just and more wise [than all the human race]. And [Cerinthus alleges] that, after the baptism [of our Lord], Christ in form of a dove came down upon him, from that absolute sovereignty which is above all things. And then, [according to this heretic,] Jesus proceeded to preach the unknown Father, and in attestation [of his mission] to work miracles. It was, however, [the opinion of Cerinthus,] that ultimately Christ departed from Jesus, and that Jesus suffered and rose again; whereas that Christ, being spiritual, remained beyond the possibility of suffering.

4.3. Eusebius, *Ecclesiastical History* 3.28. Caesarea, ca. A.D. 325.

Source: Eusebius, *History of the Church*, trans. G. Williamson, 137–39.

Eusebius makes use of sources available to him concerning Cerinthus. One is a work by Gaius of Rome (ca. A.D. 160–230), another is by Bishop Dionysius of Alexandria (ca. 190–264), and the third is by Irenaeus. The sources are critical of Cerinthus and his followers largely for their immorality.

At the time under discussion, tradition tells us, another heretical sect was founded by Cerinthus. Gaius, whose words I quoted earlier, in the *Disputation* attributed to him writes this about him:

Then there is Cerinthus, who by revelations purporting to have been written by a great apostle presents us with tales of wonder falsely alleged to have been shown to him by angels. He declares that after the Resurrection the Kingdom of Christ will be on earth, and that carnal humanity will dwell in Jerusalem, once more enslaved to lusts and pleasures. And in his enmity towards the Scriptures of God, and his anxiety to lead men astray, he foretells a period of a thousand years given up to wedding festivities.

Dionysius again, who held the bishopric of the Alexandrian see in my own time, in Book II of his *Promises* makes certain statements about the Revelation of John on the basis of very ancient tradition. He then refers to Cerinthus in the following terms.

Cerinthus: the founder of a sect called Cerinthian after him, who wished to attach a name commanding respect to his own creation. This, they say, was the doctrine he taught—that Christ's Kingdom would be on earth; and the things he lusted after himself, being the slave of his body and sensual through and through, filled the heaven of his dreams—unlimited indulgence in gluttony and lechery at banquets, drinking-bouts, and wedding-feasts, or (to call these by what he thought more respectable names) festivals, sacrifices, and the immolation of victims.

That is how Dionysius puts it. Irenaeus in Book I of his *Heresies Answered* set out some of his more revolting errors, and in Book III has placed on record a memorable story. He states on the authority of Polycarp that one day John the apostle went into a bath-house to take a bath, but when he found that Cerinthus was inside he leapt from the spot and ran for the door, as he could not endure to be under the same roof. He urged his companions to do the same, calling out: "Let us get out of here, for fear the place falls in, now that Cerinthus, the enemy of the truth, is inside."

Chapter 5

On the Origins of Gnosticism

The writings gathered here exemplify the general assessment of the anti-heretical writers toward the origins and characteristics of various Gnostic movements.

The title "gnostic" derives from the Greek word *gnosis* meaning "knowledge." It is a title commonly given a diverse set of movements that, in spite of clear differences, have common characteristics. As indicated by the hymn cited from Hippolytus below (§ 5.3), it is also a designation used by adherents to at least some of the sects in describing its "path."

The complex gnostic movement(s), while originating in the first century, came to full flower in the second century with the development of various "schools" based upon the names and teachings of such teachers as Valentinus and Basilides. There is disagreement in the scholarly community as to whether Gnosticism, as an identifiable movement, originated prior to Christianity or arose simultaneously with it. It is, however, clear that by the end of the second century Gnosticism, while retaining certain variations on Christian teachings, had become mostly separate sects and movements.

The central tenet of Gnosticism revolves around the importance of a certain revealed "knowledge" (*gnosis*) imparted through Jesus, his apostles, and/or later teachers. This knowledge is from the true God who sent Jesus, not the false or upstart god (the demiurge) who created all the physical worlds as imperfect, a prison for lost and ignorant souls. Into some selected human beings was inserted a spark of divine spiritual substance which through the enlightenment of *gnosis* was able to be rescued from the imprisonment of evil matter. Evil, then, was less an aspect of sin than it was a function of material existence.

37

The nature of the *gnosis*, imparted as the means of salvation from physical existence, took a number of forms in the various schools. The gnostic systems took the form of philosophical speculation, severe asceticism (the intentional development of virtues through self-denial), radical antinomianism (libertinism), or amalgams of secret rites and knowledge of the means to pass through layer upon layer of mythological levels of existence toward pure spiritual existence. The teachings, rites, and mythology were often borrowed from many sources (pre- and post-Christian) and were gathered and presented in a syncretistic fashion. Human beings were often divided into two or three types: the *pneumatikoi*, or spiritual; the *sarkikoi*, the merely "fleshly" or physical; and sometimes the *psychikoi*, or "psychics" who were an intermediate class. Christ is an emissary of the true God, bringing *gnosis*. Christ's humanity is at times described in the literature as truly earthly, but most often he is seen as either assuming a truly human body, only temporarily inhabiting a human body (to be abandoned in time of suffering), or having an entirely phantasmal appearance.

These last descriptions of gnostic thought form the basis for the classic response of the antiheretical writers. The heresiologists found such ideas as the following objectionable: the "lie" that Jesus Christ was not truly human and divine; that the world is not God's creation, and created for human good; that all humans cannot be saved by virtue of the fact that some are merely "fleshly"; that they continued to find new "revealers" who led them astray; their unbelievable mythological structures; their occasional libertinism; and (because of their negative view of creation) a disdain for the value of martyrdom. We shall see each of these objections rehearsed in the following chapter and throughout Part II of this collection.

The discovery of the Nag Hammadi texts (referred to in the introduction) is expected to throw more light on the origins of Gnosticism. It is clear that Jewish and Greek thought in the first century was fertile ground for gnostic ideas. Christian and purely gnostic borrowings from this environment cannot be denied. Yet, it is still important to understand just how these ideas were received in what is now termed the "orthodox" Christian movement.

5.1. Justin, *Dialogue with Trypho* 35. Rome, ca. A.D. 155–60.

Source: *Saint Justin Martyr*, trans. T. B. Falls, 200–202.

In this selection, Justin responds to Trypho's observation that some who style
themselves "Christian" see no problem with openly libertine ideas toward non-
Christian worship practices, that is, eating meat sacrificed to idols. Justin's
point does not seem to directly address the question. Rather, he sees the observa-
tion of Trypho as indicative of the antinomian character of some Gnostics. He
cites Jesus' warning regarding "spirits of error" and "false apostles." He names
them as among the Marcionites, Valentinians, Saturnilians, and Basilidians.
He concludes with words regarding suffering and martyrdom, a fate often held
in disdain by Gnostics who see no value in suffering even death for the truth.

At this point, Trypho interrupted me by saying, "I know that there are
many who profess their faith in Jesus and are considered to be Christians,
yet they claim there is no harm in their eating meats sacrificed to idols."

"The fact that there are such men," I replied, "who pretend to be Christians and admit the crucified Jesus as their Lord and Christ, yet profess not
His doctrines, but those of the spirits of error, only tends to make us
adherents of the true and pure Christian doctrine more ardent in our faith
and more firm in the hope He announced to us. As we look about us, we
see events actually taking place which He predicted would happen in His
name. Indeed, He foretold: 'Many shall come in My name, clothed out-
wardly in sheep's clothing, but inwardly they are ravening wolves' [[Matt.
7:15]]. And: 'There shall be schisms and heresies.' And: 'Beware of false
prophets, who come to you in clothing of sheep, but inwardly they are
ravening wolves' [[Matt. 7:15]]. And: 'There shall arise many false Christs
and false Apostles, and they shall deceive many of the faithful' [[Matt.
24:11]].

"My friends, there were, and still are, many men who, in the name of
Jesus, come and teach others atheistic and blasphemous doctrines and
actions; we call them by the name of the originator of each false doctrine.
(For each has his own peculiar method of teaching how to blaspheme the
Creator of the universe, and Christ, whose Advent was foretold by Him,
and the God of Abraham, and of Isaac, and of Jacob. They are all outside
of our communion, for we know them for what they are, impious atheists
and wicked sinners, men who profess Jesus with their lips, but do not worship Him in their hearts. These men call themselves Christians in much
the same way as some Gentiles engrave the name of God upon their stat-
ues, and then indulge in every kind of wicked and atheistic rite.) Some of
these heretics are called Marcionites, some Valentinians, some Basilidians,
and some Saturnilians, and others by still other names, each designated by

the name of the founder of the system, just as each person who deems himself a philosopher, as I stated at the beginning of this discussion, claims that he must bear the name of the philosophy he favors from the founder of that particular school of philosophy. Not only from these events do we conclude, as I said, that Jesus possessed foreknowledge of what would happen to Him, but also from the many other happenings which He predicted would befall those who believe and profess that He is the Messiah. He even foretold all the suffering we would have to bear when those of our own household put us to death. Consequently, we can find no fault with either His words or actions. For this reason, too, we pray for you and for everyone else who hates us, that you may repent with us, and refrain from blaspheming Jesus Christ, who is proved to be totally without blame and reproach by His own deeds and by the miracles which even now are wrought in His name by the words of His teaching and the prophecies concerning Him. We pray, also, that you may believe in Jesus Christ, and thus at His second triumphant coming you will be saved and not be condemned by Him to the fire of hell."

5.2. Eusebius, *Ecclesiastical History* 4.7. Caesarea, ca. A.D. 325.

Source: Eusebius, *History of the Church*, trans. G. Williamson, 158–60.

Eusebius carries on a tradition of seeing Simon and Menander as the "twin heads of a snake" which results in the full-blown heresies of Saturnilus, Carpocrates, and Basilides. He isolates sources, few of which are extant. Again, a critical complaint from Eusebius is the Gnostics' disdain for the preservation of true teaching, especially if they deny the value of martyrdom. Likewise he holds up the secret magical rites of the Gnostics as those acts which set them apart from the truth. These rites, he says, have led many astray to vile acts upon one another. These acts, he says, were often attributed to all Christian teaching by those who only saw the gnostic rendering of them.

Like dazzling lights the churches were now shining all over the world, and to the limits of the human race faith in our Savior and Lord Jesus Christ was at its peak, when the demon who hates the good, sworn enemy of truth and inveterate foe of man's salvation, turned all his weapons against the Church. In earlier days he had attacked her with persecutions from without; but now that he was debarred from this, he resorted to unscrupulous impostors as instruments of spiritual corruption and ministers of destruction, and employed new tactics, contriving by every possible means that impostors and cheats, by cloaking themselves with the same name as our religion, should at one and the same time bring to the abyss of destruction every believer they could entrap, and by their own actions and endeavors turn those ignorant of the Faith away from the path that leads to the message of salvation.

Thus it was that from Menander—who was mentioned above as successor to Simon—proceeded a power with the two mouths and twin heads of a snake, which set up the originators of two heresies, Saturninus, an Antiochene by birth, and Basilides of Alexandria, who—one in Syria and one in Egypt—established schools of detestable heresies. For the most part Saturnilus taught the same false doctrines as Menander, as Irenaeus makes clear; but Basilides, under the pretence of deeper mysteries, extended his fantasies into the infinite, inventing monstrous fictions to support his impious heresy. Consequently, while a great number were busy at that time fighting for the truth and eloquently championing the beliefs of the apostles and the Church, some also set down on paper for the benefit of later generations the means of defence against these very heresies.

I have in my hands, from the pen of a very well-known writer of the day, Agrippa Castor, a most effective refutation of Basilides, which unmasks the man's clever imposture. In laying bare his mysteries he says that Basilides compiled twenty-four books on the gospel and that he named as his prophets Barcabbas and Barcoph, inventing for himself several others, creatures of his imagination, and calling them by barbarous names to amaze those who gape at such things. He taught that there was no objection to eating meat offered to idols, or to cheerfully forswearing the Faith in times of persecution. Like Pythagoras he enjoined on his neophytes a five-year silence. Other facts of the same sort about Basilides are catalogued by Agrippa, who thus admirably exposed the erroneous character of this heresy.

Irenaeus also writes that contemporary with these was Carpocrates, father of another heresy known as that of the Gnostics. These claimed to transmit Simon's magic arts, not secretly like Basilides but quite openly, as if this was something marvellous, preening themselves as it were on the spells which they cast by sorcery, on dream-bringing familiar spirits, and on other goings-on of the same sort. In keeping with this they teach that all the vilest things must be done by those who intend to go through with their initiation into these "mysteries" or rather abominations; for in no other way can they escape the "cosmic rulers" than by rendering to them all the due performance of unspeakable rites.

Thus it came about that with the help of these ministers the demon that delights in evil enslaved their pitiable dupes and brought them to ruin, furnishing the unbelieving heathen with ample grounds for speaking ill of the divine message, since the talk to which they gave rise circulated widely and involved the whole Christian people in calumny. This was the main reason why that wicked and outrageous suspicion regarding us was current among the unbelievers of that time—the suspicion that we practised unlawful intercourse with mothers and sisters and took part in unhallowed feasts.

But this propaganda brought Carpocrates no lasting success, for Truth asserted herself, and with the march of time shone with increasing light. For by her activity the machinations of her foes were promptly shown up and extinguished, though one after another new heresies were invented, the earlier ones constantly passing away and disappearing, in different ways at different times, into forms of every shape and character. But the splendor of the Catholic and only true Church, always remaining the same and unchanged, grew steadily in greatness and strength, shedding on every race of Greeks and non-Greeks alike the majestic, spotless, free, sober, pure light of her inspired citizenship and philosophy. Thus the passage of time extinguished the calumnies against the whole of our doctrine, and our teaching remained alone, everywhere victorious and acknowledged as supreme in dignity and sobriety, in divine and philosophic doctrines, so that no one today could dare to subject our Faith to vile abuse or to any such misrepresentation as in the past those who conspired against us were in the habit of using.

5.3. Hippolytus, *Refutation of All Heresies* 5.1, 2, 5. Rome, ca. A.D. 230.

Source: *Ante-Nicene Fathers*, ed. A. Roberts and J. Donaldson, 5:47–49, 51, 58.

Hippolytus, in this passage, sees the origins of the Gnostics in the teachings of the Naasenes who, according to him, borrowed from a variety of ancient sources, patched pieces together, and passed it off as a new revelation. They teach a primordial "son of man" who is hermaphrodite, of three parts, rational, physical, and earthly. These three parts descended into Jesus, each speaking in the guise of the others according to their own proper quality. Human existence and sexuality are an enslavement and punishment of the "Perfect Man," the work of the demiurge. Jesus came, according to their hymn, to lead souls, through knowledge, along the right path (filled with mysteries) to salvation. Our principle sources for ideas on the Naasenes are Hippolytus, Irenaeus, and Origen.

1. For from philosophers the heresiarchs deriving starting-points, [and] like cobblers patching together, according to their own particular interpretation, the blunders of the ancients, have advanced them as novelties to those that are capable of being deceived, as we shall prove in the following books. In the remainder [of our work], the opportunity invites us to approach the treatment of our proposed subjects, and to begin from those who have presumed to celebrate a serpent, the originator of the error [in question], through certain expressions devised by the energy of his own [ingenuity]. The priests, then, and champions of the system, have been first those who have been called Naasseni, being so denominated from the Hebrew language, for the serpent is called naas [in Hebrew]. Subsequently, however, they have styled themselves Gnostics, alleging that they alone have sounded the depths of knowledge. Now, from the system of these [speculators], many, detaching parts, have constructed a heresy which, though with several subdivisions, is essentially one, and they explain precisely the same [tenets]; though conveyed under the guise of different opinions, as the following discussion, according as it progresses, will prove.

These [Naasseni], then, according to the system advanced by them, magnify, [as the originating cause] of all things else, a man and a son of man. And this man is a hermaphrodite, and is denominated among them Adam; and hymns many and various are made to him. The hymns, however — to be brief — are couched among them in some such form as this: "From thee [comes] father, and through thee [comes] mother, two names immortal, progenitors of Æons, O denizen of heaven, thou illustrious man." But they divide him as Geryon into three parts. For, say they, of this man one part is rational, another physical, another earthly. And they suppose that the knowledge of him is the originating principle of the capacity for a knowledge of God, expressing themselves thus: "The originating principle of perfection is the knowledge of man, while the knowledge of God is absolute perfection." All these qualities, however — rational, and physical, and earthly — have, [the Naassene] says, retired and descended into one man simultaneously — Jesus, who was born of Mary. And these three men [the Naassene] says, are in the habit of speaking [through Jesus] at the same time together, each from their own proper substances to those peculiarly their own. For, according to these, there are three kinds of all existent things — angelic, physical, earthly; and there are three churches — angelic, physical, earthly; and the names of these are elect, called, captive. ...

2. They ask what is the soul, and whence, and what kind in its nature, that, coming to the man and moving him, it should enslave and punish the image of the Perfect Man. They do not, however, [on this point] institute an inquiry from the Scriptures, but ask this [question] also from the mystic [rites]. And they affirm that the soul is very difficult to discover, and hard to understand; for it does not remain in the same figure or the same form invariably, or in one passive condition, that either one could express it by a sign or comprehend it substantially. ...

For [the Naassene] says, there is the hermaphrodite man. According to this account of theirs, the intercourse of woman with man is demonstrated, in conformity with such teaching, to be an exceedingly wicked and filthy [practice]. ...

That is, from the blessed man from above, or the primal man or Adam, as it seems to them, souls have been conveyed down here into a creation of clay, that they may serve the Demiurge of this creation, Ialdabaoth, a fiery God, a fourth number; for so they call the Demiurge and father of the formal world....

5. This psalm of theirs has been composed, by which they seem to celebrate all the mysteries of the error [advanced by] them in a hymn, couched in the following terms:

> The world's producing law was Primal Mind,
> And next was First-born's outpoured Chaos;
> And third, the soul received its law of toil:
> Encircl'd, therefore, with an aqueous form,
> With care o'erpowered it succumbs to death.
> Now holding sway, it eyes the light,
> And now it weeps on misery flung;
> Now it mourns, now it thrills with joy;
> Now it wails, now it hears its doom;
> Now it hears its doom, now it dies,
> And now it leaves us, never to return.
> It, hapless straying, treads the maze of ills.
> But Jesus said, Father, behold,

A strife of ills across the earth
Wanders from thy breath [of wrath];
But bitter Chaos [man] seeks to shun,
And knows not how to pass it through.
On this account, O Father, send me;
Bearing seals, I shall descend;
Through ages whole I'll sweep,
All mysteries I'll unravel
And forms of Gods I'll show:
And secrets of the saintly path,
Styled "Gnosis," I'll impart.

Part II

Second-Century Gnostics

Carpocrates and the Carpocratians

Carpocrates (second century A.D.) was a gnostic teacher in his native city of Alexandria, Egypt, in the middle of the second century. He founded a school, and his followers were called Carpocratians. He taught that the world was created by intermediaries (angels) that had been created by the Father. Moreover, he and his followers held that Jesus was the son of Joseph (and Mary) and was distinct from the rest of humanity only in the purity of his soul. But the distinction between Christ and the Gnostic becomes blurred in this system, for the Gnostic can become like Jesus. Indeed, some of the Carpocratians believed that they were even "stronger" than Jesus, and still others claimed superiority to his disciples, including Peter and Paul. Among other things, the Carpocratians also taught the transmigration of souls and a libertine ethic. The sect seems to have ceased existing sometime in the fourth century A.D.

6.1. Irenaeus, *Against Heresies* 1.25.1-6. Lyons, ca. A.D. 190.

Source: *Gnosis*, ed. W. Foerster, 1:36–38.

According to Irenaeus, the Carpocratians called themselves Gnostics. They claimed a secret tradition from Jesus that was transmitted to them (the worthy) from the apostles. Further, they claimed that Jesus was the son of Joseph, that good and evil are a matter of opinion only, and that the body is a prison from which the true Gnostic wins release.

1. Carpocrates and his disciples say that the world and what is in it was made by angels, who are much inferior to the unbegotten Father. Jesus was

born of Joseph and like the rest of men, but he was distinct from the rest in that, since his soul was strong and pure, it remembered what it had seen in the regions of the unbegotten God: and for this reason power was sent down to him that he might escape the world-creators by it. It passed through them all and was set free in all, and ascended up to him, and likewise the [souls] which embraced the like. They say that the soul of Jesus was lawfully nurtured in the traditions of the Jews, but despised them and thereby obtained powers by which he vanquished the passions which attach to men for punishment.   2. The soul which like the soul of Jesus is able to despise the creator archons likewise receives power to do the same things. Hence they have come to such presumption that some say they are like Jesus, some actually affirm that they are even stronger than he, and some [declare] that they are superior to his disciples, like Peter and Paul and the other Apostles; they are in no way inferior to Jesus himself. Their souls derive from the same surroundings, and therefore likewise despise the creators of the world and are counted worthy of the same power, and return again to the same place. But if anyone despises the things here more than he, he can be greater than he.   3. They practise magic arts and incantations, love potions and love-feasts, familiar spirits and dream-inducers, and the other evil things, saying that they already have the power to prevail over the archons and creators of this world, and not only that, but over all that is created in it. ... They live a dissipated life and hold an impious doctrine, and use the name as a cloak for their wickedness. ...   4. So abandoned are they in their recklessness that they claim to have in their power and to be able to practise anything whatsoever that is ungodly and impious. They say that conduct is good and evil only in the opinion of men. And after the transmigration the souls must have been in every kind of life and every kind of deed—if a man does not in one life do at one and the same time all that is not merely forbidden for us to speak or hear but may not even enter into the thought of our minds, nor may one believe if men in our cities do anything of the sort—so that, as their scriptures say, their souls have been in every enjoyment of life and when they depart [from the body] they are deficient in nothing; but they must labour lest perchance, because something is lacking to their freedom, they be compelled to be sent again into bodies.

That is why Jesus spoke this parable: "When you are with your adversary on the way, take pains to get free of him, lest he deliver you to the judge and the judge to his servant, and cast you into prison. Amen, I tell you, you will not come out thence until you have paid the last farthing"

[Matt. 5:25f. par.]. The adversary, they say, is one of the angels who are in the world, whom they call the devil, saying that he was appointed to bring the souls which have perished from the world to the Prince. He, they say, is the first of the world-creators, and he hands over such souls to another angel who serves him, that he may shut them up in other bodies. For they say that the body is a prison. And the saying "You will not come out thence until you have paid the last farthing" they interpret to mean that one does not come out from the power of the angels who made the world.

So long must [a man] continue to be reincarnated, until he has been in absolutely every action in the world. When no more is lacking, then his soul, set free, goes to that God who is above the creator angels, and so it is saved. All souls, whether they have gone ahead to engage in every action at one coming [into the flesh], or whether they migrate from body to body or, inserted into every kind of life, fill up and pay their dues, all souls are liberated, so that they may no longer be in the body.

5. Now if these things are done among them which are godless and unrighteous and forbidden, I could not believe. But in their writings it is so written, and they themselves explain thus: Jesus, they say, spoke in a mystery to his disciples and apostles privately, and charged them to hand these things on to the worthy and those who assented. For through faith and love are [men] saved. All other things are indifferent, being accounted now good, now evil, according to the opinion of men, but nothing is evil by nature.

6. Some of them mark their own disciples by branding them on the back of the right ear-lobe. Hence also Marcellina, who came to Rome under Anicetus [ca. A.D. 154–65], since she was of this doctrine led astray many. They call themselves gnostics. They have also images, some painted, some too made of other material, and say they are the form of Christ made by Pilate in that time when Jesus was with men. These they crown, and they set them forth with the images of the philosophers of the world, Pythagoras, Plato, Aristotle, and the rest; and their other observance concerning them they carry out like the heathen.

6.2. Clement of Alexandria, *Stromateis* 3.2.5, 10. Alexandria, ca.
     A.D. 200.

Source: *Alexandrian Christianity*, ed. John E. L. Oulton and H. Chadwick, 42, 45.

Clement lived in the same city as the followers of Carpocrates, although he was not a contemporary of the founder of the movement. In this first excerpt he mentions Epiphanes, who was a son of Carpocrates and a leader of the movement, although Clement says that he died at the age of seventeen. Nevertheless, he had written a book, from which Clement derives some information.

5. But the followers of Carpocrates and Epiphanes think that wives should be common property. Through them the worst calumny has become current against the Christian name.

Clement is sarcastic in speaking of the Carpocratians as "excellent." They must have observed "love feasts" (or agape meals) as did other Christian groups, but Clement says that they should not be called that. He goes on to describe their libertine behavior at such meals.

10. These then are the doctrines of the excellent Carpocratians. These, so they say, and certain other enthusiasts for the same wickednesses, gather together for feasts (I would not call their meeting an Agape), men and women together. After they have sated their appetites ("on repletion Cypris, the goddess of love, enters," as it is said), then they overturn the lamps and so extinguish the light that the shame of their adulterous "righteousness" is hidden, and they have intercourse where they will and with whom they will. After they have practised community of use in this love-feast, they demand by daylight of whatever women they wish that they will be obedient to the law of Carpocrates—it would not be right to say the law of God.

6.3. Hippolytus, *Refutation of all Heresies* 7.20. Rome, ca. A.D. 230.

Source: *The Ante-Nicene Fathers*, ed. A. Roberts and J. Donaldson, 5:113–14.

Hippolytus gives essentially the same information about the Carpocratians as Irenaeus. He makes additional claims, however, on the Carpocratian teaching concerning Christ, who came down upon Jesus from the superior God, and who ascended to God after revealing divine secrets to his followers.

Carpocrates affirms that the world and the things in it were made by angels, far inferior to the unbegotten Father; and that Jesus was generated of Joseph, and that, having been born similar to [other] men, He was more just than the rest [of the human race]. And [Carpocrates asserts] that the soul [of Jesus], inasmuch as it was made vigorous and undefiled, remembered the things seen by it in its converse with the unbegotten God. And [Carpocrates maintains] that on this account there was sent down upon [Jesus] by that [God] a power, in order that through it He might be enabled to escape the world-making [angels]. And [he says] that this power, having passed through all, and having obtained liberty in all, again ascended to God [Himself]. And [he alleges] that in the same condition with [the soul of Jesus are all the souls] that embrace similar objects of desire with the [power just alluded to]. And they assert that the soul of Jesus, [though] according to law, it was disciplined in Jewish customs, [in reality] despised them. And [he says] that on this account [Jesus] received powers whereby He rendered null and void the passions incidental to men for their punishment. And [he argues], therefore, that the [soul], which, similarly with that soul of Christ, is able to despise the world-making Archons, receives in like manner power for the performance of similar acts. Wherefore, also, [according to Carpocrates, there are persons who] have attained unto such a degree of pride as to affirm some of themselves to be equal to Jesus Himself, whereas others among them to be even still more powerful. But [they also contend] that some enjoy an excellence above the disciples of that [Redeemer], for instance Peter and Paul, and the rest of the Apostles, and that these are in no respect inferior to Jesus. And [Carpocrates asserts] that the souls of these have originated from that supernal power, and that consequently they, as equally despising the world-making [angels], have been deemed worthy of the same power, and [of the privilege] to ascend to the same [place]. If, however, any one would despise earthly concerns more than did that [Saviour, Carpocrates says] that such a one would be able to become superior to [Jesus. The followers of this heretic] practise their magical arts and incantations, and spells and voluptuous feasts. And [they are in the habit of invoking the aid of] subordinate demons and dream-senders, and [of resorting to] the rest of the tricks [of sorcery], alleging that they possess power for now acquiring sway over the Archons and makers of this world, nay, even over all the works that are in it.

[Now these heretics] have themselves been sent forth by Satan, for the purpose of slandering before the Gentiles the divine name of the Church. [And the devil's object is,] that men hearing, now after one fashion and now after another, the doctrines of those [heretics], and thinking that all of us are people of the same stamp, may turn away their ears from the preaching of the truth, or that they also, looking, [without abjuring,] upon all the tenets of those [heretics], may speak hurtfully of us. [The followers of Carpocrates] allege that the souls are transferred from body to body, so far as that they may fill up [the measure of] all their sins. When, however, not one [of these sins] is left, [the Carpocratians affirm that the soul] is then emancipated, and departs unto that God above of the world-making angels, and that in this way all souls will be saved. If, however, some [souls], during the presence of the soul in the body for one life, may by anticipation become involved in the full measure of transgressions, they, [according to these heretics,] no longer undergo metempsychosis. [Souls of this sort,] however, on paying off at once all trespasses, will [the Carpocratians say,] be emancipated from dwelling any more in a body. Certain, likewise, of these [heretics] brand their own disciples in the back parts of the lobe of the right ear. And they make counterfeit images of Christ, alleging that these were in existence at the time [during which our Lord was on earth, and that they were fashioned] by Pilate.

6.4. Eusebius, *Ecclesiastical History* 4.7. Caesarea, ca. A.D. 325.

See 5.2 above.

6.5. Epiphanius, *Panarion* 27.3.3-4. Salamis, Cyprus, A.D. 375–78.

Source: *Panarion*, trans. P. R. Amidon, 84.

According to Epiphanius, the Carpocratians actually designated themselves "Christians." Most of what is recorded by him elsewhere in this portion of the Panarion *is similar to what has already been found in previous sources.*

[3.3] Now it is Satan who has prepared and sent them forth to be a reproach and a scandal to God's church. For they call themselves Christians, this being what Satan has planned in order to scandalize the pagans by means of them and to turn them from the benefit to be derived from God's holy church and from the true doctrine because of their lawless deeds and incurably evil works, [3.4] that the pagans, who despise their continual lawless deeds and suppose that those who belong to God's holy church are of the same sort, may be turned, as I said, from listening to the true teaching of God or may even, when they see certain people [behaving so irreligiously?], blaspheme [us] all in the same manner. For this reason most of the pagans wherever they see such people have nothing to do with us either, whether in everyday affairs or in their disposition of mind or in hearing the word of God, and they refuse to listen to us, frightened as they are by the irreligious behavior of these lawless people.

Saturninus

Saturninus (second century A.D.)—also known as Satornilus—was a gnostic teacher who originated from "Antioch by Daphne" and taught in Syria, according to Irenaeus (*Against Heresies* 1.24.1). Daphne, mentioned in 2 Maccabees 4:33, was located near Antioch of Syria and was known for its temple of Apollo. A pupil of Menander, Saturninus taught that the world was created by intermediaries (angelic beings), who had in turn been created by the Father, who was otherwise unknown. The God of the Old Testament, he claimed, was one of these intermediaries. Christ came into this world in human form to redeem those persons who have "the spark of life in them" and to destroy the "God of the Jews" (Irenaeus, *Against Heresies* 1.24.2). He also taught an ascetic ethic, renouncing marriage and the eating of meat.

7.1. Irenaeus, *Against Heresies* 1.24.1-2. Lyons, ca. A.D. 190.

Source: *Gnosis*, ed. W. Foerster, 1:40–41.

According to Irenaeus, the highest God for Saturninus is "unknown to all" and can be known only by revelation through Christ to believers—persons who have "the spark of life in them." His view of Christ is a "docetic" one, that is, that Christ simply appeared to be a human being. In these ways Saturninus can be classified as a Gnostic.

1. From these [Simon and Menander] Saturninus, who was from Antioch by Daphne, and Basilides took their impulse and taught divergent doctrines, the one in Syria, the other in Alexandria. Saturninus, like Menander, taught one Father unknown to all, who made angels,

archangels, powers, and authorities. The world and everything in it came into being from seven angels, and man also was a creation of angels. When a shining image appeared from the supreme power above, which they were not able to detain, he says, because it immediately sped back upwards, they exhorted one another, saying: "Let us make a man after the image and likeness" [Gen. 1:26]. When this was done, he says, and their creation could not stand erect because of the powerlessness of the angels, but crept like a worm, then the power above took pity on him because he had been made in his likeness, and sent a spark of life which raised the man up, equipped him with limbs, and made him live. This spark of life, he says, hastens back after death to its own kind, and the rest is resolved into that from which it came into being.

2. The Saviour he assumed to be unbegotten, incorporeal, and without form, but appeared in semblance as a man. The God of the Jews, he says, was one of the angels; and because all the archons wanted to destroy the Father, Christ came for the destruction of the God of the Jews and the salvation of those who believe in him; these are they who have the spark of life in them. He was the first to say that two kinds of men had been moulded by the angels, the one wicked, the other good. And since the demons helped the wicked, the Saviour came for the destruction of the wicked men and demons, and the salvation of the good. Marriage and procreation, he says, are of Satan. Many of his followers abstain also from animal food, and through this feigned continence they lead many astray. Of the prophecies, some were spoken by the angels who created the world and some by Satan, of whom he teaches that he was himself an angel who acted against the world-creators, and especially the God of the Jews.

7.2. Hippolytus, *Refutation of All Heresies* 7.16. Rome, ca. A.D. 230.

Source: *The Ante-Nicene Fathers*, ed. A. Roberts and J. Donaldson, 5:109–10.

More than Irenaeus, Hippolytus discusses the cosmology of Saturninus and his followers. He relates their teaching concerning the creation of the world and how even "the God of the Jews" is but one of the angels that created the world.

But one Saturninus, who flourished about the same period with Basilides, but spent his time in Antioch, [a city] of Syria, propounded opinions akin to whatever [tenets] Menander [advanced]. He asserts that there is one Father, unknown to all—He who had made angels, archangels, principalities, [and] powers; and that by certain angels, seven [in number], the world was made, and all things that are in it. And [Saturninus affirms] that man was a work of angels. There had appeared above from [the Being of] absolute sway, a brilliant image; and when [the angels] were not able to detain this, on account of its immediately, he says, returning with rapidity upwards, they exhorted one another, saying, "Let us make man in our likeness and image" [[Gen. 1:26]]. And when the figure was formed, and was not, he says, able, owing to the impotence of the angels, to lift up itself, but continued writhing as a worm, the Power above, compassionating him on account of his having been born in its own image, sent forth a scintillation of life, which raised man up, and caused him to have vitality. [Saturninus] asserts that this scintillation of life rapidly returns after death to those things that are of the same order of existence; and that the rest, from which they have been generated, are resolved into those. And the Saviour he supposed to be unbegotten and incorporeal, and devoid of figure. [Saturninus,] however, [maintained that Jesus] was manifested as man in appearance only. And he says that the God of the Jews is one of the angels, and, on account of the Father's wishing to deprive of sovereignty all the Archons, that Christ came for the overthrow of the God of the Jews, and for the salvation of those that believe upon Him; and that these have in them the scintillation of life. For he asserted that two kinds of men had been formed by the angels,—one wicked, but the other good. And, since demons from time to time assisted wicked [men, Saturninus affirms] that the Saviour came for the overthrow of worthless men and demons, but for the salvation of good men. And he affirms that marriage and procreation are from Satan. The majority, however, of those who belong to this [heretic's school] abstain from animal food likewise, [and] by this affectation of asceticism [make many their dupes]. And [they maintain] that the prophecies have been uttered, partly by the world-making angels, and partly by Satan, who is also the very angel whom they suppose to act in antagonism to the cosmical [angels], and especially to the God of the Jews. These, then, are in truth the tenets of Saturninus.

7.3. Epiphanius, *Panarion* 23.1.10—2.6. Salamis, Cyprus, A.D. 375–78.

Source: *Panarion*, trans. P. R. Amidon, 66.

Epiphanius adds little in the following passage to what has been said already in the writings of Irenaeus and Hippolytus. He does, however, explicitly say that Saturninus taught "the falsely named 'knowledge,'" thus classifying him as a Gnostic.

[1.10] The magician said that Christ himself came in human shape and appearance only, and did everything only seemingly: being born, walking about, being seen, and suffering.

[2.1] From this man the falsely named "knowledge" begins again to add to the abyss of its wickedness, having taken its origin and inspiration from Simon, but adding a great deal of other nonsense which we shall speak about later in our refutation of it. [2.2] For he says, speaking of the angels, that even the God of the Jews is one of them, that he and they separated from the upper power, that the Savior was sent from the Father without the knowledge of the powers to overthrow the God of the Jews and to save those who believed [in him], and that those are saved who are of this sect, who have the spark of the Father above. [2.3] For he says that in the beginning two men were made, one good and one bad, from whom come the two races of men in the world, good and bad. [2.4] But since the demons were helping the bad, in the last days, as I said, the Savior came to help good men and overthrow the bad and the demons. [2.5] The imposter says that marriage and procreation are from Satan, so that most of them are vegetarians in order to entice people into their deception by the way of life they affect. [2.6] The magician adds that some prophecies were made by the angels who made the world, and some by Satan. Satan himself he says is an angel who opposes the angels who made the world, and especially the God of the Jews.

Basilides and the Basilidians

Basilides (second century A.D.) may have been a Syrian by birth, since he is said to have been a disciple of Menander of Syria (Irenaeus, *Against Heresies* 1.24.1), but he taught in Alexandria, Egypt, around A.D. 120–40. Next to Valentinus he is the most prolific and influential gnostic teacher of the era. He wrote many books, which are now lost, except for a few fragments. He taught that the highest God, the Father, is unknown to ordinary humans. From this God has emanated a series of spiritual beings, the first of which was Nous (Greek for "Mind"). From Nous came Logos ("Reason" or "Word") and then three other personified powers (Phronesis, Sophia, and Dynamis) in succession, followed by the "powers, principalities, and angels" (Irenaeus, *Against Heresies* 1.24.3). This latter group created the highest heaven, followed by a series of heavens, 365 in all, created by additional angelic powers. The last group, led by the God of the Jews, created the heaven seen from earth and created the earth itself.

Redemption, according to the system of Basilides, comes through the work of Nous, also known as the Christ, who has descended from the highest heaven into the world in the appearance of a human being. However, he did not suffer, for at the crucifixion Christ and Simon of Cyrene (mentioned at Mark 15:21 and par.) in effect traded places, each being transformed, so that Simon was crucified, while Christ stood by laughing at the event. After the crucifixion had taken place, Christ ascended back to the Father, knowing from whence he had come. Salvation comes to the souls (not the bodies) of those persons who have knowledge (*gnosis*) of the system, thereby knowing their origin and destiny, for such knowledge delivers them from the power of the powers (angelic beings) that have created and govern the world. There is a spiritual elitism in this, for salvation is possible only to a few (the Gnostics) who have learned what the

Savior has revealed; these are, in number, only "one in a thousand and two in ten thousand" (Irenaeus, *Against Heresies* 1.24.6). Since the body is not saved, but subject to corruption, it is of no concern to the Gnostic; and therefore conduct, whether good or bad in the eyes of others, is a matter of indifference.

8.1. Irenaeus, *Against Heresies* 1.24.3-7. Lyons, ca. A.D. 190.

Source: *Gnosis*, ed. W. Foerster, 1:59–61.

In this passage Irenaeus first spells out the details of the system of Basilides regarding the creation of the universe through a series of emanations. Then he goes on to speak of Basilides' view of Christ and his saving work. According to Basilides, one shall not speak of Christ as crucified.

3. Basilides, so that he may appear to have discovered something higher and more like the truth, vastly extends the content of his teaching. He presents Nous [[mind]] originating first from the unoriginate Father, and Logos [[word]] originating from him, then from Logos Phronesis [prudence], from Phronesis Sophia [wisdom] and Dynamis [force], from Dynamis and Sophia the powers, principalities, and angels, who are also called the first, and by them the first heaven was made. From their emanation other angels were made, and they made another heaven like the first; and in the same way when other [angels] were made by emanation from them, copies of those who were above them, they fashioned a further, third, heaven. From the third, a fourth group of downward descending ones, and successively in the same way more and more principalities and angels were made, and 365 heavens. That is why the year has that number of days, in accordance with the number of heavens.   4. But those angels who possess the last heaven, which is the one seen by us, set up everything in the world, and divided between them the earth and the nations upon it. Their chief is the one known as the God of the Jews; because he wished to subject the other nations to his own men, that is, to the Jews, all the other principalities opposed him and worked against him. For this reason the other nations were alienated from his nation.

The unoriginate and ineffable Father, seeing their disastrous plight, sent his first-born Nous—he is the one who is called the Christ—to liberate those who believe in him from the power of those who made the world. To their [the angels'] nations he appeared on earth as a man and performed miracles. For the same reason also he did not suffer, but a certain Simon of Cyrene was compelled to carry his cross for him; and this [Simon] was transformed by him [Jesus] so that he was thought to be Jesus himself, and was crucified through ignorance and error. Jesus, however, took on the form of Simon, and stood by laughing at them. For since he was an incorporeal power and the Nous of the unborn Father, he was transformed in whatever way he pleased, and in this way he ascended to him who had sent him, laughing at them, since he could not be held and was invisible to all. Therefore those who know these things have been set free from the rulers who made the world. It is not right to confess him who was crucified, and him who came in the form of a man and was supposed to have been crucified and was called Jesus and was sent by the Father in order by this dispensation to undo the works of the creators of the world. Thus [he says] if anyone confesses the crucified, he is still a slave, and under the power of those who made the bodies; he who denies [him] has been set free from them, and knows the [saving] dispensation made by the unoriginate Father.

5. Salvation is for their soul alone; the body is by nature corruptible. He says that even the prophecies themselves came from the rulers who made the world, and that the law in particular came from their chief, him who led the people out of the land of Egypt [cf. Exod. 20:2]. They despise things sacrificed to idols and think nothing of them, but enjoy them without any anxiety at all. They also enjoy the other [pagan] festivals and all [that] appetite [prompts]. They also engage in magic, conjuring of the dead, spells, calling up of spirits, and all the other occult practices. They even invent certain angelic names, and declare that some belong to the first heaven, others to the second; and one by one they attempt to expound the names, the rulers, the angels, and the powers of the 365 false heavens. In this way the name of the world, in which they say the Saviour came down and went up again, is Caulacau [[from a Hebrew expression for "line upon line" in Isa. 28:10]].

6. Accordingly, the person who has learnt these things, and knows all the angels and their origins, becomes invisible and incomprehensible to all the angels and powers, just as it happened also to Caulacau. And just as the son was unknown to all, so they also should be recognized by none; but whereas they know them all and pass through them all, they are themselves invisible and unknown to all. "For know thou them all," they say, "but let none know thee." Thus those who are such are always ready to deny it—or rather, suffering for the name is even quite impossible for them, since they

are like everybody [else]. Not many, either, can know these [doctrines], but one in a thousand and two in [ten thousand]. They say they are no longer Jews, but not yet Christians; and their secrets must not be uttered at all, but they must keep them concealed by silence.

7. They arrange the positions of the 365 heavens in the same way as the astrologers. They accept their principles, and have transferred them to their own brand of doctrine. But the chief of those [365 heavens] is Abraxas, and for this reason [they allege] he has 365 numbers in him [i.e. his name has the numerical value 365].

8.2. Hippolytus, *Refutation of All Heresies* 7.20.1—27.13. Rome, ca. A.D. 230.

Source: *Gnosis*, ed. W. Foerster, 1:64–74.

Hippolytus discusses in detail certain aspects of the system of Basilides, particularly the thoughts of the highest God, the creation of the world, and the origination of the Son. He also discusses the understanding of the gospel as taught by Basilides, which turns out to be knowledge (gnosis) of those things taught by Basilides.

20.1. Basilides and his legitimate son and disciple Isifore say that Matthias spoke to them secret words which he heard from the Saviour in secret discourse. ...

2. There was a time, says he, when there was nothing; not even the nothing was there, but simply, clearly, and without any sophistry there was nothing at all. When I say "there was," he says I do not indicate a Being, but in order to signify what I want to express I say, says he, that there was nothing at all.

3. For that, says he, is not simply something ineffable which is named [indicated]; we call it ineffable, but it is not even ineffable. For what is not [even] inexpressible is called "not even inexpressible," but is above every name that is named. For the names do not even suffice, he says, for the world, so multiform is it, but fall short. And I do not have it in me to find correct names for everything; rather it is proper to comprehend ineffably, without using names, the characteristics of the things which are to be named. For [the existence of] the same designation[s for different things] has caused the hearers confusion and error about the things. ...

21.1. Since therefore there was nothing, no matter, no substance, nothing insubstantial, nothing simple, nothing composite, nothing non-composite, nothing imperceptible [non-subjective], no man, no angel, no god, nothing at all that can be named or can be apprehended by sense-perception, nothing of the mental things and thus [also nothing of all that which] can be simply described in even more subtle ways, the non-existent God … without intelligence, without perception, without will, without resolve, without impulse, without desire, wished to make a world.   2. I say "he wished," he says, for want of a word, wish, intelligence, and perception being excluded. By "world" [I mean] not the flat, divisible world which later divided itself, but a world-seed.   3. The world-seed had everything in it, as the mustard-seed contains everything together in a tiny space, the roots, the stem, the branches, the innumerable leaves, the grains of seed which come from the plant, which in turn again and again spread seed for yet more plants.   4. Thus the non-existent God made a non-existent world from the non-existent, inasmuch as he deposited and planted one single seed which contained in itself the whole seed-mixture of the world. Or, to make plainer what they say, just as the egg of a variegated and many-coloured [species], although it is only single, yet has within it many shapes of multiform, multicoloured, and heterogeneous things, so, says he, the non-existent seed deposited by the non-existent God has [within it] the multiform and heterogeneous seed-mixture of the world.

22.1. There was thus stored up in the seed everything that can be mentioned, or if it is not to be found can be left out, everything that was going to be suitable for the world that would arise from the seed, the world which of necessity at its own season expands by enlargement derived from a God so great and of such a kind. [It is] just as with a new-born child. We see how later the teeth and the paternal characteristics and the intelligence are acquired, and whatever else did not previously exist, but gradually comes to a man as he grows up from infancy.   2. But since it is difficult to say that the non-existent God—for Basilides shuns and abhors the essence of things produced by emanation—for what emanation was necessary, for what material was the basis present, such that God should manufacture the world as the spider takes its threads, or a mortal man when he manufactures [something] takes bronze or wood or some piece of material? 3. Rather, he says: "He spoke and it was," and that is what Moses said, so these men say: "Let there be light, and there was light" [Gen. 1:3]. Whence, says he, came the light? From nothing. For, says he, it is not written where [it came] from, but only [that it came] from the voice of him that spoke. But the speaker, says he, did not exist, so neither did what came into being exist.   4. The seed of the world, says he, came from the non-existent, the word which was spoken, "Let there be light"; and that, says he, is what is said in the Gospels, "There was the true light, which enlightens every man who comes into the world" [John 1:9].   5. It takes its origins from that seed and is enlightened. That is the seed which contains within it the whole seed-mixture, which Aristotle says is the "genus" which is divided into innumerable species, just as cow, horse, and man are subdivisions of "animal," which does not exist [which is a non-existent].

6. Given therefore the existence of the cosmic seed, they say this: Whatever I say came into existence after this, do not ask, he says where [it came from]. For it [the world-seed] had all the seeds stored and laid up within itself, since it had been previously determined by the non-existent God that the non-existent should come into being.   7. Let us therefore see what according to them was the first, what the second, and what the third thing that came into being from the cosmic seed. There was, says he, in the seed a threefold Sonship, in all respects the same in substance as the non-existent God, which came into being from the non-existent. Of this Sonship with its triple division, one part was light, another coarse, and a third in need of purification.   8. The light part, therefore, as soon as the seed was first deposited by the non-existent, was first to bubble up, and ascended and sped upwards from below with the swiftness [which the] poet [describes as] "like a wing or a thought" [Hom., *Od.* VII 36], and reached, says he, the non-existent. For every natural thing strives after him because of his extreme loveliness and beauty, one in one way, one in another. 9. But the coarser [nature], which still remained in the seed, wanted to imitate it, but could not rise upwards; for it fell very far short of the lightness of the Sonship which rose up by itself.   10. The coarser Sonship provided itself with a wing of that kind with which Plato, Aristotle's teacher, equipped the soul in Phaedrus [Plato, *Phedr.* 246a], but Basilides calls it not a wing, but Holy Spirit, on which the Sonship bestows benefit by putting it on, and receives benefit.   11. It bestows benefit, because just as a bird's wing by itself and separated from the bird would never become high or airborne, and a bird separated from its wing would never become high or airborne; the Sonship had some such relation to the Holy Spirit and the Spirit to the Sonship.   12. So the Sonship was borne aloft by the Spirit as by a wind, and bore aloft its wing, that is the Spirit; and when it came near to the light Sonship and the non-existent, it [the Sonship] could not keep it [the Spirit] with it, for it was not of the same substance and had no nature [in common] with the Sonship.   13. Rather, just as pure and

dry air is contrary to their nature and destructive for fish, so for the Holy Spirit that place of the non-existent God and the Sonship, [a place] more ineffable than the ineffable and above every name, was contrary to its nature. So the Sonship left it [the Spirit] in the vicinity of that blessed place which cannot be approached by the intellect or "defined" by any word, [but] not utterly and completely destitute and severed from the Sonship.   14. Rather it is like a vessel that has had particularly fragrant ointment poured into it; though it might be emptied with the utmost care, still the fragrance of the ointment remains and is left behind in the jar, even if it [the ointment] is removed far from the jar; and the jar has not ointment but the fragrance of ointment. In the same way the Holy Spirit remained without any part of the Sonship and separated from it, but has within itself, after the manner of the effect of the ointment, a fragrance of the Sonship.   15. This is the saying: "Like ointment on the head, which runs down on Aaron's beard" [Ps. 133 (132):2]; the fragrance which is borne by the Holy Spirit down from above to the formlessness and the place where we are, whence the Sonship began to ascend as it were carried on the wings and back of an eagle, so he says.   16. For everything, he says, hastens upwards from below, from the worse to the better. For none of those among the better things is so foolish that it may not come down. But the third Sonship, says he, which needed purification, stayed in the great heap of the world-seed, giving and receiving benefit. How it receives and gives benefit we shall describe later when we reach the proper place for it.

23.1. When therefore the first and second ascent of the Sonship had taken place and the Holy Spirit had remained there in the manner described, set as a firmament [Gen. 1:7] between the supermundane and the world—2. for the things that exist are divided by Basilides into two adjacent and principle divisions; the one is called according to him Cosmos [World], and the other the Supermundane, and the limit between the world and the Supermundane is that Spirit which both is holy and has remaining within it the fragrance of the Sonship—3. when therefore the firmament, which is above the heaven, was there, there bubbled up and was born out of the cosmic seed and the heap of the world-seed the Great Ruler, the head of the world, a beauty and a greatness and power which cannot be spoken of. For he is, says he, more ineffable than the wise, and superior to any beautiful things whatever that you might mention. 4. When he had been born, he lifted himself up and soared and was wholly carried right up to the firmament; he thought that the firmament was the end of ascent and height, and supposed that nothing whatever existed beyond, and he became wiser than all that lay below, whatever in fact was cosmic, [he became] more powerful, more excellent, more luminous, surpassing everything you might call good, excepting only the Sonship which was still left behind in the world-seed. For he did not know that it was wiser and more powerful and better than he.   5. So deeming himself to be lord and master and wise architect he turned to the detailed construction of the world. And first he thought it proper not to be alone, and he made for himself and begot from what lay below a Son much better and wiser than himself.   6. For the non-existent God had purposed all these things in advance, when he deposited the world-seed. When he [the Great Ruler] saw his Son, he was filled with astonishment, admiration, and consternation. Such did the beauty of the Son appear to the Great Ruler; and the Ruler made him sit on the right [Ps. 110 (109) 1].   7. That is what is known among them as the Ogdoad, where the Great Ruler sits. The whole celestial, that is, the etherial, creation was the achievement of the great and wise Demiurge himself. But the Son born from him was effective in this and proposed it to him, being much wiser than the Demiurge himself.

24.1. This is Aristotle's entelechy of the physical, organic body, the soul which is effective in it, without which the body can achieve nothing, greater, more splendid, more powerful, and wiser than the body. The thought, therefore, which Aristotle expressed previously in connection with the soul and body, Basilides stated in connection with the Great Ruler and the Son associated with him.

2. For according to Basilides the Ruler has begotten the Son, and Aristotle says that the soul is work and accomplishment, the entelechy of the physical, organic body. Thus as the entelechy manages the body, so, according to Basilides, the Son manages the God who is more ineffable than the ineffable.

3. Thus all the etherial things, which extend as far as the moon, are purposed and directed by the entelechy of the Great Ruler. For from there on the air is distinguished from the ether. So when all the etherial things had been set in order, another Ruler in turn arose from the world-seed, greater than all that lay below him, apart from the Sonship that had been left behind, but much inferior to the first Ruler. He also is called ineffable by them.   4. This locality is called the Hebdomad and is the controller and creator of all that lies beneath. He too made himself a Son from the world-seed, more prudent and wise than himself, in just the way described in the case of the first [Ruler].   5. What is in this region is the heap itself, and the seed-mixture; and what happens [there] happens naturally as some-

thing anticipated by him who contrived the future, when it should be, of what kind it should be, and in what way it should be. Controller, provider or shaper of these things there was none; for sufficient for these things was that contrivance which the non-existent contrived when he created.

25.1. When therefore the whole world and the supermundane things were, in their account, finished, and nothing was lacking, there remained [still] in the world-seed the third Sonship, which had been left in the seed to give and receive benefit, and it was necessary for the Sonship that was left behind to be revealed and restored to that place above the exalted Spirit, to the light Sonship and the one that imitates it and to the non-existent, as it is written—so he says: "And the creation itself groans together and is in labour together, waiting for the revelation of the sons of God" [Rom. 8:19, 22]. 2. "Sons," he says, means us spiritual ones, who are left behind here to order, train, correct, and perfect our souls, whose nature is to stay in this region. "Up to Moses, from Adam, sin reigned," as it is written [Rom. 5:13]. 3. For there reigned the Great Ruler, whose limit extends to the firmament, in the belief that he alone was God and that there was nothing beyond him. For everything was guarded in a deep silence. That, he says, is "the mystery which was not made known to the earlier generations" [Eph. 3:3-5], but in those times, so it appears, the king and lord of the universe was the Great Ruler, the Ogdoad. 4. But there was also a king and lord over this region, the Hebdomad; the Ogdoad is ineffable, but the Hebdomad is effable. This is, he says, the Ruler of the Hebdomad who spoke to Moses and said: "I am the God of Abraham, Isaac, and Jacob, and the name of God I have not shown them" [Exod. 6:2f.]—so they suppose it is written—that is, [the name] of the ineffable God, the Ruler of Ogdoad. 5. That, therefore, is the source, he says, of what was spoken by all the prophets before the Saviour.

Since then, says he, we, the children of God, had to be revealed, [we] over whom the creation, says he, groaned and was in labour, waiting for [their] revelation, the Gospel came into the world, and passed through every rule and authority and lordship and every name that is named. 6. It really came, although nothing descended from above, nor did the blessed Sonship leave that inconceivable, blessed, non-existent God. Rather, just as Indian naphtha, if it is merely seen from a very great distance, catches fire, so from below the powers penetrate from the formlessness of the heap up to the Sonship above. 7. For the Son of the Great Ruler of the Ogdoad seized and received the thoughts like Indian naphtha, as if he were naphtha, from the blessed Sonship beyond the boundary. For the power of the Sonship, which flow and drift, with the Son of the Great Ruler. 26.1. So the Gospel came first he says, from the Sonship, through the Son who sits enthroned beside the Great Ruler, to the Ruler [himself], and the Ruler learned that he was not the God of the universe, but was begotten, and had above him, stored up, the treasure of the ineffable and unnameable non-existent and the Sonship, and he was converted and became afraid, for he perceived what ignorance he was in. 2. This is, he says, the saying: "The fear of the Lord is the beginning of wisdom" [Ps. 111(110):10; Prov. 1:7; etc]. For he [the Great Ruler] began to grow wise under the instruction of the Christ who sits beside him, as he was taught who is the non-existent, what the Sonship, what the Holy Spirit is, how the universe is arranged, and how [or where] it will be fully restored. 3. That is the wisdom spoken in a mystery, of which, says he, the Scripture says: "Not in taught words of human wisdom, but in taught [words] of the spirit" [1 Cor. 2:13]. Instructed, then, and taught, and made afraid, says he, the ruler acknowledged his sin, which he had committed in magnifying himself. 4. That, says he, is the saying: "I have recognized my sin, and I know my lawlessness, I will confess this for ever" [Ps. 32 (31):5]. When therefore the Great Ruler had been instructed and taught, and the mystery was made known to the heavenly spheres.

Then the Gospel had to come to the Sphere of the Seven, so that the Ruler of the Hebdomad might also be taught and have the Gospel brought to him. 5. So the Son of the Great Ruler shed upon the Son of the Ruler of the Sphere of the Seven the light which he had himself caught from above from the Sonship; and the Son of the ruler of the Hebdomad was illuminated, and brought the Gospel to the Ruler of the Hebdomad, and exactly as in the previous account he also became afraid and made [his] confession. 6. When therefore everything in the Sphere of the Seven had been illuminated and the Gospel had been proclaimed to them—according to them there are in the regions interminable creations and governments, powers and authorities, about which they have a very large book with many words, where they also say there are 365 heavens, and that their great Ruler is Abrasax, because his name comprises the number 365, so that the numerical value of his name comprises everything, and for that reason the year consists of that number of days—7. but when, says he, these things had happened thus, the formlessness affecting us had also lastly to be illuminated, and the mystery which had not been made known to previous generations [had] to be revealed to the Sonship which had been left in the formlessness like an abortion, as it is written, says he:

"According to a revelation the mystery was made known to me" [Eph. 3:3] and "I heard ineffable words which a man is unable to utter" [2 Cor. 12:4].

8. So from the Sphere of the Seven the light, which had descended from above from the Sphere of the Eight upon the Son of the Hebdomad, descended upon Jesus the Son of Mary, and he was illuminated and kindled by the light that shone upon him.   9. That is, he says, the saying: "Holy Spirit will come upon you," [the Spirit] which passed from the Sonship through the boundary Spirit to the Spheres of the Eight and the Seven and reached Mary, "and power of the Highest will overshadow you" [Luke 1:35], the power of separation from above, from the apex down through the demiurge as far as the creation, which is the Son's. 10. Up to this point the world has had its [present] constitution, until all the Sonship that was left behind to bestow benefit on the souls in the formlessness and to receive benefit, when it has wholly been transformed [achieved form], follows Jesus, rises upward, and arrives purified; and it becomes extremely light, so as to be able to rise up of itself like the first [Sonship]. For it possesses the whole power naturally fixed by the light which shone downwards from above.

27.1 When the whole Sonship thus arrives [above], he says, and is beyond the boundary, the Spirit, then the creation will receive pity. For up to the present it groans and is tormented and waits for the revelation of the sons of God [Rom. 8:19, 22], so that all men of the Sonship may go up from here. When that has happened, God, he says, will bring on the whole world the great ignorance, so that everything may remain in accordance with [its] nature, and nothing desire anything contrary to its nature. 2. Rather, all the souls whose nature it is to remain immortal in this region alone will stay here below, knowing nothing other than or better than this region; in the [regions] below there will be no news and no knowledge of the [regions] above, so that the souls found below may not be tormented by striving for the impossible, like a fish striving to graze on the hills with the sheep—such a desire would, he says, be for them destruction.   3. Thus everything, says he, which stays in [its] place is imperishable, but perishable if it wants to overleap and transgress the limits of [its] nature. So the Ruler of the Sphere of the Seven will know nothing of the things above. For the great ignorance will grip even him, in order that "sorrow, pain, and sighing" [Isa. 35:10; 51:11] may leave him, for he will desire nothing impossible and not feel sorrow. Similarly, this ignorance will grip even the Great Ruler of the Ogdoad and all the created things subject to him in the same way, so that they may in no way strive for what is contrary to [their] nature and feel pain. And thus will come about the restoration of all things, which were founded in the beginning according to nature in the seed of the universe, and will be restored in their proper seasons. 5. That each thing has its proper times is indicated by the Saviour when he says, "My hour has not yet come" [John 2:4], and by the Magi who saw the star; for even this was planned beforehand in the great "heap" with the birth of the stars and the times of the restoration. 6. This is what they take to be the inner, spiritual man in the psychic man [animal- or soul-man]—that is, the Sonship has left the Holy Spirit on the boundary at the proper place—the spiritual man, who at that time was wearing his own soul.

7. But so that we do not leave out any of their [thoughts], I will set out what they also say about the Gospel. The Gospel is, according to them, the knowledge of the supermundane things, as we have made plain, which the Great Ruler did not apprehend. Then when it was shown to him that the Holy Spirit exists, that is the boundary, and the Sonship and God the non-existent who is the cause of all these things, he rejoiced at [these] reports and was jubilant. That is, according to them, the Gospel. 8. Jesus was born, according to them, in the manner described. When the birth previously described had taken place, all that concerns the Saviour happened in a similar way to what is written in the gospels. These things happened, says he, so that Jesus might become the first-fruits of the "distinction of kinds" among what was confused. 9. For since the world is divided into the Sphere of Eight, which is the head of the whole world—but the head of the whole world is the Great Ruler—and the Sphere of the Seven, which is the head of that which lies beneath—but the head is the Demiurge—and this region round us, where the formlessness is, it was therefore necessary that what was confused should be "distinguished into kinds" through the separation which happened to Jesus. 10. There suffered, therefore, that bodily part of him which derived from the formlessness, and it returned to formlessness. There rose up that psychic part of him [which derived form the Sphere of the Seven], and returned to the Sphere of the Seven. He roused [!] what belonged to the pinnacle of the Great Ruler, and it stayed with the Great Ruler. He bore aloft what was from the boundary Spirit, and it stayed in the boundary Spirit. 11. But the third Sonship was quite purified through him, [the Sonship] which had been left behind to give and receive benefit, and it went up to the blessed Sonship, when it had passed through all these. Their whole system is as it were a confusion of the world-seed, a distinction of kinds and the restoration [return] of the con-

fused things to what is proper to them.   12. Jesus became the first-fruit of the distinction of kinds, and the suffering of Jesus took place with no other object than the distinction into kinds of what had been confused. For he says the whole Sonship which was left behind in the formlessness to give and receive benefit must be distinguished into kinds in the very way in which Jesus also was distinguished into kinds.

13. This then is what Basilides made up while he tarried in Egypt, and from them [the Egyptians?] he learned this mighty wisdom and bore such fruits.

8.3. Epiphanius, *Panarion* 24.4.1; 24.5.4-5. Salamis, Cyprus,
A.D. 375–78.

Source: *Panarion*, trans. P. R. Amidon, 70–71.

From what he says at 1.4 of his work, Epiphanius claims that the sect of Basilides (a person of the second century) continued to exist in Egypt during the days of Epiphanius (late fourth century). Epiphanius provides a summary of the teachings of this sect in his writings (too extensive to reproduce here) and says that the sect emphasized great secrecy. According to him, furthermore, the members of the sect claimed that "they are no longer Jews and have not yet become Christians" (24.5.5; cf. the same in Irenaeus, Against Heresies *1.24.6 in §8.1 above). That they would not speak of themselves forthrightly as Christians must indicate the strength of "orthodox" Christianity in Egypt at the time. Furthermore, that the people of this sect would not undergo martyrdom is, of course, a judgment against their allegiance to Christ.*

[4.1] He teaches something else that he allows, namely, that one should not undergo martyrdom. ...

[5.4] He says that his followers [should] reveal the teaching about the Father and his cult to no one at all, but keep it in silence in themselves, revealing it to one out of a thousand and two out of ten thousand. He lays down a principle for his disciples: "Know everyone, but let no one know you."   [5.5] He and those of his sect when asked say that they are no longer Jews, and have not yet become Christians but always deny it; he says that he keeps the faith in himself in silence and reveals it to no one, but he is detected in his shame because of his lack of frankness about his shameful deeds and evil teaching.

Cerdo

Cerdo (second century A.D.)—also known as Cerdon—was of Syrian origin. According to Irenaeus (*Against Heresies* 1.27.1), he was a follower of the Simonian sect; and according to Epiphanius (*Panarion* 41.1.1), he had also come under the influence of Saturninus (a Syrian Gnostic). He moved to Rome around A.D. 140 and taught there. Irenaeus reports that he was one of Marcion's teachers (*Against Heresies* 1.27.2); this claim is echoed by other writers (see texts below). One of Cerdo's major teachings, which was shared by Marcion, was a radical distinction between the God of the Old Testament, revealed by Moses and the prophets, and the Father of Jesus Christ. The Father of Jesus Christ, he claimed, was unknown and totally good; he had to be revealed by Jesus. Cerdo denied that Christ truly appeared in the flesh, and taught that the soul, but not the body, will participate in the resurrection.

9.1. Irenaeus, *Against Heresies* 1.27.1. Lyons, ca. A.D. 190.

Source: *Gnosticism*, ed. R. M. Grant, 44.

In this account Irenaeus claims that Cerdo arrived in Rome while Hyginus was bishop, which was around A.D. 138. He also sets forth the basic tenets of his teachings.

And a certain Cerdo, originating from the Simonians, came to Rome under Hyginus [who held the office of bishop ninth in succession from the apostles] and taught that the one who was proclaimed as God by the law and the prophets is not the Father of our Lord Jesus Christ. The [Old Testament] God is known; the Father is unknown. The former is just, while the latter is good.

9.2. Hippolytus, *Refutation of All Heresies* 7.25. Rome, ca. A.D. 230.

Source: *The Ante-Nicene Fathers*, ed. A. Roberts and J. Donaldson, 5:115.

Like Irenaeus before him, Hippolytus speaks about Cerdo's theology, in which there is a distinction between the God of the Old Testament and the God proclaimed and revealed by Jesus. He mentions Marcion and a person named Lucian. Both were disciples of Cerdo. Concerning Marcion, see chapter 12. The Lucian mentioned was a contemporary of Marcion, and his views are discussed by Epiphanius in his Panarion *43.*

But one Cerdon himself also, taking occasion in like manner from these [heretics] and Simon, affirms that the God preached by Moses and the prophets was not Father of Jesus Christ. For [he contends] that this [Father] had been known, whereas that the Father of Christ was unknown, and that the former was just, but the latter good. And Marcion corroborated the tenet of this [heretic] in the work which he attempted to write, and which he styled *Antitheses*. And he was in the habit, [in this book,] of uttering whatever slanders suggested themselves to his mind against the Creator of the universe. In a similar manner likewise [acted] Lucian, the disciple of this [heretic].

9.3. Eusebius, *Ecclesiastical History* 4.10-11. Caesarea, ca. A.D. 325.

Source: Eusebius, *History of the Church*, trans. G. Williamson, 163.

In this section of his work Eusebius locates Cerdo within the time of Emperor Antoninus Pius (A.D. 138–61) and the beginning of the episcopacy of Hyginus (A.D. 138). Further, drawing from the writings of Irenaeus, he indicates that Cerdo and Valentinus arrived in Rome about the same time. In the selection below there is reference to Anicetus. This man was Bishop of Rome after Hyginus, and the years of his episcopacy were approximately A.D. 154–

65. The second quotation from the writings of Irenaeus is much like the one directly from Irenaeus at 9.1 above.

10. When Hadrian, after twenty-one years, paid the debt of nature, Antoninus called Pius succeeded to the Roman Empire. In his first year, Telesphorus departed this life in the eleventh year of his ministry, and Hyginus took over the office of Bishop of Rome. Irenaeus notes that Telesphorus died nobly as a martyr. In the same chapter he states that while Hyginus was bishop, Valentinus, who introduced a heresy of his own, and Cerdo, who was responsible for the Marcionite error, were both prominent in Rome. He writes:

11. Valentinus arrived in Rome in the time of Hyginus, reached his heyday under Pius, and remained till Anicetus. Cerdo, who preceded Marcion, also joined the Roman church and declared his faith publicly, in the time of Hyginus, the ninth bishop; then he went on in this way—at one time he taught in secret, at another he again declared his faith publicly, at another he was convicted of mischievous teaching and expelled from the Christian community.

This comes from Book III of Heresies Answered. *In Book I we find this additional information about Cerdo:*

One Cerdo, whose notions stemmed from the followers of Simon, had settled in Rome in the time of Hyginus, who held the ninth place in the episcopal succession from the apostles. He taught that the God proclaimed by the Law and the Prophets was not the Father of our Lord Jesus Christ; for the one was known, the other unknown; the one was righteous, the other gracious. He was succeeded by Marcion of Pontus, who inflated his teaching, blaspheming unblushingly.

9.4. Epiphanius, *Panarion* 41.1.1; 41.1.6-9; 41.3.1. Salamis, Cyprus, A.D. 375–78.

Source: *Panarion*, trans. P. R. Amidon, 143.

Much of what Epiphanius relates concerning Cerdo is familiar from previous sources. But there are some additional matters. According to him, Cerdo and his followers rejected Jesus' birth from Mary and the incarnation. At most Christ appeared as a human being (so a "docetic" Christology). Like Marcion after him, he rejected the Old Testament as Scripture for the church.

[1.1] One Cerdo succeeds Heracleon and these others. He is of the same school and is influenced by Simon and Saturnilus. He moved from Syria, came to Rome, and ruined himself and those who put their faith in him. ...

[1.6] He too preached that the world has two principles and indeed two gods, one who is good and unknown to all, whom he also called the father of Jesus, and one who is the Demiurge and is wicked and known. He it is who spoke in the law, appeared to the prophets, and often made himself visible. [1.7] Christ was not born of Mary, nor did he appear in the flesh, but seemed to exist, seemed to appear, and seemed to do everything. He rejects the resurrection of the flesh and refuses to accept the Old Testament given through Moses and the prophets as foreign to God. [1.8] Christ came, he says, from the regions above, from the unknown Father, to abolish the rule and tyranny of the demiurge here who made the world, just as many of the sects have said. [1.9] Having spent a short while in Rome, he imparted his poison to Marcion, who thus succeeded him....

[3.1] The silly man says that the law and the prophets belong to the evil and opposing principle, but Christ to the good.

Chapter 10

Apelles

Apelles (second century A.D.) was Marcion's most important disciple. After years of study with Marcion, however, there seems to have been conflict. Apelles moved to Alexandria in Egypt, only to return to Rome after Marcion's death.

Although he was a Gnostic and had affinities to Marcion, it is obvious that Apelles disagreed with his master on at least two significant points. First, Apelles had a more complicated theology. Like Marcion, he claimed that there is a superior God who was revealed by Christ. But he was willing to grant that the demiurge—a second god, the creator of the world—is also good and just, and he claimed that there were still two other gods: the one who spoke through Moses (which for Marcion had been the demiurge), and the one who is the source of evil.

Second, Apelles rejected Marcion's extreme docetism. While Marcion maintained that Christ had not truly come in the flesh, but only in an appearance of it, Apelles maintained that Christ had truly come in a body of flesh and had suffered. He agreed with Marcion that this body was not born; specifically, he claimed that Christ himself formed the body as he descended to earth from the elements that make up the universe. In death, his body was returned to the elements.

Apelles agreed with Marcion regarding the status of the Old Testament, going even further in his condemnation of it. While Marcion saw no religious value in the Old Testament, Apelles went so far as to call it a lying book, totally worthless.

The known works of Apelles were *The Syllogisms* (many passages of which are preserved in Ambrose's *De Paradiso*) and *The Revelations*, a collection of prophetic utterances of Philumene, which no longer exists.

10.1. Hippolytus, *Refutation of All Heresies* 7.26. Rome, ca. A.D. 230.

Source: *The Ante-Nicene Fathers*, ed. A. Roberts and J. Donaldson, 5:115–16.

This selection from Hippolytus sets forth the basic teachings of Apelles and points especially to those ideas of Apelles which differed from his master Marcion. Hippolytus seems to have maintained that Apelles agreed with Marcion that there was one good God, but designated three other god-figures as somehow lesser entities, that is, angels, who create and produce evil results. Apelles also seems to have taught that Jesus indeed had a human body, but it was formed from created elements, and returned to those elements when no longer used. He, as emissary of the good God, is not properly associated with created elements. Hippolytus indicates that Apelles, like Marcion, also selects only portions of the Gospels and the epistles of Paul as authoritative. He also mentions the "discourses" of Philumene, a prophetess and contemporary of Apelles. Apparently Apelles himself wrote them down as authoritative for him and his followers, but they have not been preserved.

But Apelles, sprung from these, thus expresses himself, [saying] that there is a certain good Deity, as also Marcion supposed, and that he who created all things is just. Now he, [according to Apelles,] was the Demiurge of generated entities. And [this heretic also maintains] that there is a third [Deity], the one who was in the habit of speaking to Moses, and that this [god] was of a fiery nature, and that there was another fourth god, a cause of evils. But these he denominates angels. He utters, however, slanders against law and prophets, by alleging that the things that have been written are [of] human [origin], and are false. And [Apelles] selects from the Gospels or [from the writings of] the Apostle [Paul] whatever pleases himself. But he devotes himself to the discourses of a certain Philumene as to the revelations of a prophetess. He affirms, however, that Christ descended from the power above; that is, from the good [Deity], and that he is the son of that good [Deity]. And [he asserts that Jesus] was not born of a virgin, and that when he did appear he was not devoid of flesh. [He maintains,] however, that [Christ] formed his body by taking portions of it from the substance of the universe: that is, hot and cold, and moist and dry. And [he says that Christ], on receiving in this body cosmical powers, lived for the time he did in [this] world. But [he held that Jesus] was subsequently crucified by the Jews, and expired, and that, being raised up after three days, he appeared to his disciples. And [the Saviour] showed them, [so Apelles taught,] the prints of the nails and [the wound] in his side, desirous of persuading them that he was in truth no phantom, but was present in the flesh. After, says [Apelles], he had shown them his flesh, [the Saviour] restored it to earth, from which substance it was [derived. And this he did because] he coveted nothing that belonged to another. [Though indeed Jesus] might use for the time being [what belonged to another], he yet in due course rendered to each [of the elements] what peculiarly belonged to them. And so it was, that after he had once more loosed the chains of his body, he gave back heat to what is hot, cold to what is cold, moisture to what is moist, [and] dryness to what is dry. And in this condition [our Lord] departed to the good Father, leaving the seed of life in the world for those who through his disciples should believe in him.

10.2. Hippolytus, *Refutation of All Heresies* 10.16. Rome, ca. A.D. 230.

Source: *The Ante-Nicene Fathers*, ed. A. Roberts and J. Donaldson, 5:147.

In this section Hippolytus claims that the system of Apelles comprised five gods, not four, for Christ was the fifth. Again he mentions the discourses (here called the "Revelations") of the prophetess Philumene. Finally, it is said that Apelles considered the Old Testament books to contain falsehoods.

But Apelles, a disciple of this heretic, was displeased at the statements advanced by his preceptor, as we have previously declared, and by another theory supposed that there are four gods. And the first of these he alleges to be the "Good Being," whom the prophets did not know, and Christ to be His Son. And the second God, he affirms to be the Creator of the universe, and Him he does not wish to be a God. And the third God, he states to be the fiery one that was manifested; and the fourth to be an evil one. And Apelles calls these angels; and by adding [to their number] Christ likewise, he will assert Him to be a fifth God. But this heretic is in the habit of devoting his attention to a book which he calls, "Revelations" of a certain Philumene, whom he considers a prophetess. And he affirms that Christ did not receive his flesh from the Virgin, but from the adjacent substance of the world. In this manner he composed his treatises against the law and the prophets, and attempts to abolish them as if they had spoken falsehoods, and had not known God. And Apelles, similarly with Marcion, affirms that the different sorts of flesh are destroyed.

10.3. Epiphanius, *Panarion* 44.1.1-3; 44.2.1-6; 44.4.1. Salamis, Cyprus, A.D. 375–78.

Source: *Panarion*, trans. P. R. Amidon, 162–63.

Epiphanius repeats Hippolytus' claim that Apelles differed in some ways from his teacher Marcion. He also maintains that Apelles taught that Christ was not born of the virgin Mary, but rather, in disdain for the work of the demiurge, formed his body from the elements of the demiurge's creation in order to reveal himself to humans. While Apelles does acknowledge a real body and a real suffering and resurrection for Christ, the physical is not properly a focus for salvation—only the vehicle for revelation. Likewise, for Apelles there is no resurrection of the body, again because the physical is not the proper focus for salvation. Epiphanius surveys the teachings of Apelles and indicates that in the system of Apelles salvation comes by way of knowledge (2.1), a basic teaching of every form of Gnosticism.

Epiphanius also mentions Lucian, who was a contemporary of Marcion, and Apelles, who was a contemporary of the apostle Paul (mentioned at Romans 16:10). Hippolytus makes it clear that he is not speaking of the latter.

[1.1] Apelles succeeded the Lucian just mentioned; he is not the holy man recommended by the holy apostle, but someone else, from whom the Apelleians derive. He was a fellow student of Lucian and disciple of the Marcion mentioned earlier.... [1.2] But his doctrines differ from those of the others; he takes up arms against his own master and against the truth, and so that he too may gather to himself a school of men gone astray, he teaches the following sort of things. [1.3] He says that Marcion is wrong, and that things did not happen as he said....

[2.1] He says that Christ has come in the last times, the son of the good God above, and his Holy Spirit likewise for the salvation of those coming to a knowledge of him. [2.2] When he came, he did not just seem to appear, but truly took flesh, not from the Virgin Mary, but he had true flesh and a body, [although] it was not from a man's seed or from a virgin woman. [2.3] He had, however, true flesh, [but] in the following way: in coming from the heavenly regions he arrived on earth and gathered a body for himself from the four elements.... [2.5] From dryness [he took] dryness, from heat heat, from wetness wetness, and from cold cold, and thus, having fashioned himself a body, he truly appeared in the world and taught us the supernal knowledge. [2.6] He taught us to despise the demiurge and to deny his works, showing us in which book of scripture which things were really said by him, and which are from the demiurge. "For, he says, this is what he said in the gospel: become good bankers. For I make use of every book of scripture, choosing what is useful.".…

[4.1] His teaching about other kinds of flesh and about other things is like that of his master Marcion: he says that there is no resurrection of the flesh, and in everything else which [he taught in disparaging the things?] of earth, his doctrine is similar.

Valentinus and the Valentinians

Valentinus (ca. A.D. 115–65) was born in Egypt and educated at Alexandria. He is regarded as the most important of the gnostic teachers of the second century. He moved from Alexandria to Rome and resided there from about 135 to 165. He had many followers, and according to Hippolytus (*Refutation of All Heresies* 6.30), they formed two branches—a western one (called "Italian"), which included such leaders as Heracleon and Ptolemaeus, and an eastern one (called "Oriental"), which included Axionicus and Bardesianes. Valentinus produced many writings, and it is possible that *The Gospel of Truth* discovered at Nag Hammadi in 1945 was written by him or one of his followers. Other Nag Hammadi texts usually considered to have originated with Valentinians include *The Tripartite Tractate, The Interpretation of Knowledge*, and *A Valentinian Exposition*.

Valentinus taught an elaborate theology. According to him, there is a higher spiritual world, the Pleroma (Greek for "Fullness"), made up of thirty aeons (or spiritual powers) that exist in pairs. Still others emanate from these. The world came into being due to the fall of the youngest of the aeons, Sophia, who is the mother of the demiurge, who is the equivalent to the God of the Old Testament. Redemption has come about by the descent of another of the aeons, Christ, from the Pleroma to unite with the man Jesus at his baptism (according to the Italian branch) or at his conception (according to the Oriental branch) to bring knowledge (*gnosis*) to persons concerning their origin and destiny. This *gnosis* is given, however, only to the "pneumatics" (spiritual ones), who thereupon enter into the Pleroma at death. The pneumatics are Valentinians alone. The rest of humanity is divided into two other groups. First, there are the "psychics" (persons with souls, but who are not spiritual). These are ordinary (or catholic) Christians, who can attain a middle range of salvation by faith and good works. Second, there are the "hylics" (materialists). These are the rest of humanity, and there is no possibility of salvation for them at all.

11.1. Irenaeus, *Against Heresies* 1.1.1-3; 1.5.2-3; 1.7.2-5; 1.11.1
       Lyons, ca. A.D. 190.

Source: Irenaeus, *Against the Heresies*, trans. D. Unger, 23–24, 33–34, 39–40, 51–52.

Except for the primary texts from Nag Hammadi associated with the Valentinians, Irenaeus is the principal source of our knowledge of Valentinus and his followers. In these excerpts from his writings Irenaeus sets forth the main teachings of Valentinus, including his elaborate doctrine of the thirty aeons, the seven heavens, the nature of Christ, and the three classes of humanity.

1.1.1. They claim that in the invisible and unnameable heights there is a certain perfect Aeon that was before all, the First-Being, whom they also call First-Beginning, First-Father, and Profundity. He is invisible and incomprehensible. And, since he is incomprehensible and invisible, eternal and ingenerate, he existed in deep quiet and stillness through countless ages. Along with him there existed Thought, whom they also name Grace and Silence. At one time this Profundity decided to emit from himself the Beginning of all things. This emission would be as a "seed" which he decided to emit and deposit as it were in the womb of Silence, who coexisted with him. After she had received this "seed" and had become pregnant, she gave birth to Mind, who was both similar and equal to his Father who emitted him; and he alone comprehended his [Father's] greatness. This Mind they also call Only-begotten, Father and Beginning of all things. Truth was emitted at the same time he [Mind] was. Thus these four constitute the first and principal Pythagorean Tetrad, for there are Profundity and Silence, then Mind and Truth. This [Tetrad] they also style the root of all things. But when this Only-begotten perceived for what things he was emitted, he in turn emitted Word and Life, since he was Father of all who were to come after him and the beginning and formation of the entire Fullness. Thereupon by the conjugal union of Word and Life, Man and Church were emitted. That is the principal Ogdoad, the root and the substance of all things, known among them by four names, Profundity, Mind, Word, and Man, because each of these is male and female; thus, in the first case, First-Father was united in marriage to Thought whom they call Grace and Silence; then Only-begotten, that is, Mind, to Truth; next Word, to Life; finally Man, to Church.

1.1.2. Since these Aeons themselves were emitted for their Father's glory, they in turn wished to glorify the Father by something of their own. So they sent forth emissions through conjugal unions. After Man and Church had been emitted, Word and Life emitted ten other Aeons, whose names are these: Profound and Mingling, Ageless and Union, Self-producing and Pleasure, Immobile and Blending, Only-begotten and Happiness. These are the ten Aeons which they assert were emitted by Word and Life. Moreover, Man himself, together with Church, emitted twelve Aeons, to whom they give these names: Advocate and Faith, Paternal and Hope, Maternal and Love, Praise and Understanding, Ecclesiastic and Blessedness, Desired and Wisdom.

1.1.3. Such are the thirty Aeons of their erroneous system. They are enveloped in silence and are known to no one. This indivisible and spiritual Fullness of theirs is tripartite, being divided into an Ogdoad, a Decad, and a Dodecad. And for this reason Savior—for they do not wish to call him Lord—did not work in public for thirty years, thus manifesting the mystery of these Aeons. They also assert that these thirty Aeons are most plainly indicated in the parable of the laborers sent into the vineyard [[Matthew 20:1-16]]; for some are sent about the first hour, others about the third hour, others about the sixth hour, others about the ninth hour, others about the eleventh hour. Now if the hours mentioned are added up, the sum total will be thirty; for one, three, six, nine, and eleven make thirty. Thus they hold that the Aeons have been indicated by these hours. Besides, they claim that these are great and wonderful and unutterable mysteries, which they themselves bear as fruit. And if anywhere anything of the many things mentioned in the Scriptures can [be drawn to these things, they wish to] accommodate and adapt them to their fabrication....

1.5.2. Accordingly, they assert that he became Father and God of all things outside the Fullness, inasmuch as he is the Maker of all the ensouled and material beings. For it was he who distinguished the two substances that were confused and made corporeal out of incorporeal things. He made the heavenly and earthly things, and became the Maker of the material and ensouled beings, of the right-handed and the left-handed, of the light and the heavy, of those that tend upwards and of those that tend downwards. He made also seven heavens, above which he himself exists. On this account they style him the Hebdomad, but his Mother Achamoth is the Ogdoad, since she preserves the number of the original and primary Ogdoad of the Fullness. They affirm that the seven heavens are intelligent, and they opine that they are Angels, and even Demiurge himself they opine is an Angel like God. Likewise, paradise is above the third heaven, and is a fourth Archangel with power. From him Adam received something while he dwelt in it.

1.5.3. Demiurge imagines, they assert, that he made the totality of these things by himself, whereas he made them inasmuch as Achamoth [his Mother] emitted them. He made the heavens without knowing the heavens; he fashioned man without knowing Man; he brought the earth to light without understanding the Earth. In like manner, they assert, he was ignorant of the images of the things he made, even of his Mother herself. He imagined that he himself was all things. His Mother, they say, was the cause of that false notion of his, because she wished thus to promote him as the head and beginning of her own substance and Lord over all affairs. This Mother they also call Ogdoad, Wisdom, Earth, Jerusalem, Holy Spirit, and Lord, in the masculine gender. Her dwelling is the intermediate region. She is indeed above Demiurge, but below or outside the Fullness until the consummation....

1.7.2. There are those who say that Demiurge produced even Christ as his own son but also of an ensouled nature, and that he spoke of him [Christ] through the prophets. Moreover, this is he who passed through Mary just as water passes through a tube. It was on him that Savior, who belonged to the Fullness and was made from all the Aeons, descended in the shape of a dove at his baptism. In him, too, was the spiritual "seed" of Achamoth itself. Our Lord, then, as they assert, was composed of these four elements—having preserved, however, the type of the original and primary Tetrad: first, of the spiritual element, which was from Achamoth; second, of the ensouled element, which was from Demiurge; third, of Economy, who was prepared with ineffable art; and fourth, of Savior, who was the dove that descended on him [Jesus]. He remained impassible— inasmuch as he is inapprehensible and invisible it would be impossible for him to suffer—consequently, when he was led to Pilate, Christ's Spirit, who had been deposited in him, was taken away. But neither did the "seed" that he received from his Mother suffer, for it too was impassible, being spiritual and invisible even to Demiurge. For the rest, according to them, the ensouled element in Christ suffered, as also he [Jesus] who was prepared by way of mystery because of the Economy, in order that through him the Mother might display the type of the Christ on high, of him, namely, who extended himself beyond Stake and made Achamoth's formation according to substance. All these things they say are types of the things above.

1.7.3. They assert, furthermore, that the souls which possess the "seed" of Achamoth are superior to the rest. For this reason they are also loved more than the others by Demiurge, who, being ignorant of the real reason, thinks they are such because of himself. Consequently, he also classified souls as prophets, priests, and kings. They explain, too, that this offspring spoke many things through the prophets, inasmuch as it was of a more exalted nature. The Mother, too—rather she through Demiurge and through the souls made by him—spoke many things about the Aeons on high. Moreover, they divide the prophecies into various classes: one portion they hold was spoken by the Mother, another by the offspring, and still another by Demiurge. In the same manner, Jesus had his prophecies partly from Savior, partly from his Mother, partly from Demiurge, as we shall show as our work proceeds.

1.7.4. Furthermore, Demiurge, inasmuch as he was ignorant of the things that were above him, was moved in regard to the things that were spoken, but treated them with contempt, thinking that various things were the causes: either the prophetic spirit— which possessed a certain motion all its own—or mere man, or the admixture of the baser materials. Thus he remained ignorant of those things until Savior's coming. But when Savior came, Demiurge learned from him all the things, and with all his strength gladly drew near to him. He is the centurion of the Gospel who said to Savior: *For I too have soldiers and slaves under my authority, and whatever I command, they do [[Matthew 8:9]]*. He will carry out the Economy relative to this world until the time appointed, mostly because of his concern for Church, but also because he is aware of the prize in store for him, namely, that he will advance to his Mother's region.

1.7.5. They suppose that there are three classes of people—the spiritual, the ensouled, and the earthly—as Cain, Abel, and Seth were; and from these [one arrives at] the three natures by considering them no longer as individuals but as a class. The earthly indeed goes into corruption; but the ensouled, if it chooses the better things, will rest in the intermediate region; if, however, it chooses the worse things, it too will go to regions similar [to the worse things]. Moreover, they dogmatize that the spiritual people whom Achamoth has planted as "seeds" from then until now in just souls, and which have been disciplined and nourished here below—

because they were sent forth immature—and have finally become worthy of perfection, will be given brides to the Angels of Savior, while their souls will of necessity rest forever in the intermediate region together with Demiurge. Again, subdividing the souls, they say that some are good by nature and some evil by nature. The good are those that are capable of receiving the "seed," whereas those evil by nature are never capable of receiving that "seed." . . .

1.11.1. Now let us look at the unstable doctrine of these men and how, since there are two of them, they do not say the same things about the same subject, but contradict themselves in regard to things and names. For example, Valentinus, the foremost, having adapted the principles from the so-called Gnostic heresy to his peculiar system of doctrine, defined it as follows. There is an unnameable Duality, whose one part is called Unutterable, and the other Silence. Next, out of this Duality a second Duality was emitted whose one part he named Father [Mind] and the other Truth. Now from this Tetrad were produced Word and Life, Man and Church. So there existed the first Ogdoad. He says that from Word and Life ten powers were emitted, as we have said before; but from Man and Church, twelve. One of these, having gone astray and become degenerate, was the cause of the rest of the affairs. He explained that there were two Limits, the one between Profundity and the rest of the Fullness, separating the Aeons who were generated from Father who was ingenerate; the other separating their Mother [Wisdom] from the Fullness. But Christ was not emitted by the Aeons within the Fullness; he was brought forth by the Mother, after she had gone out of the Fullness, with some shadow, because of her memory of better things. He, being masculine, severed the shadow from himself and entered the Fullness; but his Mother, though she was left with shadow and was devoid of the spiritual substance, brought forth another son. This is Demiurge, whom he also calls the all-powerful of all things under him. Together with him, he dogmatized, was emitted also a left-handed ruler. In this he agrees with those falsely called Gnostics, of whom we shall speak later. As for Jesus, at times he says that he was emitted by him who was separated from their Mother and united with all the rest, that is, by Desired; at times, by him who reentered the Fullness, that is, by Christ; at times, by Man and Church. Holy Spirit, he claims, was emitted by Truth for the purpose of testing the Aeons and making them productive, and for this he enters them in an invisible manner. So through him the Aeons produce the plants of truth.

11.2. Hippolytus, *Refutation of All Heresies* 6.16. Rome, ca. A.D. 230.

Source: *The Ante-Nicene Fathers*, ed. A. Roberts and J. Donaldson, 5:81–82.

In this passage Hippolytus claims that Valentinus borrowed heavily from Greek philosophical traditions, including those of the Pythagoreans (followers of the sixth–fifth century B.C. philosopher Pythagoras) and Plato (ca. 429–347 B.C.).

The heresy of Valentinus is ... connected with the Pythagorean and Platonic theory.... [Valentinus took his opinions] from these, because, although he has suppressed the truth regarding his obligations to [the Greek philosophers], and in this way has endeavoured to construct a doctrine, [as it were,] peculiarly his own, yet, in point of fact, he has altered the doctrines of those [thinkers] in names only, and numbers, and has adopted a peculiar terminology [of his own]. Valentinus has formed his definitions by measures, in order that he may establish an Hellenic heresy, diversified no doubt, but unstable, and not connected with Christ.

Hereafter (chapters 17–23) Hippolytus describes the philosophical systems of the Pythagoreans and Plato.

11.3. Hippolytus, *Refutation of All Heresies* 6.24-31. Rome, ca. A.D. 230.

Source: *The Ante-Nicene Fathers*, ed. A. Roberts and J. Donaldson, 5:85–90.

In this section Hippolytus identifies major disciples of Valentinus, namely, Heracleon and Ptolemaeus, and later on discusses the essential differences between two wings of Valentinians—the Italian (which includes Heracleon and Ptolemaeus) and the Oriental. He discusses the elaborate theology of the Valentinians, beginning with the "originating cause" of the universe, a Monad (or Father) who is self-generating, and the aeons that have been produced by it. Among them are Nous (Mind) and Aletheia (Truth), from which come Logos (Word), Zoe (Life), Christ, and the Holy Spirit. A number of other aeons have come into being, including Sophia (Wisdom), the demiurge, and the devil.

Jesus has been produced by the demiurge in terms of his body, and by the Holy Spirit (or Sophia) in terms of his "essence" (the indwelling Logos).

24. Of some such nature ... is the opinion of Pythagoras and Plato. And from this [system], not from the Gospels, Valentinus, as we have proved, has collected the [materials of] heresy—I mean his own [heresy]—and may [therefore] justly be reckoned a Pythagorean and Platonist, not a Christian. Valentinus, therefore, and Heracleon, and Ptolemaeus, and the entire school of these [heretics], as disciples of Pythagoras and Plato, [and] following these guides, have laid down as the fundamental principle of their doctrine the arithmetical system. For, likewise, according to these [Valentinians], the originating cause of the universe is a Monad, unbegotten, imperishable, incomprehensible, inconceivable, productive, and a cause of the generation of all existent things. And the aforesaid Monad is styled by them Father. There is, however, discoverable among them some considerable diversity of opinion. For some of them, in order that the Pythagorean doctrine of Valentinus may be altogether free from admixture [with other tenets], suppose that the Father is unfeminine, and unwedded, and solitary. But others, imagining it to be impossible that from a male only there could proceed a generation at all of any of those things that have been made to exist, necessarily reckon along with the Father of the universe, in order that he may be a father, Sige as a spouse. But as to Sige, whether at any time she is united in marriage [to the Father] or not, this is a point which we leave them to wrangle about among themselves. We at present, keeping to the Pythagorean principle, which is one, and unwedded, unfeminine, [and] deficient in nothing, shall proceed to give an account of their doctrines, as they themselves inculcate them. There is, says [Valentinus], not anything at all begotten, but the Father is alone unbegotten, not subject to the condition of place, not [subject to the condition of] time, having no counsellor, [and] not being any other substance that could be realized according to the ordinary methods of perception. [The Father,] however, was solitary, subsisting, as they say, in a state of quietude, and Himself reposing in isolation within Himself. When, however, He became productive, it seemed to Him expedient at one time to generate and lead forth the most beautiful and perfect [of those germs of existence] which He possessed within Himself, for [the Father] was not fond of solitariness. For, says he, He was all love, but love is not love except there may be some object of affection. The Father Himself, then, as He was solitary, projected and produced Nous and Aletheia, that is, a duad which

became mistress, and origin, and mother of all the Aeons computed by them [as existing] within the Pleroma. Nous and Aletheia being projected from the Father, one capable of continuing generation, deriving existence from a productive being. [Nous] himself likewise, in imitation of the Father, projected Logos and Zoe; and Logos and Zoe project Anthropos and Ecclesia. But Nous and Aletheia, when they beheld that their own off-spring had been born productive, returned thanks to the Father of the universe, and offer unto Him a perfect number, viz., ten Aeons. For, he says, Nous and Aletheia could not offer unto the Father a more perfect [one] than this number. For the Father, who is perfect, ought to be celebrated by a perfect number, and ten is a perfect number, because this is first of those [numbers] that are formed by plurality, [and therefore] perfect. The Father, however, being more perfect, because being alone unbegotten, by means of the one primary conjugal union of Nous and Aletheia, found means of projecting all the roots of existing things.

25. Logos himself also, and Zoe, then saw that Nous and Aletheia had celebrated the Father of the universe by a perfect number; and Logos himself likewise with Zoe wished to magnify their own father and mother, Nous and Aletheia. Since, however, Nous and Aletheia were begotten, and did not possess paternal [and] perfect uncreatedness, Logos and Zoe do not glorify Nous their father with a perfect number, but far from it, with an imperfect one. For Logos and Zoe offer twelve Aeons unto Nous and Aletheia. For, according to Valentinus, these—namely, Nous and Aletheia, Logos and Zoe, Anthropos and Ecclesia—have been the primary roots of the Aeons. But there are ten Aeons proceeding from Nous and Aletheia, and twelve from Logos and Zoe....

At this point Hippolytus provides a list of the names of the various Aeons. Among them is Sophia (Wisdom).

But [the] youngest of all the ... Aeons, being a female, and called Sophia, observed the multitude and power of the begetting Aeons, and hurried back into the depth of the Father. And she perceived that all the rest of the Aeons, as being begotten, generate by conjugal intercourse. The Father, on the other hand, alone, without copulation, has produced [an offspring]. She wished to emulate the Father, and to produce [offspring] of herself without a marital partner, that she might achieve a work in no wise inferior to [that of] the Father. [Sophia, however,] was ignorant that the Unbegotten One, being an originating principle of the universe, as well as root and depth and abyss, alone possesses the power of self-generation. But Sophia, being begotten, and born after many more [Aeons], is not able to acquire possession of the power inherent in the Unbegotten One. For in the Unbegotten One, he says, all things exist simultaneously, but in the begotten [Aeons] the female is projective of substance, and the male is formative of the substance which is projected by the female. Sophia, therefore, prepared to project that only which she was capable [of projecting], viz., a formless and undigested substance. And this, he says, is what Moses asserts: "The earth was invisible, and unfashioned" [[Gen. 1:2]]. This [substance] is, he says, the good [and] the heavenly Jerusalem, into which God has promised to conduct the children of Israel, saying, "I will bring you into a land flowing with milk and honey" [[Exod. 3:17]].

26. Ignorance, therefore, having arisen within the Pleroma in consequence of Sophia, and shapelessness in consequence of the offspring of Sophia, confusion arose in the Pleroma. [For all] the Aeons that were begotten [became overwhelmed with apprehension, imagining] that in like manner formless and incomplete progenies of the Aeons should be generated; and that some destruction, at no distant period, should at length seize upon the Aeons. All the Aeons, then, betook themselves to supplication of the Father, that he would tranquillize the sorrowing Sophia; for she continued weeping and bewailing on account of the abortion produced by her,—for so they term it. The Father, then, compassionating the tears of Sophia, and accepting the supplication of the Aeons, orders a further projection. For he did not, [Valentinus] says, himself project, but Nous and Aletheia [projected] Christ and the Holy Spirit for the restoration of Form, and the destruction of the abortion, and [for] the consolation and cessation of the groans of Sophia. And thirty Aeons came into existence along with Christ and the Holy Spirit....

27. After, then, there ensued some one [treaty of] peace and harmony between all the Aeons within the Pleroma, it appeared expedient to them not only by a conjugal union to have magnified the Son, but also that by an offering of ripe fruits they should glorify the Father. Then all the thirty Aeons consented to project one Aeon, joint fruit of the Pleroma, that he might be [an earnest] of their union, and unanimity, and peace. And he alone was projected by all the Aeons in honour of the Father. This [one] is styled among them "Joint Fruit of the Pleroma." These [matters], then, took place within the Pleroma in this way. And the "Joint Fruit of the Pleroma" was projected, [that is,] Jesus,—for this is his name,—the great High Priest....

28. As, therefore, the primary and greatest power of the animal essence came into existence [[i.e., the soul]], an image [of the only begotten Son]; so also the devil, who is the ruler of this world, constitutes the power of the material essence, as Beelzebub is of the essence of demons which emanates from anxiety. [In the consequence of this,] Sophia from above exerted her energy from the Ogdoad to the Hebdomad. For the Demiurge, they say, knows nothing at all, but is, according to them, devoid of understanding, and silly, and is not conscious of what he is doing or working at. But in him, while thus in a state of ignorance that even he is producing, Sophia wrought all sorts of energy, and infused vigour [into him]. And [although Sophia] was really the operating cause, he himself imagines that he evolves the creation of the world out of himself: whence he commenced, saying, "I am God, and beside me there is no other" [[Isa. 45:5]].

29. Sophia is called "Spirit," and the Demiurge "Soul," and the Devil "the ruler of this world," and Beelzebub "the [ruler] of demons." These are the statements which they put forward. But further, ... [they determine] that the thirty Aeons within the Pleroma have again, in addition to these, projected other Aeons, according to the [numerical] proportion [adopted by the Pythagoreans], in order that the Pleroma might be formed into an aggregate, according to a perfect number. For how the Pythagoreans divided [the celestial sphere] into twelve and thirty and sixty parts, and how they have minute parts of diminutive portions, has been made evident.

In this manner these [followers of Valentinus] subdivide the parts within the Pleroma. Now likewise the parts in the Ogdoad have been sub-divided, and there has been projected Sophia, which is, according to them, mother of all living creatures, and the "Joint Fruit of the Pleroma," [who is] the Logos, [and other Aeons,] who are celestial angels that have their citizenship in Jerusalem which is above, which is in heaven. For this Jerusalem is Sophia, she [that is] outside [the Pleroma], and her spouse is the "Joint Fruit of the Pleroma." And the Demiurge projected souls. This [Demiurge], according to them, is Abraham, and these [souls] the children of Abraham. From the material and devilish essence the Demiurge fash-ioned bodies for the souls. This is what has been declared: "And God formed man, taking clay from the earth, and breathed upon his face the breath of life, and man was made into a living soul" [[Gen. 2:7]]. This, according to them, is the inner man, the natural [man] residing in the material body. Now a material [man] is perishable, incomplete, [and] formed out of the devilish essence. And this is the material man, as it were, according to them an inn or domicile, at one time of soul only, at another time of soul and demons, at another time of soul and Logoi. And these are the Logoi that have been dispersed from above, from the "Joint Fruit of the Pleroma" and [from] Sophia, into this world. And they dwell in an earthly body, with a soul, when demons do not take up their abode with that soul....

30. All the prophets, therefore, and the law, spoke by means of the Demiurge,—a silly god, he says, [and themselves] fools, who knew nothing....When, therefore, the creation received completion, and when after [this] there ought to have been the revelation of the sons of God—that is, of the Demiurge, which up to this had been concealed, and in which obscurity the natural man was hid, and had a veil upon the heart;—when [it was time], then, that the veil should be taken away, and that these mysteries should be seen, Jesus was born of Mary the virgin, according to the declaration [in Scripture], "The Holy Ghost will come upon thee"— Sophia is the Spirit—"and the power of the Highest will overshadow thee,"—the Highest is the Demiurge,—"wherefore that which shall be born of thee shall be called holy" [[Luke 1:35]]. For he has been generated not from the highest alone, as those created in [the likeness of] Adam have been created from the highest alone—that is, [from] Sophia and the Demiurge. Jesus, however, the new man, [has been generated] from the Holy Spirit—that is, Sophia and the Demiurge—in order that the Demiurge may complete the conformation and constitution of his body, and that the Holy Spirit may supply his essence, and that a celestial Logos may proceed from the Ogdoad being born of Mary.

Concerning this [Logos] they have a great question amongst them—an occasion both of divisions and dissension. And hence the doctrine of these has become divided: and one doctrine, according to them, is termed Oriental, and the other Italian. They from Italy, of whom is Heracleon and Ptolemaeus, say that the body of Jesus was [an] animal [one]. And on account of this, [they maintain] that at his baptism the Holy Spirit as a dove came down—that is, the Logos of the mother above, [I mean Sophia]—and became [a voice] to the animal [man], and raised him from the dead....The Orientals, on the other hand, of whom is Axionicus and Bardesianes, assert that the body of the Saviour was spiritual; for there came upon Mary the Holy Spirit—that is, Sophia and the power of the highest. This is the creative art, [and was vouchsafed] in order that what was given to Mary by the Spirit might be fashioned.

At the outset of chapter 31 Hippolytus says that Sophia taught the demiurge
that he is not himself the only God, and she instructed him concerning the
Father and the Aeons; then he goes on to say that the "trespasses" on earth had
to be rectified.

31. On this account Jesus the Saviour was born of Mary, that he might
rectify [the trespasses committed] here; as the Christ who, having been
projected additionally from above by Nous and Aletheia, had corrected the
passions of Sophia—that is, the abortion [who was] outside [the Pleroma].
And, again, the Saviour who was born of Mary came to rectify the passions
of the soul. There are therefore, according to these [heretics], three Christs:
[the first the] one additionally projected by Nous and Aletheia, along with
the Holy Spirit; and [the second] the "Joint Fruit of the Pleroma," spouse
of Sophia, who was outside [the Pleroma]. And she herself is likewise
styled Holy Spirit, but one inferior to the first [projection]. And the third
[Christ is] He who was born of Mary for the restoration of this world of
ours.

11.4. Hippolytus, *Refutation of All Heresies* 10.9. Rome, ca. A.D. 230.

Source: *The Ante-Nicene Fathers*, ed. A. Roberts and J. Donaldson,
5:144.

As in the previous selection (11.3), Hippolytus here indicates a distinction
among the Valentinians and discusses the views of one branch of them. They
hold that the originating principle is the Father, or Bythus (Depth), and his
spouse Sige (Silence), and that their immediate projections are Nous (Mind),
Aletheia (Truth), Logos (Word), Zoe (Life), Anthropos (Man), and Ecclesia
(Church). These eight form the Ogdoad (the Group of Eight) and are within
the Pleroma (Fullness). Christ has descended into the world from within this
company to save the indwelling spirit within human beings. Salvation consists
of release of the spirit from the flesh.

Valentinus ... and the adherents of this school, though they agree in
asserting that the originating principle of the universe is the Father, still
they are impelled into the adoption of a contrary opinion respecting Him.
For some of them maintain that [the Father] is solitary and generative;
whereas others hold the impossibility, [in His as in other cases,] of procre-

ation without a female. They therefore add Sige as the spouse of this Father, and style the Father Himself Bythus. From this Father and His spouse some allege that there have been six projections,—viz., Nous and Aletheia, Logos and Zoe, Anthropos and Ecclesia,—and that this constitutes the procreative Ogdoad. And the Valentinians maintain that those are the first projections which have taken place within the limit, and have been again denominated "those within the Pleroma"; and the second are "those without the Pleroma"; and the third, "those without the Limit." ... And [[Valentinus asserts]] that Christ came down from within the Pleroma for the salvation of the spirit who has erred. This spirit, [according to the Valentinians,] resides in our inner man; and they say that this inner man obtains salvation on account of this indwelling spirit. Valentinus, however, [to uphold the doctrine,] determines that the flesh is not saved, and styles it "a leathern tunic," and the perishable portion of man.

11.5. Epiphanius, *Panarion* 31.2.2-10; 31.7.3-11. Salamis, Cyprus,
 A.D. 375–78.

Source: *Panarion,* trans. P. R. Amidon, 108–9, 113.

Epiphanius claims that Valentinus received some of his teachings from Hesiod, an early Greek poet (date unknown, some placing him as early as the eighth century B.C.). He recounts the names for the various aeons and provides translations for them. According to him, Valentinus was originally orthodox but departed from orthodoxy while living on Cyprus on his way to Rome. His followers deny the resurrection of the dead, divide humanity into three classes, and call themselves Gnostics.

[2.2] Most people, then, do not know his homeland or where he was born, for hardly any writer has been concerned to show where he was from. But we have heard a sort of rumor, so we will not pass over it without indicating where he was from. The matter is somewhat in doubt (to tell the truth), but we will not fail to report what we have heard. [2.3] Some, that is, have said that he was born a Phrebonite, on the coast of Egypt, and received the sort of education which the Greeks do in Alexandria. [2.4] So in imitation of Hesiod's *Theogony* [and] of the thirty gods spoken of by Hesiod, he also, having absorbed the poetry of the Greek myths, acquired the outlook of those who with him and before him had fallen from the truth, and, altering what was in Hesiod by changing the names, he wished to delude the world. [2.5] For he too wants to introduce thirty gods and aeons and heavens, of which the first is Depth, as he says with his lack of sense, just as Hesiod, the one responsible for his ideas, certainly said: "Chaos is the very first of gods." Now who does not realize that "Chaos" and "Depth" mean the same thing?

[2.6] ... He wishes to produce thirty aeons, which he also calls "gods," saying that there are fifteen male and as many female. [2.7] He and his followers say that each aeon is masculofeminine and a couple. They say that there are fifteen dyads, which they call "pairs." In number there are thirty aeons, each female one engendering from the male the ones that follow. They are as follows, each male name paired with a female one: Ampsiou Auraan Boukoua Thardouou Ouboukoua Thardeddein Merexa Atar Barba Oudouak Esten Ouananin Lamertarde Athames Soumin Allora Koubiatha Danadaria Dammo Oren Lanaphek Oudinphek Emphiboche Barra Assiou Ache Belim Dexariche Masemon. [2.9] This is how they have been arranged as male-female pairs, but the order of their succession is as follows: Ampsiou Auraan Boukoua Thardouou Ouboukoua Thardeddein Merexa Atar Barba Oudouak Esten Ouananin Lamertarde Athames Soumin Allora Koubiatha Danadaria Dammo Oren Lanaphek Oudinphek Emphiboche Barra Assiou Ache Belim Dexariche Masemon. [2.10] The meanings of the names are as follows: Depth [and] Silence, Mind and Truth, Logos and Life, Man and Church, Paraclete and Faith, Paternal and Hope, Maternal and Charity, Ever-Mind and Intelligence, Willed (also called Light) and Beatitude, Ecclesiasticus and Wisdom, Deep and Combination, Ageless and Union, Self-Originate and Blending, Only-Begotten and Unity, Unmoved and Pleasure....

[7.3] He and his disciples say that our Lord Jesus Christ, as I said, is Savior, Christ, Logos, Cross, Conveyer, Boundary-Setter, and Boundary. [7.4] They say that he brought down from above the body and like water through a channel came through the Virgin Mary, but took nothing from the virginal womb; he has the body from above, as I said. [7.5] He is not the first Logos or the Christ after the Logos who is above among the Aeons above, but, they say, he was emitted for no other reason but to come and save the spiritual race which is from above.

[7.6] They deny the resurrection of the dead, uttering some senseless fable about it not being this body that rises, but another one which comes from it and which they call "spiritual." But [salvation belongs?] only to those among them who are spiritual, and to those called "natural"—if, that is, the natural ones act justly; but those called "material," "carnal," and "earthly" perish utterly and are in no way saved. [7.7] Each substance proceeds to what emitted it: the material is given over to matter and what is carnal and earthly to the earth. [7.8] For they teach the existence of three classes of human beings, spiritual, natural, and carnal, saying that they are the spiritual class as well as the "gnostic," and that they do not need to labor, but need only knowledge and the incantations of their rites. Each of them does anything whatsoever without fear or concern, for, they say, their class, being spiritual, will be saved from everything. [7.9] But the next class of humans in the world, which they call "natural," cannot be saved on its own, unless it saves itself by labor and just deeds. The material class of humans in the world, they say, is incapable of knowledge and cannot receive it, even if someone from that class wanted it, but it perishes, body and soul together. [7.10] Their class, however, being spiritual, is saved with another body, something interior, which they fancifully call a spiritual body. [7.11] But the "natural ones," having labored much and ascended above the Demiurge, will he given above to the angels who are with Christ. They recover nothing of their bodies, but only the souls found to be in the fullness of their knowledge and to have ascended above the Demiurge are given as brides to the angels with Christ.

Part III

Other Teachers and Sects of the Second Century

Chapter 12

Marcion and Marcionism

Marcion (second century, died ca. A.D. 160) was the founder of a major, independent church that rivaled the Catholic church and continued to exist until at least the middle of the fifth century. The son of a bishop, Marcion was born at Sinope, a city in Pontus on the southern coast of the Black Sea. He arrived in Rome around A.D. 130, joined the church there, and presented it with a large gift. In time Marcion came under the influence of the gnostic teacher Cerdo, and in 144 he founded his own church (and received his contribution to the Catholic church back). His church had an organizational pattern similar to that of the Catholic church. When Justin wrote his *First Apology* (ca. A.D. 155), he said that Marcion's followers could be found in every nation (1.26).

Marcion taught a radical separation between the law and the gospel, contending that the God revealed by Jesus Christ is one of absolute goodness and devoid of wrath. The God revealed in the Hebrew Scriptures, the Creator of the world (sometimes called by Marcion and his followers the *Demiurge*), is other than this God. Accordingly, for Marcion there are two Gods—the highest of them being a God of love, gospel, and peace; the lower of them a God of wrath, law, and judgment. Christ, who reveals the former, did not come in the flesh, but only in the appearance of it. The flesh, being material, is to be considered evil.

Marcion was the first Christian to designate a collection of books as a standard (or "canon") of Christian teaching, and this consisted of an abridged edition of the Gospel of Luke and ten expurgated letters of the apostle Paul (his collection did not include 1 and 2 Timothy and Titus of the thirteen letters attributed to Paul in our present New Testament); the Old Testament was rejected altogether. Marcion and his followers (who did not hesitate to call themselves "Christians") followed a strict, ascetic pattern of behavior which prohibited marriage, the eating of meat, and the drinking of wine. Marcion and Marcionites are mentioned and discussed by several early Christian writers, including Justin, Irenaeus, Hippolytus, Tertullian, Clement of Alexandria, Origen, Eusebius, and Epiphanius. These writers give the impression that Marcionism was a powerful movement. Often it is classified as a form of Gnosticism, and there are major likenesses. But Marcion differs from the gnostic leaders and movements in general by his insistence on a literal rather than an allegorical interpretation of the Scriptures, his view that the human being is wholly the handiwork of the Creator rather than a being that also contains a divine spark, and his organizational ability and the networking among his churches. His churches lasted in the West until the end of the third century and in the East until the middle of the fifth.

12.1. Justin, *Apology* 1.26. Rome, ca. A.D. 155.

See reading 1.2 above.

12.2. Irenaeus, *Against Heresies* 1.27.2-3. Lyons, ca. A.D. 190.

Source: *Gnosticism*, ed. R. M. Grant, 45.

Irenaeus provides a brief introduction to Marcion's thought, including some of its major tenets: the God of the Old Testament is less than the superior God whom Jesus revealed; an abbreviated Gospel of Luke and an abridged edition of the epistles of Paul alone are authoritative; and he himself is more trustworthy than the apostles.

Marcion of Pontus succeeded Cerdo and developed his doctrine, shamelessly blaspheming him who was proclaimed as God by the law and the prophets and calling him the creator of evil things [Is. 45:7], desirous of wars, inconstant in purpose [Gen. 6:6], and inconsistent with himself. From the Father, who is above the God who made the world, Jesus came to Judaea in the time of the governor Pontius Pilate, procurator for Tiberius Caesar, and was manifested in the form of a man to those who were in Judaea; he destroyed the prophets and the law [cf. Matt. 5:17] and all the works of that God who made the world, whom Marcion calls Cosmocrator [world-ruler]. Furthermore, Marcion circumcises the gospel according to Luke and takes out everything written about the generation of the Lord [Luke 1:1—2:52], as well as many items about the teaching of the Lord's words in which the Lord is most plainly described as acknowledging the Creator of this universe as his Father. He persuaded his disciples that he himself was more trustworthy than the apostles who transmitted the gospel; but he delivered to them not the gospel but a particle of the gospel. Similarly he abridged the epistles of the apostle Paul, taking out whatever was clearly said by the apostle concerning that God who made the world [since this God is the Father of our Lord Jesus Christ] as well as whatever the apostle taught when he mentioned passages from the prophetic writings which foretell the Lord's coming.

12.3. Hippolytus, *Refutation of All Heresies* 7.17-19. Rome, ca. A.D. 230.

Source: *The Ante-Nicene Fathers*, ed. A. Roberts and J. Donaldson, 5:110, 112–14.

In this passage Hippolytus claims that Marcion took some of his teachings from the pagan philosopher Empedocles (493-433 B.C.), particularly some of his asceticism (forbidding marriage, dissolving those that exist, and forbidding the eating of meat). According to Hippolytus, Marcion also taught a docetic view of Christ, denying that he came in the flesh "unbegotten," which means, in this case, not born of Mary.

17. But Marcion, a native of Pontus, far more frantic than these [heretics], omitting the majority of the tenets of the greater number [of speculators], [and] advancing into a doctrine still more unabashed, supposed [the existence of] two originating causes of the universe, alleging one of them to be a certain good [principle], but the other an evil one. And himself imagining that he was introducing some novel [opinion], founded a school full of folly, and attended by men of a sensual mode of life, inasmuch as he himself was one of lustful propensities.

18. When, therefore, Marcion or some one of his hounds barks against the Demiurge, and adduces reasons from a comparison of what is good and bad, we ought to say to them, that neither Paul the apostle nor Mark, he of the maimed finger, announced such [tenets]. For none of these [doctrines] has been written in the Gospel according to Mark. But [the real author of the system] is Empedocles, son of Meto, a native of Agrigentum.

And [Marcion] despoiled this [philosopher], and imagined that up to the present would pass undetected his transference, under the same expressions, of the arrangement of his entire heresy from Sicily into the evangelical narratives. For bear with me, O Marcion: as you have instituted a comparison of what is good and evil, I also to-day will institute a comparison following up your own tenets, as you suppose them to be. You affirm that the Demiurge of the world is evil—why not hide your countenance in shame, [as thus] teaching to the Church the doctrines of Empedocles? You say that there is a good Deity who destroys the works of the Demiurge: then do not you plainly preach to your pupils, as the good Deity, the Friendship of Empedocles. You forbid marriage, the procreation of children, [and] the abstaining from meats which God has created for participation by the faithful, and those that know the truth. [Thinkest thou, then,] that thou canst escape detection, [while thus] enjoining the purificatory rites of Empedocles? For in point of fact you follow in every respect this [philosopher of paganism], while you instruct your own disciples to refuse meats, in order not to eat any body [that might be] a remnant of a soul which has been punished by the Demiurge. You dissolve Marriages that have been cemented by the Deity. And here again you conform to the tenets of Empedocles, in order that for you the work of Friendship may be perpetuated as one [and] indivisible. For, according to Empedocles, Matrimony separates unity, and makes [out of it] plurality, as we have proved.

19. Marcion, adopting these sentiments, rejected altogether the generation of our Saviour. He considered it to be absurd that under the [category of a] creature fashioned by destructive Discord should have been the Logos that was an auxiliary to Friendship—that is, the Good Deity. [His doctrine,] however, was that, independent of birth, [the Logos] Himself descended from above in the fifteenth year of the reign of Tiberius Caesar, and that, as being intermediate between the good and bad Deity, He proceeded to give instruction in the synagogues. For if He is a Mediator, He has been, he says, liberated from the entire nature of the Evil Deity. Now, as he affirms, the Demiurge is evil, and his works. For this reason, he affirms, Jesus came down unbegotten, in order that He might be liberated from all [admixture of] evil. And He has, he says, been liberated from the nature of the Good One likewise, in order that He may be a Mediator, as Paul states, and as Himself acknowledges: "Why call ye me good? There is one good" [[Mark 10:18]]. These, then, are the opinions of Marcion, by means of which he made many his dupes, employing the conclusions of Empedocles. And he transferred the philosophy invented by that [ancient

speculator] into his own system of thought, and [out of Empedocles] constructed his [own] impious heresy.

12.4. Hippolytus, *Refutation of All Heresies* 10.15. Rome, ca. A.D. 230.

Source: *The Ante-Nicene Fathers*, ed. A. Roberts and J. Donaldson, 5:146.

Hippolytus here speaks of Marcion's views concerning Christ, such as his view that Christ only appeared to be human and to suffer, and the reason why Marcion opposed marriage.

[[Marcion says]] that Christ is the Son of the good Being, and was sent for the salvation of souls by him whom he styles the inner man. And he asserts that he appeared as a man though not being a man, and as incarnate though not being incarnate. And he maintains that his manifestation was only phantastic, and that he underwent neither generation nor passion except in appearance. And he will not allow that flesh rises again; but in affirming marriage to be destruction, he leads his disciples towards a very cynical life. And by these means he imagines that he annoys the Creator, if he should abstain from the things that are made or appointed by Him.

12.5. Tertullian, *Against Marcion*, 1.1.6; 1.2.1-3; 1.19.4-5; 1.24.5; 1.26.1-4; 1.29.1-2; 3.8.2-7; 4.2.1-5; 4.3.2; 4.6.1-4. Carthage, North Africa, A.D. 207–8.

Source: *Tertullian Adversus Marcionem*, trans. E. Evans, 1:5, 7, 49–51, 67, 73–75, 81, 193–95; 2:261–65, 275.

Of all the ancient writers Tertullian has provided the fullest account of Marcion and his teachings. The work of Tertullian, written in Latin, is an extremely important source because it is relatively early and ample. It consists of five books in its third edition (he was dissatisfied with his first draft, and the second was stolen). In the selections recorded here, Tertullian attacks Marcion's views as a departure from earlier orthodoxy (which undercuts any claim that Marcion taught a version of Christianity that is earlier and more faithful), his theology (the two gods), his separation of law and gospel, his denial of the incarnation, his opposition to marriage, and his rejection of the Old Testament.

1.1.6 [[Marcion's]] followers cannot deny that his faith at first agreed with ours, for his own letter proves it: so that without further ado that man can be marked down as a heretic, or "chooser," who, forsaking what had once been, has chosen for himself that which previously was not. For that which is of later importation must needs be reckoned heresy, precisely because that has to be considered truth which was delivered of old and from the beginning.

1.2.1-3 This man of Pontus presents us with two gods, as it were the two Clashing Rocks on which he suffers shipwreck: the one the Creator, whom he cannot deny, which is our God: the other, whom he cannot prove, a god of his own. The unhappy man became afflicted with the idea of this wild guess in consequence of that plain statement which our Lord made, which applies to men, not to gods, the example of the good tree and the bad, that neither does the good tree bring forth bad fruit nor the bad tree good fruit [[Luke 6:43]]—that is, that a good mind or a good faith does not produce evil actions, nor an evil mind and faith good ones. For, like many even in our day, heretics in particular, Marcion had an unhealthy interest in the problem of evil—the origin of it—and his perceptions were numbed by the very excess of his curiosity. So when he found the Creator declaring, *It is I who create evil things* [[Isa. 45:7]], in that he had, from other arguments which make that impression on the perverse, already assumed him to be the author of evil, he interpreted with reference to the Creator the evil tree that creates evil fruit—namely, evil things in general—and assumed that there had to be another god to correspond with the good tree which brings forth good fruits. Discovering then in Christ as it were a different dispensation of sole and unadulterated benevolence, an opposite character to the Creator's, he found it easy to argue for a new and hitherto unknown divinity revealed in its own Christ, and thus with a little leaven has embittered with heretical acidity the whole mass of the faith. He was acquainted also with a certain Cerdo, who gave shape to this outrage. And so the blind were easily led to think they had a clear prospect of two gods, in that they had no accurate view of the one God. To the blear-eyed a single lamp looks double. So then the one God, whose existence he was forced to admit, Marcion has overthrown by slandering him as responsible for evil: the other, whom he constrained himself to invent, he has set up on a scaffolding of goodness. My own answers will make it clear in what specific terms he has portioned out these two sets of attributes.

1.19.4-5 The separation of Law and Gospel is the primary and principal exploit of Marcion. His disciples cannot deny this, which stands at the head of their document, that document by which they are inducted into and confirmed in this heresy. For such are Marcion's *Antitheses*, or Contrary Oppositions, which are designed to show the conflict and disagreement of the Gospel and the Law, so that from the diversity of principles between those two documents they may argue further for a diversity of gods. Therefore, as it is precisely this separation of Law and Gospel which has suggested a god of the Gospel, other than and in opposition to the God of the Law, it is evident that before that separation was made, [that] god was still unknown who has just come into notice in consequence of the argument for separation: and so he was not revealed by Christ, who came before the separation, but was invented by Marcion, who set up the separation in opposition to that peace between Gospel and Law which previously, from the appearance of Christ until the impudence of Marcion, had been kept unimpaired and unshaken by virtue of that [sound] reasoning which refused to contemplate any other god of the Law and the Gospel than that Creator against whom after so long a time, by a man of Pontus, separation has been let loose.

1.24.5 Now although, in the view of your heresy, Christ did not clothe himself with the verity of flesh, yet he did vouchsafe to take upon him the appearance of it. The very fact that he made a false pretence of it has given it some claim upon him. Yet what else is man if not flesh?

1.26.1-4 At present it is enough to have shown their god to be thoroughly inconsistent, even in their laudation of goodness as his one and only attribute: for because of this they refuse to impute to him those emotions of mind which they object to in the Creator. For if he displays neither hostility nor wrath, if he neither condemns nor disdains, if, that is, he never makes himself a judge, I cannot see how his moral law, that more extensive moral law, can have stability. To what purpose does he lay down commands if he will not require performance, or prohibit transgressions if he is not to exact penalties, if he is incapable of judgement, a stranger to all emotions of severity and reproof? Why does he forbid the commission of an act he does not penalize when committed? It would have been much more honest of him not to forbid an act he was not going to penalize, than to refrain from penalizing what he had forbidden. In fact he ought openly to have allowed it: for if he was not going to penalize it he had no reason to forbid it. In real life an act forbidden without sanctions is tacitly permitted: and in any case one only forbids the commission of acts one dislikes to see being done. So this [god] is exceptionally dull-witted if he is not offended by the doing of that which he dislikes to see being done: for offence is attendant upon wishes set at naught. Or else, if he does take offence, he ought to be displeased, and if displeased he ought to punish. For punishment is the outcome of displeasure, as displeasure is the due reward of offence, and offence, as I have said, is attendant upon wishes set at naught. But as he does not punish, it is plain that he is not offended: and as he is not offended it is plain that his wishes suffer no hurt when that is done which he has desired should not be done: and in that case the wrongdoing takes place in accordance with his will, seeing that anything which does no injury to his will is in no opposition to his will.

1.29.1-2 Among that god's adherents no flesh is baptized except it be virgin or widowed or unmarried, or has purchased baptism by divorce: as though even eunuch's flesh was born of anything but marital intercourse. Of course this regulation can justify itself if matrimony stands condemned. We have to inquire whether it is justly condemned: not that we intend to demolish the blessedness of chastity, as do certain Nicolaitans, advocates of vice and wantonness; but as those who, without condemning marital intercourse, recognize and seek after chastity, giving it preference, not as a good thing over a bad one, but as a better thing over a good one. For we do not repudiate marital intercourse, but give it lower rank: nor do we demand chastity, but advise it, retaining both the good thing and the better, to be followed according to each man's powers. But we vigorously defend matrimony when, under the charge of indecency, it suffers hostile attack to the discredit of the Creator: for he, in consideration of the honour of that estate, blessed matrimony for the increase of mankind, even as he blessed the whole of creation for wholesome and advantageous uses.

3.8.2-7 So Marcion, even more of an antichrist, seized upon this assumption, being better equipped in fact for denial of Christ's corporal substance, in that he had postulated that even Christ's god was neither the creator of flesh nor would raise it to life again—in this too supremely good, and entirely divergent from the lies and deceptions of the Creator. And that is why his Christ, so as not to tell lies, or to deceive, and in this fashion perhaps be accounted as belonging to the Creator, was not that which he appeared to be, and told lies about what he was—being flesh and not flesh, man and not man, and in consequence a Christ [who was] god and not god. For why should he not also have been clothed in a phantasm of god? Or can I believe what he says of his more recondite substance, when he has deceived me about that which was more evident? How shall he be accounted truthful about the secret thing, who has been found so deceptive about the obvious? How can it have been that by confusing within himself truth of the spirit with deceit of the flesh, he conjoined that fellowship of light, which is truth, and deception, which is darkness, that the apostle says is impossible? Also, now that it is found to be a lie that Christ [was made] flesh, it follows that all things that were done by means of Christ's flesh were done by a lie, his meetings with people, his touching of them, his partaking of food, his miracles besides. For if by touching someone, or being touched by someone, he gave freedom from sickness, the act performed by the body cannot be credited as truly performed apart from the verity of the body itself. It was not feasible for anything solid to be performed by that which is void, anything full by that which is empty. Putative constitution, putative activity: imaginary operator, imaginary operations. Thus also the sufferings of Marcion's Christ will fail to find credence: one who has not truly suffered, has not suffered at all, and a phantasm cannot have truly suffered. Consequently God's whole operation is overthrown. There is a denial of Christ's death, the whole weight and value of the Christian name, that death which the apostle so firmly insists on, because it is true, declaring it the chief foundation of the gospel, of our salvation, and of his own preaching. *For I delivered unto you,* he says, *first of all, that Christ died for our sins, and that he was buried, and that he rose again the third day* [[1 Cor. 15:3-4]]. But if his flesh is denied, how can his death be affirmed? For death is the particular experience of flesh, which by means of death is turned downwards into the earth from which it was taken: such is the law of its own Creator. But if the death is denied, as it is when the flesh is denied, neither can there be assurance of the resurrection. By whatever reasoning he did not die, by the same reasoning he did not rise again: which was that he had not the substance of flesh, to which death appertains, and likewise resurrection. But further, if doubt is cast upon Christ's resurrection, ours also is overthrown: for if Christ's is not valid, neither can that be valid for the sake of which Christ came. For just as those who said there was no resurrection of the dead are confuted by the apostle from the resurrection of Christ, so also, if Christ's resurrection fails, the resurrection of the dead is also taken away. And so also our faith is vain, and vain is the apostles' preaching. They are also found false witnesses of God, because they have borne witness that he has raised up Christ, whom he has not raised up. And we are yet in our sins. And those who are fallen asleep in Christ, have perished—no doubt they will rise again, but in a phantasm perhaps, as Christ did.

4.2.1-5 You have there my short and sharp answer to the *Antitheses.* I pass on next to show how his gospel—certainly not Judaic but Pontic—is in places adulterated: and this shall form the basis of my order of approach. I lay it down to begin with that the documents of the gospel have the apostles for their authors, and that this task of promulgating the gospel was imposed upon them by our Lord himself. If they also have for their authors apostolic men, yet these stand not alone, but as companions of apostles or followers of apostles: because the preaching of disciples might be made suspect of the desire of vainglory, unless there stood by it the authority of their teachers, or rather the authority of Christ, which made the apostles teachers. In short, from among the apostles the faith is introduced to us by John and by Matthew, while from among apostolic men Luke and Mark give it renewal, [all of them] beginning with the same rules [of belief], as far as relates to the one only God, the Creator, and to his Christ, born of a virgin, the fulfilment of the law and the prophets. It matters not that the arrangement of their narratives varies, so long as there is agreement on the essentials of the faith—and on these they show no agreement with Marcion. Marcion, on the other hand, attaches to his gospel no author's name,—as though he to whom it was no crime to overturn the whole body, might not assume permission to invent a title for it as well. At this point I might have made a stand, arguing that no recognition is due to a work which cannot lift up its head, which makes no show of courage, which gives no promise of credibility by having a fully descriptive title and the requisite indication of the author's name. But I prefer to join issue on all points, nor am I leaving unmentioned anything that can be taken as being in my favour. For out of those authors whom we possess, Marcion is seen to have chosen Luke as the one to mutilate. Now Luke was not an apostle but an apostolic man, not a master but a disciple, in any case less than his master, and assuredly even more of lesser account as being a follower of a later apostle, Paul, to be sure: so that even if Marcion had introduced his gospel under the name of Paul in person, that one single document would not be adequate for our faith, if destitute of the support of his predecessors. For we should demand the production of that gospel also which Paul found [in existence], that to which he gave his assent, that with which shortly afterwards he was anxious that his own should agree: for his intention in going up to Jerusalem to know and to consult the apostles, was lest perchance he had run in vain—that is, lest perchance he had not believed as they did, or were not preaching the gospel in their manner. At length, when he had conferred with the original [apostles], and there was agreement concerning the rule of the faith, they joined the right hands [of fellowship], and from thenceforth divided their spheres of preaching, so that the others should go to the Jews, but Paul to Jews and gentiles. If he therefore who gave the light to Luke chose to have his predecessors' authority for his faith as well as his preaching, much more must I require for Luke's gospel the authority which was necessary for the gospel of his master.

4.3.2 But Marcion has got hold of Paul's epistle to the Galatians, in which he rebukes even the apostles themselves for not walking uprightly according to the truth of the gospel, and accuses also certain false apostles of perverting the gospel of Christ: and on this ground Marcion strives hard to overthrow the credit of those gospels which are the apostles' own and are published under their names, or even the names of apostolic men, with the intention no doubt of conferring on his own gospel the repute which he takes away from those others.

4.6.1-4 Certainly the whole of the work he has done, including the pre-fixing of his *Antitheses*, he directs to the one purpose of setting up opposi-tion between the Old Testament and the New, and thereby putting his Christ in separation from the Creator, as belonging to another god, and having no connection with the law and the prophets. Certainly that is why he has expunged all the things that oppose his view, that are in accord with the Creator, on the plea that they have been woven in by his partisans; but has retained those that accord with his opinion. These it is we shall call to account, with these we shall grapple, to see if they will favour my case, not his, to see if they will put a check on Marcion's pretensions. Then it will become clear that these things have been expunged by the same disease of heretical blindness by which the others have been retained. Such will be the purpose and plan of my treatise, on those precise terms which have been agreed by both parties. Marcion lays it down that there is one Christ who in the time of Tiberius was revealed by a god formerly unknown, for the salvation of all the nations; and another Christ who is destined by God the Creator to come at some time still future for the re-establishment of the Jewish kingdom. Between these he sets up a great and absolute opposi-tion, such as that between justice and kindness, between law and gospel, between Judaism and Christianity. From this will also derive my statement of claim, by which I lay it down that the Christ of a different god has no right to have anything in common with the Creator; and again, that Christ must be adjudged to be the Creator's if he is found to have administered the Creator's ordinances, fulfilled his prophecies, supported his laws, given actuality to his promises, revived his miracles, given new expression to his judgements, and reproduced the lineaments of his character and attributes.

12.6. Eusebius, *Ecclesiastical History* 4.11. Caesarea, ca. A.D. 325.

Source: Eusebius, *History of the Church*, trans. G. Williamson, 164–65.

In this selection Eusebius quotes from the Apology *of Justin Martyr, a contemporary of Marcion. This corresponds closely with the text from Justin printed earlier at chapter 1.2. It is of interest that Marcion and his followers accepted the term "Christians" for themselves.*

In their time Justin was at his most active; wearing the garb of a philosopher he proclaimed the divine message, and contended by means of his writings on behalf of the Faith. In a pamphlet which he wrote against Marcion he mentions that at the time when he was composing it the man was alive and in the public eye:

There was one Marcion of Pontus, who is still busy teaching his adherents to believe in some other god greater than the Creator. All over the world, with the help of the demons, he has induced many to speak blasphemously, denying that the Maker of this universe is the Father of Christ, and declaring that the universe was made by another, greater than He. All who base their belief on such doctrines are, as I said, called Christians, just as philosophers, even if they have no common principles, yet have one thing in common—the name "philosopher."

12.7. Epiphanius, *Panarion* 42.1.1-2; 42.3.1—4.6; 42.9.1-4; 42.11.1-5; 42.11.9-11. Salamis, Cyprus, A.D. 375-78.

Source: *Panarion*, trans. P. R. Amidon, 144–46, 148–49, 154–55.

In his discussion of Marcion, Epiphanius discusses his theology but also provides considerable information about which New Testament books he accepted as authoritative and ways in which he altered them. Excerpts of the longer discussion are included in this selection.

[1.1] Marcion, the founder of the Marcionists, was influenced by the aforementioned Cerdo and himself came forth as a great snake into the world. He deceived, and continues to deceive, many people in many different ways, and opened a school. [1.2] The sect may still be found in Rome and in Italy, in Egypt and in Palestine, in Arabia and in Syria, in Cyprus and the Thebaid, and even in Persia and other places....

[3.1] He was influenced by the aforementioned Cerdo, a magician and deceiver. He too proclaimed two principles, but he added further to him, to Cerdo that is, and taught something different than he. He said that there are three principles: one the unnameable and invisible one, which he wants to call as well the good God and which has created nothing in the world, [3.2] another the visible God who is creator and demiurge, and the third the devil, who is as it were between the two others, the visible and the invisible. The creator and demiurge and visible God is of the Jews, and is judge. [3.3] Marcion also preaches virginity, and fasting on Saturday. He celebrates the sacraments with the catechumens looking on. He uses water in the sacraments. [3.4] He says to fast on Saturday for this reason: since it is the time of rest for the God of the Jews who made the world and rested on the seventh day, we should fast on that day, lest we do what befits the God of the Jews. [3.5] He rejects the resurrection of the flesh, like many of the sects. Resurrection, life, and salvation belong to the soul only, he says. [3.6] But he gives not just one sacred bath; it is allowed by them to give up to three baths and more to those who want them, as I have heard from many people. [3.7] It came about that he allowed three or more baths to be given because of the mockery he suffered from his disciples who knew him, on account of his lapse and his seduction of the virgin. [3.8] Because he seduced the virgin in his own city, fled, and was detected in his great lapse, the imposter thought up for himself a second bath, saying that it is allowed to give up to three baths, that is three baptisms, to take away sins, so that if one lapses after the first and repents, he receives a second, and a third likewise if he lapses after the second. [3.9] In order to save himself from ridicule, he offers as proof that after his fall he was once again purified and is now among the innocent, a text which he argues wrongly is persuasive, one which can deceive although it does not have the meaning he gives it. [3.10] He says that the Lord, who had been baptized by John, used to say to his disciples, "I have a baptism with which to be baptized, and how I wish that I had accomplished it," and again, "I have a cup to drink, and my only wish is to fill it." And thus he taught the giving of several baptisms.

[4.1] Not only that, but he also rejects the law and all the prophets, saying that such people prophesied under the influence of the archon who made the world. [4.2] He says that Christ came down from above from the invisible and unnameable Father for the salvation of souls and the refutation of the God of the Jews, the law, the prophets, and suchlike. [4.3] The Lord descended to the netherworld to save those associated with Cain, Korah, Dathan and Abiram, as well as Esau and all the nations who did not know the God of the Jews. [4.4] But those associated with Abel, Enoch, Noah, Abraham, Isaac, Jacob and Moses, David and Solomon he left there, because, he says, they knew the God of the Jews, who is maker and creator, and did what he commanded, and did not dedicate themselves to the invisible God. [4.5] He also allows women to baptize. For with them all is ridicule and nothing else, since they dare even to celebrate the sacraments in the sight of catechumens. [4.6] He says also, as I mentioned, that resurrection is not of bodies but of souls, and he restricts salvation to them; he does not allow it for the bodies. And he talks likewise about transmigrations of souls and reincarnations from bodies to bodies....

[9.1] I will now proceed to his writings, or rather to his mischief. He has as a gospel only Luke's, with the beginning removed because of the Savior's conception and incarnation. [9.2] But he cut off not just the beginning...but removed as well much of the conclusion and of the words of truth that come between, and added other things to what was written. But this is the only writing he accepts: Luke's Gospel. [9.3] He has as well ten letters of the holy apostle, which are all he accepts; but he does not accept everything written in them. Some of their passages he removes, and some he alters. These are the two books he accepts, but he composed other writings of his own for those whom he led astray.

[9.4] The letters mentioned by him are: first, to the Galatians, second, to the Corinthians, third, the second letter to the Corinthians, fourth, to the Romans, fifth, to the Thessalonians, sixth, the second letter to the Thessalonians, seventh, to the Ephesians, eighth, to the Colossians, ninth, to Philemon, and tenth, to the Philippians. He also has parts of the letter called "to the Laodiceans."...

[11.1] Those who make it their practice to obtain accurate information about the spurious ideas of the deceiver Marcion and to distinguish the devices fabricated by his herd will not be slow to peruse this collection. [11.2] For we have devoted ourselves to arranging here those passages from his gospel which may be used in refutation of his cunning villainy, so that those who desire to peruse this work may use it as an exercise in acuity, with a view to refuting the strange utterances dreamed up by him. [11.3] For although the document containing Luke's Gospel [does contain the text of that Gospel?], because it is mutilated and has no beginning, middle, or end, it is like a garment eaten by many moths. [11.4] For at the very outset, everything written by Luke at the beginning, where he says, "Inasmuch as many have undertaken" and so forth, and about Elizabeth and the angel bringing the good news to the Virgin Mary, about John and Zechariah and the birth in Bethlehem, the genealogy and the account of the baptism—[11.5] All this he removes and skips over, and puts as the beginning of the gospel: "In the fifteenth year of Tiberius Caesar" and so forth....

[11.9] Such is Marcion's spurious composition, which contains the text and wording of Luke's gospel and the incomplete writings of the apostle Paul, meaning not all of his letters, [11.10] but only Romans, Ephesians, Colossians, Laodiceans, Galatians, First and Second Corinthians, First and Second Thessalonians, Philemon, and Philippians. [11.11] [But he includes none?] of First and Second Timothy, Titus, and Hebrews [and even?] those he includes [are mutilated?], so that they are not complete, but are as though corrupted.

Chapter 13 ——————————————————————

Ebionites

The Ebionites were a Jewish Christian sect of the second century that, according to Epiphanius, traced themselves back to the church at Jerusalem. While there is no direct evidence of this lineage by Epiphanius, the Ebionites were a named entity by the time of Irenaeus (ca. A.D. 190). The name "Ebionites" comes from the Greek *Ebionaioi, Ebionitai,* or *Ebionaei.* These terms were Greek forms of the Hebrew *Ebionim,* meaning "the poor." Although Origen uses the term simply to refer to early Jewish converts to Christianity (*Against Celsus* 2.1), he also gives it the unfavorable meaning (*Against Celsus* 4.1.22) later reflected in Eusebius' remark that the Ebionites were characterized by their "poor and mean opinions" regarding Christ (see 13.4). While Hippolytus and Tertullian had heard that the name "Ebionite" was derived from a founder named Ebion (*Refutation* 7.35.1; *De Praescriptione hereticorum* 33, respectively), this is most likely a confusion on their part.

According to Eusebius (cf. entry 13.4 below) the name "Ebionite" referred to at least two basic groups of Jewish Christians who differed regarding the nature of Jesus as the Christ. According to one group (perhaps initially referred to as the "Nazarenes"), the birth of Christ took place by means of the Holy Spirit through Mary. The other group affirmed the paternity of Jesus through Joseph, which tended toward an adoptionist-messianic view that ultimately circumvented the divinity of Jesus. Both strands were known, however, to share a conviction regarding the importance of adhering to the Jewish law. They differed, apparently, with regard to the question of the necessity of adhering to the law for salvation.

As can be seen in the following excerpts ranging from Justin to Eusebius, it is the christological question that becomes more and more the

116

focus for identification of the Ebionites, while the New Testament question regarding the relationship of the Christian to the law, spoken of by Justin in particular, recedes into the background.

13.1. Justin, *Dialogue with Trypho* 47. Rome, ca. A.D. 155–60.

Source: *Saint Justin Martyr*, trans. T. B. Falls, 218–19.

Justin is discussing with Trypho a question of enduring importance in the early church, namely, the relationship of the Christian to the law. Note that Justin will neither condemn nor judge negatively those who, of their own choice, seek to follow the precepts of the Jewish law. He does, however, roundly condemn those who would seek to influence other Christians to do the same, based upon the argument that salvation demands it.

"But," Trypho again objected, "if a man knows that what you say is true, and, professing Jesus to be the Christ, believes in and obeys Him, yet desires also to observe the commandments of the Mosaic Law, shall he be saved?"

"In my opinion," I replied, "I say such a man will be saved, unless he exerts every effort to influence other men (I have in mind the Gentiles whom Christ circumcised from all error) to practice the same rites as himself, informing them that they cannot be saved unless they do so. You yourself did this at the opening of our discussion, when you said that I would not be saved unless I kept the Mosaic precepts."

"But why," pressed Trypho, "did you say, 'In my opinion such a man will be saved?' There must, therefore, be other Christians who hold a different opinion."

"Yes, Trypho," I conceded, "there are some Christians who boldly refuse to have conversation or meals with such persons. I don't agree with such Christians. But if some [Jewish converts], due to their instability of will, desire to observe as many of the Mosaic precepts as possible—precepts which we think were instituted because of your hardness of heart—while at the same time they place their hope in Christ, and if they desire to perform the eternal and natural acts of justice and piety, yet wish to live with us Christians and believers, as I already stated, not persuading them to be circumcised like themselves, or to keep the Sabbath, or to perform any other similar acts, then it is my opinion that we Christians should receive them and associate with them in every way as kinsmen and brethren. But if any of your people, Trypho, profess their belief in Christ, and at the same time force the Christian Gentiles to follow the Law instituted through Moses, or refuse to share in communion with them this same common life, I certainly will also not approve of them. But I think that those Gentiles who have been induced to follow the practices of the Jewish Law, and at the same time profess their faith in the Christ of God, will probably be saved. Those persons, however, who had once believed and publicly acknowledged Jesus to be the Christ, and then later, for one reason or another, turned to the observance of the Mosaic Law, and denied that Jesus is the Christ, cannot be saved unless they repent before their death. The same can be said of those descendants of Abraham, who follow the Law and refuse to believe in Christ to their very last breath. Especially excluded from eternal salvation are they who in their synagogues have cursed and still do curse those who believe in that very Christ in order that they may attain salvation and escape the avenging fires of Hell. God in His goodness, kindness, and infinite richness considers the repentant sinner to be just and innocent, as He declared through the Prophet Ezechiel, and the one who turns from the path of piety and justice to follow that of injustice and impiety God judges to be an impious and unjust sinner. Thus has our Lord Jesus Christ warned us: 'In whatsoever things I shall apprehend you, in them also shall I judge you.'"

13.2. Irenaeus, *Against Heresies* 1.26.2. Lyons, ca. A.D. 190.

Source: *Gnosticism*, ed. R. M. Grant, 42.

Irenaeus points to another characteristic of the Ebionites, namely, the tie with gnostic thinking. He also reveals a penchant on the part of the Ebionites for the Gospel of Matthew and the rejection of Paul.

Those who are called Ebionites acknowledge that the world was made by God, but their attitude towards the Lord is like that of Cerinthus and Carpocrates. They use only the gospel which is according to Matthew, and they reject the apostle Paul, calling him an apostate from the law. They endeavour to interpret the prophet writings in a rather speculative way. They are circumcised and they persevere in the practices of the law and in a Jewish manner of life to such an extent that they venerate Jerusalem as the house of God.

13.3. Hippolytus, *Refutation of All Heresies* 7.22. Rome, ca. A.D. 230.

Source: *The Ante-Nicene Fathers*, ed. A. Roberts and J. Donaldson, 5:114.

Hippolytus brings out another feature of Ebionite thought that corresponds to their emphasis on obedience to the law—a corresponding Christology. The designation "Christ" is not by virtue of a form of incarnation, but a designation bestowed in virtue of obedience.

The Ebioneans, however, acknowledge that the world was made by Him Who is in reality God, but they propound legends concerning the Christ similarly with Cerinthus and Carpocrates. They live conformably to the customs of the Jews, alleging that they are justified according to the law, and saying that Jesus was justified by fulfilling the law. And therefore it was, [according to the Ebioneans,] that [the Saviour] was named [the] Christ of God and Jesus, since not one of the rest [of mankind] had observed completely the law. For if even any other had fulfilled the commandments [contained] in the law, he would have been that Christ. And the [Ebioneans allege] that they themselves also, when in like manner they fulfil [the law], are able to become Christs; for they assert that our Lord Himself was a man in a like sense with all [the rest of the human family].

13.4. Eusebius, *Ecclesiastical History* 3.27. Caesarea, ca. A.D. 325.

Source: Eusebius, *History of the Church*, trans. G. Williamson, 136–37.

The issue of a lack of incarnational theology and a denial of Jesus' divinity is revisited by Eusebius in the following excerpt. It seems, according to Eusebius' account, that the Ebionites differed among themselves regarding the divine origin of the birth of Jesus, but were of one mind regarding the necessity of obedience to and observation of the law.

There were others whom the evil demon, unable to shake their devotion to the Christ of God, caught in a different trap and made his own. Ebionites they were appropriately named by the first Christians, in view of the poor and mean opinions they held about Christ. They regarded Him as plain and ordinary, a man esteemed as righteous through growth of character and nothing more, the child of a normal union between a man and Mary; and they held that they must observe every detail of the Law—by faith in Christ alone, and a life built upon that faith, they would never win salvation.

A second group went by the same name, but escaped the outrageous absurdity of the first. They did not deny that the Lord was born of a virgin and the Holy Spirit, but nevertheless shared their refusal to acknowledge His pre-existence as God the Word and Wisdom. Thus the impious doctrine of the others was their undoing also, especially as they placed equal emphasis on the outward observance of the Law. They held that the epistles of the Apostle ought to be rejected altogether, calling him a renegade from the Law; and using only the "Gospel of the Hebrews," they treated the rest with scant respect. Like the others, they observed the Sabbath and the whole Jewish system; yet on the Lord's Day they celebrated rites similar to our own in memory of the Saviour's resurrection. It is then because of such practices that they have been dubbed with their present name: the name of Ebionites hints at the poverty of their intelligence, for this is the way in which a poor man was referred to by the Hebrews.

13.5. Eusebius, *Ecclesiastical History* 6.17. Caesarea, ca. A.D. 325.

Source: Eusebius, *History of the Church*, trans. G. Williamson, 256–57.

Eusebius also refers to the significance of a certain Symmachus among the Ebionites, referring to a work that Origen was believed to have seen. Symmachus was a late-second-century translator of the Hebrew Scriptures into Greek. His translation was used by Origen. Both Eusebius and Jerome called Symmachus an Ebionite.

Of these translators it should be observed that Symmachus was an Ebionite. The adherents of what is known as the Ebionite heresy assert that Christ was the son of Joseph and Mary, and regard Him as no more than a man. They insist also that the law ought to be kept more in the Jewish manner, as I mentioned earlier in this history. Pamphlets also by Symmachus are still extant, in which he inveighs against the Gospel according to Matthew, apparently in order to bolster up his heresy. These, together with other comments on Scripture by Symmachus, Origen states that he received from a woman called Juliana, on whom, he says, Symmachus had himself bestowed them.

13.6. Epiphanius, *Panarion* 30.1.1; 30.2.1-8; 30.3.7; 30.16.1; 30.26.1-2; 30.34.6. Salamis, Cyprus, A.D. 375–78.

Source: *Panarion*, trans. P. R. Amidon, 94–95, 103, 106–7.

Epiphanius follows an earlier tradition concerning a person by the name of "Ebion" who was the founder of Ebionite theories. It is not likely that any such person existed, but rather that certain particular early Ebionite theories came to be attributed to a single source. According to Epiphanius, the Ebionites occupied a wide-ranging spectrum regarding Jesus on the one hand as mere man with an adopted divine Spirit, and on the other as a sometimes-incarnate archangel (following a Gnostic thread). In the following passages, we see Epiphanius hold up for scrutiny Ebionite views on the observance of the law, multiple baptisms, the efficacy of circumcision, sex and marriage, the use of Scripture, and the nature of Jesus as the Christ.

[1.1] Next comes Ebion, the founder of the Ebionites. He held doctrines like those of the Nazoraeans…being from their sect, although what he taught and preached differed from what they did.…

[2.1] Ebion was a contemporary of these others, [was] with them and came from them. [2.2] First of all, he says that Christ was engendered from sexual intercourse and the seed of a man, namely Joseph. As we have already said, he has the same views as the others in everything, but differs in this alone, that he observes the Jewish law of the Sabbath and circumcision and everything else kept by the Jews and Samaritans.

[2.3] Like the Samaritans, he practices customs in addition to what the Jews do. He adds this, that he keeps from touching any foreigner, [2.4] and each day, if he has intercourse with a woman and departs from her, he bathes in water, if there is plenty of seawater anywhere or other kinds of water. [2.5] Not only that, but if he meets anyone when he is coming up from bathing and immersing himself in water, he likewise returns to bathe, and he even does so often in his clothes. [2.6] At present they strictly forbid virginity and continence, as is true also of the other sects like theirs.

They used to pride themselves on their virginity because of James, the brother of the Lord. [Thus] they even address their writings to elders and virgins.

[2.7] Their sect began after the capture of Jerusalem. For when all those who believed in Christ settled at that time for the most part in Peraea, in a city called Pella belonging to the Decapolis mentioned in the gospel, which is next to Batanaea and the land of Bashan, then they moved there and stayed, and that provided an opportunity for Ebion. [2.8] He took up residence in a village called Cocaba by the region of Karnaim, which is also called Ashteroth, in the land of Bashan, as the report which we received has it. From there he began his evil teaching, and there also the Nazoraeans began, as I explained earlier....

[3.7] They too accept the Gospel of Matthew, and like the followers of Cerinthus and Merinthus, they also use it alone. They call it the Gospel according to the Hebrews, to tell the truth, because Matthew alone in the New Testament expounded and declared the gospel in Hebrew and in Hebrew letters....

[16.1] They too practice a baptism apart from their daily baths. They also practice rites in imitation of the holy ceremonies in the church year after year by means of unleavened bread, and the other part of the rite by means of water alone....

[26.1] They are also proud of being circumcised, and boast that it is a seal and mark of the patriarchs and of the just who lived according to the law. Through it they think that they are their equals. Indeed, they wish to find confirmation for it with Christ himself, as do the followers of Cerinthus. [26.2] For they too say in their nonsensical way, "It is enough for the disciple to be like his master." "Christ was circumcised," they say, "so you be circumcised."...

[34.6] I have already explained that each of them has his own variant theory about Christ; Ebion himself once said that he was begotten a mere human being from sexual intercourse, while at another time the Ebionites deriving from him said that the Son acquired from God a supernal power, and that upon a time he put Adam on and took him off.

Encratites

The Encratites can only loosely be called an identifiable sect, having more of the characteristics of a movement that transcends many sects. The name "Encratite" is rooted in Paul's allusions to the necessity for self-control (*enkrateia*) with regard to the life in Christ (Acts 24:25). When the emphasis on self-control was combined with Jesus' sayings regarding the status of marriage in the kingdom of heaven (Matt. 22:30) and Paul's, at best, ambivalent attitude toward marriage (1 Cor. 7:28), a way of life emerged that regarded sexual relations as a primary means for the world to entrap the unwary believer. Strict asceticism and sexual continence were the only answer. This was the primary means by which the believer lived in separation from the world and the means of living the life that is to come.

A legitimacy of sorts was given this complex of ideas through their embrace by Tatian after he left the influence of Justin. The encratite position was also ultimately open to strong gnostic influences, especially the degradation of the flesh and the view that this world could not possibly be the creation of the same God that redeems it. For this reason, gnostic teachers such as Saturninus, as well as Marcion, are numbered among its adherents.

The thinkers and groups that were known as Encratites normally used that corpus of works known as the apocryphal "Acts" of various apostles, particularly the *Acts of Thomas*, the *Acts of Andrew*, and the *Acts of John*.

14.1. Irenaeus, *Against Heresies* 1.28.1. Lyons, ca. A.D. 190.

Source: *Gnosticism*, ed. R. M. Grant, 47.

Irenaeus sees a close connection of the encratite philosophy with the Gnosticism of Saturninus and the teachings of Marcion. Gnostic thought ran the spec-

trum from antinomian (or libertine) to ascetic. The Encratites were seen as representing the latter type. Irenaeus is quick, however, to point out that ascetic attitudes did not translate into humility on the part of Tatian, whom he charges with an inflated self-worth. Personal attacks are clearly a part of the heresiologist's arsenal.

The references to the "salvation of the first-formed man" are specific to Tatian, who moved in the direction of the Encratites after leaving the influence of Justin. Tatian became very pessimistic about human nature and tended toward gnostic exegesis regarding the creation of humankind, seeing creation as the work of an alien force or evil God. In this sense, he began to see Adam as actually damned and unable to be redeemed.

From Saturninus and Marcion the so-called Encratites [continent ones] have proclaimed celibacy, rejecting the ancient work of God in forming mankind and implicitly blaming him for making male and female for the generation of men. And they introduced abstinence from eating what they call "animate" food, ungrateful to the God who made all. They deny the salvation of the first-formed man—this is now their new discovery! A certain Tatian first introduced this blasphemy; he had been a hearer of Justin, and as long as he was with him he expressed nothing of this sort; but after Justin's martyrdom [c. 165] he left the church. He was inflated by the idea of being a teacher and by the notion that he was superior to others, so he established his own form of doctrine. He invented certain invisible Aeons like those of Valentinus, attacked marriage as corruption and fornication [like Marcion and Saturninus], and denied the salvation of Adam.

14.2. Hippolytus, *Refutation of All Heresies* 8.13. Rome, ca. A.D. 230.

Source: *The Ante-Nicene Fathers*, ed. A. Roberts and J. Donaldson, 5:124.

Hippolytus seeks, in the following excerpt, to refute encratite strictures regarding food, marriage, and social life by reference to the very Paul whom they cite as, at best, ambivalent to marriage.

Others, however, styling themselves Encratites, acknowledge some things concerning God and Christ in like manner with the Church. In respect, however, of their mode of life, they pass their days inflated with pride. They suppose that by meats they magnify themselves, while abstaining from animal food, [and] being water-drinkers, and forbidding to marry, and devoting themselves during the remainder of life to habits of asceticism. But persons of this description are estimated Cynics rather than Christians, inasmuch as they do not attend unto the words spoken against them through the Apostle Paul. Now he, predicting the novelties that were to be hereafter introduced ineffectually by certain [heretics], made a statement thus: "The Spirit speaketh expressly, In the latter times certain will depart from sound doctrine, giving heed to seducing spirits and doctrines of devils, uttering falsehoods in hypocrisy, having their own conscience seared with a hot iron, forbidding to marry, to abstain from meats, which God has created to be partaken of with thanksgiving by the faithful, and those who know the truth; because every creature of God is good, and nothing to be rejected which is received with thanksgiving; for it is sanctified by the word of God and prayer" [[I Tim. 4:1-5]]. This voice, then, of the blessed Paul, is sufficient for the refutation of those who live in this manner, and plume themselves on being just; [and] for the purpose of proving that also, this [tenet of the Encratites] constitutes a heresy.

14.3. Epiphanius, *Panarion* 46.1.4-5; 46.1.8-9. Salamis, Cyprus, A.D. 375–78.

Source: *Panarion*, ed. P. R. Amidon, 166.

In his discussion of Tatian and his followers, much of what Epiphanius provides repeats what is recorded in earlier sources. More information is given, however, on Tatian's preaching and the encratite use of a certain Gospel according to the Hebrews, better known as Tatian's Diatessaron. The Gospel according to the Hebrews mentioned by Eusebius (see 13.4 above) is most likely a different document from this.

[1.4] Tatian…at first led a good life and was strong in faith so long as he was with the martyr St. Justin. [1.5] But when St. Justin died, then like a blind man led by the hand [who] is abandoned by his guide and, left alone, walks over a precipice in his blindness and plunges down without being able to stop until he falls to his death, so also was he.…

[1.8] Most of what he preached prevailed from Antioch-by-Daphne to Cilicia, but was especially influential in Pisidia. For the so-called

Encratites have partaken of his poison by way of succession. [1.9] They also say that the gospel Diatessaron was made by him, which some call "According to the Hebrews."

14.4. Epiphanius, *Panarion* 47.1.3; 47.1.5-8. Salamis, Cyprus, A.D. 375–78.

Source: *Panarion*, ed. P. R. Amidon, 168.

Epiphanius reports how widely the Encratites were to be found. He speaks here of their teachings and practices regarding celibacy, sacraments, and abstinence from wine, and their use of apocryphal books.

[1.3] They exist as well in parts of Asia, in Isauria, Pamphylia, Cilicia, and Galatia. This sect was also long ago [sown?] [in] part of the region of Rome, to say nothing of Antioch in Syria, but not everywhere....

[1.5] They accept primarily the writings called the *Acts of Andrew, of John, and of Thomas*, certain apocryphal works, and the parts of the Old Testament which they wish. [1.6] They quite definitely teach that marriage is from the devil. They abhor animal flesh, rejecting it not for the sake of continence or asceticism, but out of fear and for the sake of appearance, lest they be condemned for partaking of animal flesh. [1.7] They too celebrate the sacraments with water. They never partake of wine, saying that it is of the devil and that those who drink it and use it are lawless folk and sinners. [1.8] They also believe in the resurrection of the dead.

Chapter 15 ──────────────────

Montanus and the Montanists

The controversies surrounding the teachings of an early church presbyter, Montanus of Phrygia, resulted in one of the earliest schisms to rock the church. We know little of Montanus' direct teachings or his life. As with so many early schismatic personalities and teachings, the works of his catholic opponents are our main source of information about him and his followers. His work and teaching can be dated anywhere between A.D. 135 and 175.

Montanus' teachings centered upon the fundamental importance of the return of Christ and the immediate work of the Holy Spirit. All church doctrine and teaching, according to Montanus, were to evolve from the expectation of Christ's immediate return. Any theological enterprise, any preaching, any teaching on the various aspects of Christian life and relationship to the world was to presuppose no permanent form or historical development. The immediate relationship to Christ and the parousia dominates the teaching. This emphasis makes Montanism the first large-scale movement in the church to call attention to Christian living and worldly relations from an eschatological perspective.

The Montanist movement arose in an environment where a decline in the intensity of Christian charismatic experience corresponded with an increasing turn toward a structured episcopate. It therefore had the character of a reaction to the loss of intense apocalyptic and eschatological hope.

It appears that Montanus claimed both to be a unique fulfillment of the work of the Paraclete promised by Jesus in John 14:26, and to be able to pass that power on to his adherents. He and his two principal followers (both women) were reported to speak in strange sounds with angels and sometimes with Jesus himself. The content of these visions had less to do with doctrine than with the call for increased ethical vigor in anticipation of the Lord's coming. The call for increased ethical vigor led to increased dependence upon ascetic practice in preparation for the Lord's coming.

While it is likely that Montanus and his immediate followers regarded themselves as mere instruments for the declarations of the Paraclete, later Montanism seems to have begun to identify Montanus with the Holy Spirit itself.

The most famous later adherent to Montanist tendencies was the theologian Tertullian. Tertullian's ethical turn of mind was impressed by the strong call of Montanist visionary experiences for the repentance of the church. Tertullian, however, lived at least two generations after the initial strong showing of Montanus and his immediate followers. Tertullian's Montanism may have been the basis of the advanced nature of his trinitarian thinking; that is, he was able to see the Holy Spirit in more personal, interrelational terms.

15.1. *The Montanist Oracles.* Asia Minor, second century A.D.

Source: *New Testament Apocrypha,* ed. E. Hennecke and W. Schneemelcher, 2:686–87.

The following oracles of Montanus, Priscilla, and Maximilla are from the earliest Montanist period. The only sources we have for these sayings are the antiheresy writers (with the exception of Tertullian, who ultimately embraces a later form of Montanism).

1. [Montanus says:] I am the Father and I am the Son and I am the Paraclete. (Didymus, *De Trin.* 3.41.1.)
2. [Montanus speaks:] I the Lord, the Almighty God, remain among men. (Epiphanius, *Haer.* 48.11.1.)
3. [Montanus says:] Neither angel, nor ambassador, but I, the Lord God the Father, am come. (Epiphanius, *Haer.* 48.11.9.)
4. [Montanus says:] Behold man is like a lyre and I rush thereon like a plectrum. Man sleeps and I awake. Behold, the Lord is he who arouses the hearts of men [throws them into ecstasy] and gives to men a new heart. (Epiphanius, *Haer.* 48.4.1.)
5. [Montanus says:] Why dost thou call the super-man [?] saved? For the righteous man, he says, will shine a hundred times more strongly than the sun, but the little ones who are saved among you will shine a hundred times stronger than the moon. (Epiphanius, *Haer.* 48.10.3.)

6. [The Paraclete in the new prophets says:] The church can forgive sins but I will not do it, lest they sin yet again. (Tertullian, *De Pud.* 21.7.)

7. [The Spirit says:] Thou wilt be publicly displayed: that is good for thee; for whosoever is not publicly displayed before men will be publicly displayed before God. Let it not perplex thee! Righteousness brings thee into the midst [of men]. What perplexes thee about winning glory? Opportunity is given, when thou art seen by men. (Tertullian, *De Fuga* 9.4.)

8. [The Spirit speaks:] Desire not to die in bed, nor in delivery of children, nor by enervating fevers, but in martyrdom, that He may be glorified who has suffered for you. (Tertullian, *De Fuga* 9.4; cf. Tertullian, *De Anima* 55.5.)

9. [The Paraclete says through the prophetess Prisca:] They are flesh and [yet] they hate the flesh. (Tertullian, *De Resurr. Mort.* 11.2.)

10. [The holy prophetess Prisca proclaims:] A holy minister must understand how to minister holiness. For if the heart gives purification [?], says she, they will also see visions [visiones], and if they lower their faces, then they will perceive saving voices, as clear as they were obscure. (Tertullian, *De Exhort. Cast.* 10.5.)

11. [Quintilla or Priscilla says:] In the form of a woman, says she, arrayed in shining garments, came Christ to me and set wisdom upon me and revealed to me that this place [= Pepuza] is holy and that Jerusalem will come down hither from heaven. (Epiphanius, *Haer.* 49.1.2-3.)

12. [Maximilla says:] After me, says she, there will be no more prophets, but [only] the consummation. (Epiphanius, *Haer.* 48.2.4.)

13. [Maximilla says:] Listen not to me, but listen to Christ. (Epiphanius, *Haer.* 48.12.4.)

14. [Maximilla says:] The Lord has sent me as adherent, preacher and interpreter of this affliction and this covenant and this promise; he has compelled me, willingly or unwillingly, to learn the knowledge of God. (Epiphanius, *Haer.* 48.13.1.)

15. [The Spirit says through Maximilla:] I am chased like a wolf from [the flock of] sheep; I am not a wolf; I am word and spirit and power. (Eusebius, *HE* 5.16.17.)

15.2. Hippolytus, *Refutation of All Heresies* 8.12. Rome, ca. A.D. 230.

Source: *The Ante-Nicene Fathers*, ed. A. Roberts and J. Donaldson, 5:123–24.

The main thrust of the critique of Hippolytus in what follows is what today might be termed a "personality cult." The women who accompany Montanus come in for particular complaint. Their ecstatic revelations are accounted as more relevant than the Scriptures or Christ. They are accused of leading many into error, especially into strict forms of asceticism regarding food and festivals. Despite the personal invective, the complaint surrounds competing revelations and asceticism.

But there are others who themselves are even more heretical in nature [than the foregoing], and are Phrygians by birth. These have been rendered victims of error from being previously captivated by [two] wretched women, called a certain Priscilla and Maximilla, whom they supposed [to be] prophetesses. And they assert that into these the Paraclete Spirit had departed; and antecedently to them, they in like manner consider Montanus as a prophet. And being in possession of an infinite number of their books, [the Phrygians] are overrun with delusion; and they do not judge whatever statements are made by them, according to [the criterion of] reason; nor do they give heed unto those who are competent to decide; but they are heedlessly swept onwards, by the reliance which they place on these [impostors]. And they allege that they have learned something more through these, than from law, and prophets, and the Gospels. But they magnify these wretched women above the Apostles and every gift of Grace, so that some of them presume to assert that there is in them a something superior to Christ. These acknowledge God to be the Father of the universe, and Creator of all things, similarly with the Church, and [receive] as many things as the Gospel testifies concerning Christ. They introduce, however, the novelties of fasts, and feasts, and meals of parched food, and repasts of radishes, alleging that they have been instructed by women. And some of these assent to the heresy of the Noetians, and affirm that the Father himself is the Son, and that this [one] came under generation, and suffering, and death. Concerning these I shall again offer an explanation, after a more minute manner; for the heresy of these has been an occasion of evils to many. We therefore are of opinion, that the statements made concerning these [heretics] are sufficient, when we shall have briefly proved to all that the majority of their books are silly, and their attempts [at reasoning] weak, and worthy of no consideration. But it is not necessary for those who possess a sound mind to pay attention [either to their volumes or their arguments].

15.3. Hippolytus, *Refutation of All Heresies* 10.21-22. Rome, ca. A.D. 230.

Source: *The Ante-Nicene Fathers*, ed. A. Roberts and J. Donaldson, 5:147–48.

In addition to attacks against competing revelations, Hippolytus here extends his critique of the Montanists to the heresy of Noetus (for further information see chapter 17). Essentially the critique is that God and Christ are seen as one principle. There is, in the opinions of the Montanists, not a hint of what later will become the doctrine of the Trinity.

21. The Phrygians, however, derive the principles of their heresy from a certain Montanus, and Priscilla, and Maximilla, and regard these wretched women as prophetesses, and Montanus as a prophet. In respect, however, of what appertains to the origin and creation of the universe, *the Phrygians* are supposed to express themselves correctly; while in the tenets which they enunciate respecting Christ, they have not irrelevantly formed their opinions. But they are seduced into error in common with *the heretics* previously alluded to, and devote their attention to the discourses of these above the Gospels, thus laying down regulations concerning novel and strange fasts.

22. But others of them, being attached to the heresy of the Noetians, entertain similar opinions to those relating to the silly women *of the Phrygians*, and to Montanus. As regards, however, the truths appertaining to the Father of the entire of existing things, they are guilty of blasphemy, because they assert that He is Son and Father, visible and invisible, begotten and unbegotten, mortal and immortal. These have taken occasion from a certain Noetus *to put forward their heresy*.

15.4. Tertullian, *On Monogamy* 1. Carthage, North Africa, ca. A.D. 217.

Source: *The Ante-Nicene Fathers*, ed. A. Roberts and J. Donaldson, 4:59.

Tertullian became a latter-day Montanist as he became more pessimistic about human nature. His concern for sanctification and eschatological moral-

ity seemed to play a large role in his shift to Montanist sentiments. The follow-
ing passage is from his Montanist period. Note that he chooses what might be
called a middle path, rejecting the heresy of severe asceticism, but checking all
the libertine freedoms of the "psychics." He seems to be opting for the spirit-led
existence of the Montanists without its excesses on the side of asceticism or an
insistence on a psychical special status.

Heretics do away with marriages; Psychics accumulate them. The former marry not *even* once; the latter not *only* once. What dost thou, Law of
the Creator? Between alien eunuchs and thine own grooms, thou com-
plainest as much of the over-obedience of thine own household as of the
contempt of strangers. They who abuse thee, do thee equal hurt with them
who use thee not. In fact, neither is such continence laudable because it is
heretical, nor such licence defensible because it is psychical. The former is
blasphemous, the latter wanton; the former destroys the God of marriages,
the latter puts Him to the blush. Among *us,* however, whom the recognition of spiritual gifts entitles to be deservedly called Spiritual, continence is
as religious as licence is modest; since both the one and the other are in
harmony with the Creator. Continence honours the law of marriage,
licence tempers it; the former is not forced, the latter is regulated; the former recognizes the power of free choice, the latter recognizes a limit. We
admit one marriage, just as we do one God. The law of marriage reaps an
accession of honour where it is associated with shamefastness. But to the
Psychics, since they receive not the Spirit, the things which are the Spirit's
are not pleasing. Thus, so long as the things which are of the Spirit's please
them not, the things which are of the flesh will please, as being the con-
traries of the Spirit. "The flesh," saith [the apostle], "lusteth against the
Spirit, and the Spirit against the flesh" [[Gal. 5:17]]. But what will the
flesh "lust" after, except what is more *of* the flesh? For which reason withal,
in the beginning, it became estranged from the Spirit.

15.5. Eusebius, *Ecclesiastical History* 5.14-16, 18-19. Caesarea,
       ca. A.D. 325.

   Source: Eusebius, *History of the Church,* trans. G. Williamson, 217–19,
223, 226.

   In typical fashion Eusebius piles up references to descriptions and refutations
of the Montanists in works available to him. The citations are interesting as

historical references. The critique centers on the notion of false prophesy, given without reference to Scripture, in an ecstatic state, by those who claim divine status. These people are denounced for asceticism, denial of marriage, lies about the status of virginity, and the acceptance of personal gain for prophetic leadership.

14. Filled with hatred of good and love of evil the enemy of God's Church left no trick untried in his machinations against mankind, and did his best to make a fresh crop of heretical sects spring up to injure the Church. Some members of these crawled like poisonous reptiles over Asia and Phrygia, boasting of Montanus 'the Paraclete' and his female adherents Priscilla and Maximilla, alleged to have been his prophetesses. 15. Others flourished at Rome, led by Florinus, an unfrocked presbyter, along with Blastus who had been disgraced in the same way. Between them they led many churchmen astray and got them under their thumb, each trying in his own way to pervert the truth.

Montanus and his band of false prophets

16. To counter the so-called Phrygian heresy, the Power which fights for truth raised up an effective and invincible weapon at Hierapolis, in the person of Apolinarius, already referred to in these pages. With him were associated many learned men of the day, who have left us ample material for reconstructing the history. At the beginning of his polemic against these heretics, one of these writers first indicates that he had also argued with them orally to refute their pretensions. His preface runs as follows: ....

There is, it appears, a village near the Phrygian border of Mysia called Ardabau. There it is said that a recent convert named Montanus, while Gratus was proconsul of Syria, in his unbridled ambition to reach the top laid himself open to the adversary, was filled with spiritual excitement and suddenly fell into a kind of trance and unnatural ecstasy. He raved, and began to chatter and talk nonsense, prophesying in a way that conflicted with the practice of the Church handed down generation by generation from the beginning. Of those who listened at that time to his sham utterances some were annoyed, regarding him as possessed, a demoniac in the grip of a spirit of error, a disturber of the masses. They rebuked him and tried to stop his chatter, remembering the distinction drawn by the Lord, and His warning to guard vigilantly against the coming of false prophets [[Matt. 7:15]]. Others were elated as if by the Holy Spirit or a prophetic gift, were filled with conceit, and forgot the Lord's distinction. They welcomed a spirit that injured and deluded the mind and led the people astray: they were beguiled and deceived by it, so that it could not now be reduced to silence. By some art, or rather by methodical use of a malign artifice, the devil contrived the ruin of the disobedient, and was most undeservedly honoured by them. Then he secretly stirred up and inflamed minds closed to the true Faith, raising up in this way two others—women whom he filled with the sham spirit, so that they chattered crazily, inopportunely, and wildly, like Montanus himself. On those who were elated and exultant about him the spirit bestowed favours, swelling their heads with his extravagant promises. Sometimes it reproved them pointedly and convincingly to their faces, to avoid appearing uncritical—though few of the Phrygians were deceived. They were taught by this arrogant spirit to denigrate the entire Catholic Church throughout the world, because the spirit of pseudo-prophecy received neither honour nor admission into it; for the Asian believers repeatedly and in many parts of Asia had met for this purpose, and after investigating the recent utterances pronounced them profane and rejected the heresy. Then at last its devotees were turned out of the Church and excommunicated....

18. While the so-called Phrygian sect was still flourishing in Phrygia itself, an orthodox writer named Apollonius embarked on a refutation, and produced a special polemic against them, proving point by point the fraudulent character of their "prophecies" and revealing the sort of life lived by the leaders of the sect. Listen to his actual words about Montanus:

What sort of person this upstart teacher is, his own actions and teaching show. This is the man who taught the dissolution of marriages, who laid down the law on fasting, who renamed Pepuza and Tymion, insignificant towns in Phrygia, as Jerusalem, in the hope of persuading people in every district to gather there; who appointed agents to collect money, who contrived to make the gifts roll in under the name of "offerings," and who has subsidized those who preach his message, in order that gluttony may provide an incentive for teaching it.

This is his summing-up of Montanus. A little farther on he has this to say of his prophetesses:

It is thus evident that these prophetesses, from the time they were filled with the spirit, were the very first to leave their husbands. How then could they lie so blatantly as to call Priscilla a virgin?

Next he goes on to say:

Don't you agree that all scripture debars a prophet from accepting gifts and money? When I see that a prophetess has accepted gold and silver and expensive clothing, am I not justified in keeping her at arm's length?

19. The polemics of Apolinarius against the Phrygian heresy are referred to by Serapion, who, we have good reason to believe, was Bishop of Antioch in succession to Maximin in the period under discussion. He mentions him in a personal letter to Caricus and Pontius, in which he gives his own answer to the same heresy, and adds this:

In order that you may know this, that the working of the so-called New Prophecy of this fraudulent organization is held in detestation by the whole brotherhood throughout the world, I am sending you the writings of Claudius Apolinarius, Bishop of Hierapolis in Asia, of most blessed memory.

In this letter of Serapion's are preserved the signatures of various bishops.

Chapter 16 ———————————————————

Adoptionists
(Dynamic Monarchians)

Dynamic Monarchianism (or Adoptionism) was the first of two movements that appealed to the "uniqueness of the first principle" (in Greek, *monarchia*) in order to establish the principle of monotheism in the face of the perceived movement toward polytheism in the early attempts to explicate a Logos theology on the part of Justin Martyr, Tertullian, and other Apologists. The primary exponent of dynamic Monarchianism was Theodotus (ca. A.D. 190), a tanner from Byzantium. The second movement, modalistic Monarchianism, is the subject of the next chapter.

Dynamic Monarchianism holds the view that Jesus was a mere man, who was indeed born of Mary and the Holy Spirit, but to whom a great power (*dynamis*) was given at his baptism. At his resurrection, Jesus was "adopted" into the divine sphere. By means of appeal to inspiration and adoption of the human element into the divine, the Monarchians of this stripe believed they could overcome the potentially insidious consequences of the Logos doctrine in favor of a doctrine of God's simplicity and unity. Dynamic Monarchianism is viewed primarily as a Christian heresy concerned with a unitarian doctrine of God. The theological cost of this unitarian doctrine was seen to be soteriological in nature—that is, if Jesus is not seen as "Word," the union of divine and human in Christ is ultimately denied and traditional atonement theories cannot account for salvation.

One of the Adoptionists most frequently referred to throughout the history of the church was Paul of Samosata (condemned at Antioch in A.D. 268), who did not see the "Word of God" as the person of Christ, but as a command or ordinance of God that achieves its end in the obedience of Jesus.

16.1. Eusebius, *Ecclesiastical History* 5.28. Caesarea, ca. A.D. 325.

Source: Eusebius, *History of the Church*, trans. G. Williamson, 235–36.

Eusebius, in this passage, seeks to refute arguments by the Monarchians to the effect that the ancient church did not teach the divinity of Jesus Christ. He not only points out the origins of the dynamic monarchian point of view in the works of Theodotus (late second century A.D.) and Paul of Samosata (ca. A.D. 260–70), but argues from early writers, hymns, psalms, and papal pronouncements and edicts that it could not have ever been a prevalent viewpoint.

In a polemic composed by one of these against Artemon's heresy, which again in my own day Paul of Samosata has tried to revive, there is extant a discussion pertinent to the historical period under review. For the assertion of the heresy in question, that the Saviour was merely human, is exposed in this book as a recent invention, because those who introduced it were anxious to represent it as ancient and therefore respectable. After adducing many other arguments to refute their blasphemous falsehood, the writer continues:

They claim that all earlier generations, and the apostles themselves, received and taught the things they say themselves, and that the true teaching was preserved till the times of Victor, the thirteenth Bishop of Rome after Peter: from the time of his successor Zephyrinus the truth was deliberately perverted. This suggestion might perhaps have been credible if in the first place Holy Scripture had not presented a very different picture; and there are also works by Christian writers published before Victor's time, written to defend the truth against both pagan criticism and current heresies—I mean works by Justin, Miltiades, Tatian, Clement, and many more. In every one of these Christ is spoken of as God. For who does not know the books of Irenaeus, Melito, and the rest, which proclaim Christ as God and man, and all the psalms and hymns written from the beginning by faithful brethren, which sing of Christ as the Word of God and address Him as God? How then can it be true that when the mind of the Church had been proclaimed for so many years, Christians up to the time of Victor preached as these people say they did? And are they not ashamed to slander Victor in this way, knowing perfectly well that it was Victor who excommunicated Theodotus the shoemaker, the prime mover and father of this God-denying apostasy, when he became the first to declare that Christ was merely human? If Victor regarded their views in the way their slanderous statements suggest, how could he have thrown out Theodotus, the inventor of this heresy?

16.2. Eusebius, *Ecclesiastical History* 7.30. Caesarea, ca. A.D. 325.

Source: Eusebius, *History of the Church*, trans. G. Williamson, 315–19.

Eusebius is unsparing in his personal invective against Paul of Samosata. According to Eusebius, Paul is arrogant, accepting of praise reserved for God, while denying that God's Son is divine. Paul was deposed in an ignominious fashion even by the civil authorities. We have little way of knowing how far these diatribes match historical reality, but very often Eusebius counters the denial of Christ's divinity with personal attacks against those who teach such ideas.

Accordingly, a single letter expressing their united judgement was drafted by the assembled pastors: nominally addressed to Bishop Dionysius of Rome and Maximus of Alexandria, it was sent out to all the provinces of the Empire. In it they made clear to all the trouble they had taken, the perverse heterodoxy of Paul, and the arguments and questions they had put to him; they also gave a survey of his whole life and character. To make sure that the facts are not forgotten, it would be well at this point to reproduce what they said:....

Whereas he has forsaken the canon and deviated to spurious and bastard doctrines, there is no need to judge the actions of one who is outside the Church, even in the case of a man who once was nearly penniless, having neither inherited a competence from his forbears nor acquired one by the labour of hand or brain, but who now has amassed immense wealth by committing illegalities, robbing churches, and blackmailing his fellow-Christians. He deprives the injured of their rights, promising them help if they will pay for it but breaking his word to them, and makes easy money out of the readiness of those entangled in court proceedings to buy relief from their persecutors. In fact, he regards religion as a way of making money.

Nor need we judge him because he is ambitious and arrogant, decking himself out with worldly honours and anxious to be called *ducenarius* rather than bishop, and swaggers in city squares, reading letters aloud or dictating them as he walks in public surrounded by a numerous bodyguard, some in front and some behind. The result is that the Faith is regarded with distaste and hatred because of his self-importance and inflated pride.

Nor need we judge the way this charlatan juggles with church assemblies, courting popularity and putting on a show to win the admiration of simple souls, as he sits on the dais and lofty throne he has had constructed for him (how unlike a disciple of Christ!) or in the *secretum*, as he calls it, which he occupies in imitation of the rulers of the world. He slaps his thigh and stamps on the dais. Some do not applaud and wave their handkerchiefs as in a theatre, or shout and spring to their feet like his circle of partisans, male and female, who form such a badly behaved audience: they listen, as in God's house, in a reverent and orderly manner. These he scolds and insults. Those who have departed this life, but once preached the word, he assails in a drunken, vulgar fashion in public, while he boasts about himself as if he were not a bishop but a trickster and mountebank.

All hymns to our Lord Jesus Christ he has banned as modern compositions of modern writers, but he arranges for women to sing hymns to himself in the middle of the church on the great day of the Easter festival: one would shudder to hear them! And he allows the fawning bishops of the neighbouring districts and towns, and presbyters too, to talk in the same way when preaching to the people. He will not admit that the Son of God came down from heaven—as we shall explain more fully later, not merely stating the fact but proving it from passage after passage of the attached notes, especially where he says that Jesus Christ is "from below." Yet those who sing hymns and praises to him in the congregation say that their blasphemous teacher is an angel come down from heaven; and he allows this to go on even when he is there to hear, such is his vanity. And what of his "spiritual brides," as the Antioch people call them? and those of his presbyters and deacons, with whom he joins in concealing this and their other incurable sins, though he knows all about them, so as to have them under his thumb, too frightened on their own account to accuse him of his offenses in word and deed? He has even enriched them, thus securing the loyalty and admiration of those who are the same way inclined....

When Paul had lost both the orthodoxy of his faith and his bishopric, Domnus, as already stated, took over the ministry of the Antioch church. But Paul absolutely refused to hand over the church building; so the Emperor Aurelian was appealed to, and he gave a perfectly just decision on the course to be followed: he ordered the building to be assigned to those to whom the bishops of the religion in Italy and Rome addressed a letter.

In this way the man in question was thrown out of the church in the most ignominious way by the secular authority.

16.3. Epiphanius, *Panarion* 65.1.5-10; 65.3.2-4. Salamis, Cyprus, A.D. 375–78.

Source: Epiphanius, *Panarion*, trans. P. R. Amidon, 218–19.

While Paul of Samosata flourished later than the second century (ca. 260–70), he falls in line with the adoptionist tendencies that began with Theodotus. In many respects, dynamic Monarchianism is more closely related to his name than to any other. Since he is much better known throughout church history than Theodotus, we include the remarks about him from Epiphanius.

Like all dynamic Monarchians, Paul is concerned to establish the absolute primacy of God as a single principle. Unlike the modalistic Monarchians (who are taken up in the next chapter), who denied a distinct status to the Son and believed that it was God the First Principle who suffered and died on the cross, Paul of Samosata denied that the Word of God could subsist outside the transcendent First Principle. The unity of the First Principle was preserved, then, for Paul of Samosata by the denial of divine status to Christ as a separate person, begotten or otherwise. As Epiphanius points out, Paul of Samosata believed that "God together with the Word is one person, as a human being and his word are one" (65.3.4). Epiphanius, appealing to the Scriptures (especially John 1), counters Paul by maintaining the truth of the eternal nature of the Logos as begotten—as a distinct person in the Godhead. Human words are indeed not self-subsisting, but the divine Word, once spoken, is begotten and eternally with God (not in God) and made flesh. Jesus, as the Christ, is not, therefore, "mere man" (65.7.4).

The dynamic Monarchians were concerned to preserve God's unity at all costs. Epiphanius' argument is designed to show that the Trinity is not polytheistic as the dynamic Monarchians feared.

[1.5] He says that God, Father and Son and Holy Spirit, are one God, and that in God are always his Word and his Spirit, just as in a man's heart is his own word. [1.6] The Son of God is not a subsistent entity, but is in God himself, as indeed Sabellius, Novatus, Noetus, and others as well taught; his doctrine, however, was not the same as theirs, but different from theirs. [1.7] He taught that the Word came and dwelt in the human being Jesus, [was active in him, and ascended again to the Father?]. [1.8] Thus, he says, God is one; the Father is not Father nor the Son Son nor the Holy Spirit Holy Spirit, but rather, the Father and his Son in him are one God, like the word in a human being. [1.9] He bases his heresy upon the following proof texts, namely, from Moses' saying "The Lord your God is one Lord." [1.10] But he does not, like Noetus, say that the Father suffered, but rather that the Word which came was alone active and ascended to the Father....

[3.2] The reason why he speaks of only one God is not because the Father is source, but [in speaking of him as] only one God, he destroys as far as he can the divinity and subsistence of the Son and of the Holy Spirit, [3.3] holding that the Father himself is the one God, who has not begotten a son. As a result, the two are incomplete, Father and Son, the Father having begotten no son, and the Word of the living God and of true wisdom having produced no fruit. [3.4] For they suppose that the Word is like that in the heart, and wisdom like that prudence in the human soul which each human being has acquired from God. For this reason they say that God together with the Word is one person, as a human being and his word are one.

Patripassionists
(Modalistic Monarchians)

The second of the monarchian theories, modalistic Monarchianism, or Patripassionism, arrived in Rome about A.D. 200 through the work of one Noetus of Smyrna (late second century A.D.). Unlike Theodotus, Noetus and the Patripassionists did not deny the fullness of the incarnation. Their theory did, however, deny Jesus Christ any distinct status as either Son or Logos. God, the first principle, is the one who is incarnate, suffers, and dies (hence the name "patripassionist").

The other term used to describe this form of Monarchianism is "Modalism." Modalism emerges most distinctly from the thought of one Sabellius, who flourished around A.D. 220 (hence, it is also frequently called "Sabellianism"). Sabellius sought to preserve the triadic baptismal formula of the church by denying the distinct realities of Father, Son, and Holy Spirit by speaking of their roles as "modes" in which the first principle shows itself in relationship to the world (for example, Creator, Redeemer, Sanctifier). The error in this view was considered to consist not in the nomenclature but in the insistence that the Trinity was to be viewed solely in terms of how God manages creation, that is, in terms of God's *oikonomia*, not in terms of God's nature.

17.1. Justin, *Dialogue with Trypho* 128–129. Rome, ca. A.D. 155–60.

Source: *Saint Justin Martyr*, trans. T. B. Falls, 347–49.

In the following remarks Justin contends with the fundamental tenet of monarchian thinking, namely, that any numerical division of God as first principle is contrary to Scripture and logic. His arguments take two forms. First, the idea of number in the divine nature is not to be taken as "abscission," thereby dividing divine substance, but as generation of power, as when one fire ignites another. This argument, by the standards of later trinitarian argumentation, is rather unsophisticated, but it recognizes that trinitarian thinking demands thinking in terms of diversity in unity without modalistic implications. The second argument augments the first in that the Scriptures speak of just such begetting in power in terms of Christ, Wisdom, and God's own plural self-designation in Genesis.

128. But some teach that this power is indivisible and inseparable from the Father, just as the light of the sun on earth is indivisible and inseparable from the sun in the skies; for, when the sun sets, its light disappears from the earth. So, they claim, the Father by His will can cause His power to go forth and, whenever He wishes, to return again. In this manner, they declare, God also made the angels. But it has been proved that the angels always exist and are not reduced again into that from which they were created. It has also been shown at length that this power which the prophetic word also calls God and Angel not only is numbered as different by its name (as is the light of the sun), but is something distinct in real number, [[as]] I have already briefly discussed. For I stated that this power was generated from the Father, by His power and will, but not by abscission, as if the substance of the Father were divided; as all other things, once they are divided and severed, are not the same as they were before the division. To illustrate this point, I cited the example of fires kindled from a fire; the enkindled fires are indeed distinct from the original fire which, though it ignites many other fires, still remains the same undiminished fire.

129. To prove this point, I will not repeat some of the Scriptural passages I already quoted. When the word of the prophecy says, "The Lord rained fire from the Lord out of heaven" [Gen. 19:24], it indicates that they are two in number: One on earth, who came down to witness the cry of Sodom, and One in Heaven, who is the Lord of that Lord on earth, and as His Father and God was the cause of His being the Mighty One and Lord and God. And when the Scripture states that in the beginning God said, "Behold Adam has become as one of Us" [Gen. 3:22], the phrase, "as one of Us," is in itself an evidence of number, and cannot be interpreted in a metaphorical sense, as the sophists attempt to do, who neither can know nor speak the truth. And the Book of Wisdom says: "If I should tell you the daily events, I would have to enumerate them from the beginning. The

Lord made Me as the beginning of His ways for His works. From eternity
He set Me up, in the beginning, before He made the earth, and before the
fountains of water came forth, before the mountains were established; and
before all the hills He begets Me" [Prov. 8:21-25].

At this point I said, "Gentlemen, if you have followed me closely, you
can see that Scripture declares that the Son was begotten of the Father
before all creatures, and everybody will admit that the son is numerically
distinct from the Father."

17.2. Hippolytus, *Refutation of All Heresies* 10.23. Rome, ca. A.D. 230.

Source: *The Ante-Nicene Fathers*, ed. A. Roberts and J. Donaldson,
5:148.

*Hippolytus takes both Noetus and Callistus (fl. ca. A.D. 217–22) to account
in the following passage. His explication of the thought of Noetus reveals the
central tenet of Monarchianism, that God in all forms or modes is one only.
This tenet, if rigidly adhered to, leads to the idea that when suffering and death
occur in a mode of divine existence, the divine person (being only one) suffers
and dies—hence, Patripassionism.*

*In the case of Callistus, Hippolytus refers to the nominalist tendency of
modalist and unitarian thought. However, it is the nominalist tendency that
causes confusion in Callistus because he at one point is patripassionist (when
not speaking nominally) and adoptionist at the other point (when he speaks of
only the Word, as divine command or ordinance, becoming incarnate).*

But in like manner, also, Noetus, being by birth a native of Smyrna, and
a fellow addicted to reckless babbling, as well as crafty withal, introduced
[among us] this heresy which originated from one Epigonus. It reached
Rome, and was adopted by Cleomenes, and so continued to this day
among his successors. *Noetus* asserts that there is one Father and God of
the universe, and that He made all things, and was imperceptible to those
that exist when He might *so* desire. *Noetus maintained that the Father* then
appeared when He wished; and He is invisible when He is not seen, but
visible when He is seen. And *this heretic also alleges that the Father* is unbegotten when He is not generated, but begotten when He is born of a virgin; as also that He is not subject to suffering, and is immortal when He
does not suffer or die. When, however, His passion came upon Him,

Noetus allows that the Father suffers and dies. And *the Noetians* suppose that this Father Himself is called Son, [and *vice versa*,] in reference to the events which at their own proper periods happen to them severally.

Callistus corroborated the heresy of these *Noetians*, but we have *already* carefully explained the details of his life. And *Callistus* himself produced likewise a heresy, and derived its starting-points from these *Noetians*,— namely, so far as he acknowledges that there is one Father and God, viz., the Creator of the universe, and that this [God] is spoken of, and called by the name of the Son, yet that in substance He is one Spirit. For Spirit, *as* the Deity, is, he says, not any *being* different from the Logos, or the Logos from the Deity; therefore this one person, [according to Callistus,] is divided nominally, but substantially not so. He supposes this one Logos to be God, and affirms that there was *in the case of the Word* an incarnation. And he is disposed [to maintain], that He who was seen in the flesh and was crucified is Son, but that the Father it is who dwells in Him. *Callistus thus* at one time branches off into the opinion of Noetus, but at another into that of Theodotus, and holds no sure doctrine. These, then, are the opinions of Callistus.

17.3. Hippolytus, *Refutation of All Heresies* 9.5. Rome, ca. A.D. 230.

Source: *The Ante-Nicene Fathers*, ed. A. Roberts and J. Donaldson, 5:127–28.

Hippolytus outlines, in what follows, the central tenets of Noetus, as well as of modalistic Monarchianism. First, there is the denial of separate and distinct status to the incarnate Son of God; therefore, the Father became incarnate, suffered, died, and resurrected himself (hence, Patripassionism). Second, while Noetus does not deny the names "Father" and "Son," these names do not indicate separate persons, but "modes" of the same person, "according to the vicissitude of times."

Now, that *Noetus* affirms that the Son and the Father are the same, no one is ignorant. But he makes his statement thus: "When indeed, then, the Father had not been born, He *yet* was justly styled Father; and when it pleased Him to undergo generation, having been begotten, He Himself became His own Son, not another's." For in this manner he seeks to establish the sovereignty *of God*, alleging that the Father and Son, *so* called, are one and the same [substance], not one individual produced from a different one, but Himself from Himself; and that He is styled by name Father and Son, according to the vicissitude of times. But that he is one who has appeared [amongst us], both having submitted to generation from a virgin, and as a man having held converse among men. And, on account of the birth that had taken place, He confessed Himself to those beholding Him a Son, no doubt; yet He made no secret to those who could comprehend Him of His being a father. That this person suffered by being fastened to a tree, and that he commended His Spirit unto Himself, having died *to appearance,* and not being [in reality] dead. And He raised Himself up the third day, after having been interred in a sepulchre, and wounded with a spear, and perforated with nails.

17.4. Hippolytus, *Against the Heresy of One Noetus,* 1–5, 7–8, 10–11, 14, 18. Rome, ca. A.D. 230.

Source: *The Ante-Nicene Fathers,* ed. A. Roberts and J. Donaldson, 5:223–28, 230.

Hippolytus seeks to establish three things in his refutation of Noetus, and what was later to be called "Patripassionism": first, that Noetus claims that God and Jesus Christ are one and that it is the single principle, God, who suffers, dies, and raises himself. Hippolytus maintains that Noetus, like others, comes to this conclusion by the use of only one type of Scripture. Second, he moves to those passages of Scripture which clearly show that Christ himself spoke of himself as coming down from heaven. The inference is that Christ had always been distinct from the Father. Third, Hippolytus counters the claim that the Trinity speaks of three Gods.

The whole treatise ends with a magnificent passage that treats of the willingness of the Son of God to suffer and die for humanity ("thus, then, too, though demonstrated as God, He does not refuse the conditions proper to Him as man"), claiming it was indeed the will of the Son that maintains connection with the Father, not the personhood.

1. [[Noetus]] alleged that Christ was the Father Himself, and that the Father Himself was born, and suffered, and died....

2. Now [[the followers of Noetus]] seek to exhibit the foundation for their dogma by citing the word in the law, "I am the God of your fathers;

ye shall have no other gods beside me" [[Exod. 3:6; 20:3]]; and again in another passage, "I am the first," He saith, "and the last; and beside me there is none other" [[Isa. 44:6]]. Thus they say they prove that God is one. And then they answer in this manner: "If therefore I acknowledge Christ to be God, He is the Father Himself, if He is indeed God; and Christ suffered, being Himself God; and consequently the Father suffered, for He was the Father Himself." But the case stands not thus; for the Scriptures do not set forth the matter in this manner. ...

3. In this way, then, they choose to set forth these things, and they make use only of one class of passages; just in the same one-sided manner that Theodotus employed when he sought to prove that Christ was a mere man. But neither has the one party nor the other understood the matter rightly, as the Scriptures themselves confute their senselessness, and attest the truth. See, brethren, what a rash and audacious dogma they have introduced, when they say without shame, the Father is Himself Christ, Himself the Son, Himself was born, Himself suffered, Himself raised Himself. But it is not so. The Scriptures speak what is right; but Noetus is of a different mind from them....

4. And it is not simply that I say this, but [[Christ]] Himself attests it who came down from heaven; for He speaketh thus: "No man hath ascended up to heaven, but He that came down from heaven, even the Son of man which is in heaven" [[John 3:13]]. What then can he seek beside what is thus written? Will he say, forsooth, that flesh was in heaven? Yet there is the flesh which was presented by the Father's Word as an offering,—the flesh that came by the Spirit and the Virgin, [and was] demonstrated to be the perfect Son of God. It is evident, therefore, that He offered Himself to the Father. And before this there was no flesh in heaven. Who, then, was in heaven but the Word unincarnate, who was dispatched to show that He was upon earth and was also in heaven? For He was Word, He was Spirit, He was Power. The same took to Himself the name common and current among men, and was called from the beginning the Son of man on account of what He was to be, although He was not yet man, as Daniel testifies when he says, "I saw, and behold one like the Son of man came on the clouds of heaven" [[Daniel 7:13]]. Rightly, then, did he say that He who was in heaven was called from the beginning by this name, the Word of God, as being from the beginning.

5. But what is meant, says he, in the other passage: "This is God, and there shall none other be accounted of in comparison of Him" [[Baruch 3:35]]? That said he rightly. For in comparison of the Father who shall be

accounted of? But he says: "This is our God; there shall none other be accounted of in comparison to Him. He hath found out all the way of knowledge, and hath given it unto Jacob His servant, and to Israel His beloved" [[Baruch 3:35-36]]. He hath said well. For who is Jacob His servant, Israel His beloved, but He of whom He crieth, saying, "This is my beloved Son, in whom I am well pleased: hear ye Him" [[Matt. 17:5]]? Having received, then, all knowledge from the Father, the perfect Israel, the true Jacob, afterward did show Himself upon earth, and conversed with men. And who, again, is meant by Israel but *a man who sees God?* and there is no one who sees God except the Son alone, the perfect man who alone declares the will of the Father....

7. If, again, if [[Noetus]] allege [[Christ's]] own word when He said, "I and the father are one," let [[Noetus]] attend to the fact, and understand that He did not say, "I and the Father *am one*, but *are one*." For the word *are* is not said of one person, but it refers to *two persons*, and one power. He has Himself made this clear, when He spake to His father concerning the disciples, "The glory which Thou gavest me I have given them; that they may be one even as we are one: I in them, and Thou in me, that they may be made perfect in one; that the world may know that Thou hast sent me" [[John 17:22-23]]. What have the Noetians to say to these things? Are all one body with respect of substance, or is it that we become one in the power and disposition of unity of mind? In the same manner the Son, who was sent and was not known of those who are in the world, confessed that He was in the Father in power and disposition. For the Son is the one mind of the Father. We who have the Father's mind believe so [in Him]; but they who have it not have denied the Son ....

8. Many other passages, or rather all of them, attest the truth. A man, therefore, even though he will not, is compelled to acknowledge God the Father Almighty, and Christ Jesus the Son of God, who, being God, became man, to whom also the Father made all things subject, Himself excepted, and the Holy Spirit; and these, therefore, are three. But if he desires to learn how it is shown still that there is one God, let him know that His power is one. As far as regards the power, therefore, God is one. But as far as regards the economy there is a three-fold manifestation, as shall be proved afterwards when we give account of the true doctrine.... For there is one God in whom we must believe, but unoriginated, impassible, immortal, doing all things as He wills, in the way He wills, and when He wills. What, then, will this Noetus, who knows nothing of the truth,

dare to say to these things? And now, as Noetus has been confuted, let us turn to the exhibition of the truth itself, that we may establish the truth, against which all these mighty heresies have arisen without being able to state anything to the purpose....

10. God, subsisting alone, and having nothing contemporaneous with Himself, determined to create the world. And conceiving the world in mind, and willing and uttering the word, He made it; and straightway it appeared, formed as it had pleased Him. For us, then, it is sufficient simply to know that there was nothing contemporaneous with God. Beside Him there was nothing; but He, while existing alone, yet existed in plurality. For He was neither without reason, nor wisdom, nor power, nor counsel. And all things were in Him, and He was the All. When He willed, and as He willed, He manifested His word in the times determined by Him, and by Him all things were made. When He wills, He does; and when He thinks, He executes; and when He speaks, He manifests; when He fashions, He contrives in wisdom. For all things that are made He forms by reason and wisdom—creating them in reason, and arranging them in wisdom. He made them, then, as He pleased, for He was God. And as the Author, and fellow-Counsellor, and Framer of the things that are in formation, He begat the Word; and as He bears this Word in Himself, and that, too, as [yet] invisible to the world which is created, He makes Him visible; [and] uttering the voice first, and begetting Him as Light of Light, He set Him forth to the world as its Lord, [and] His own mind; and whereas He was visible formerly to Himself alone, and invisible to the world which is made, He makes Him visible in order that the world might see Him in His manifestation, and be capable of being saved.

11. And thus there appeared another beside Himself. But when I say *another*, I do not mean that there are two Gods, but that it is only as light of light, or as water from a fountain, or as a ray from the sun. For there is but one power, which is from the All; and the Father is the All, from whom cometh this Power, the Word....

14. For the Father indeed is One, but there are two Persons, because there is also the Son; and then there is the third, the Holy Spirit. The Father decrees, the Word executes, and the Son is manifested, through whom the Father is believed on. The economy of harmony is led back to one God; for God is One. It is the father who commands, and the Son who obeys, and the Holy Spirit who gives understanding: the Father who is *above all*, and the Son who is *through all*, and the Holy Spirit who is *in*

all. And we cannot otherwise think of one God, but by believing in truth in Father and Son and Holy Spirit.… For it is through this Trinity that the Father is glorified. For the Father willed, the Son did, the Spirit manifested. The whole Scriptures, then, proclaim this truth.…

18. Thus, then, too, though demonstrated as God, He does not refuse the conditions proper to Him as man, since He hungers and toils and thirsts in weariness, and flees in fear, and prays in trouble. And He who as God has a sleepless nature, slumbers on a pillow. And He who for this end came into the world, begs off from the cup of suffering. And in an agony He sweats blood, and is strengthened by an angel, who Himself strengthens those who believe in Him, and taught men to despise death by His work. And He who knew what manner of man Judas was, is betrayed by Judas. And He, who formerly was honoured by him as God, is condemned by Caiaphas. And He is set at nought by Herod, who is Himself to judge the whole earth. And He is scourged by Pilate, who took upon Himself our infirmities. And by the soldiers He is mocked, at whose behest stand thousands of thousands and myriads of myriads of angels and archangels. And He who fixed the heavens like a vault is fastened to the cross by the Jews. And He who is inseparable from the Father cries to the Father, and commends to Him His spirit; and bowing His head, He gives up the ghost, who said, "I have power to lay down my life, and I have power to take it again" [[John 10:18]]; and because He was not overmastered by death, as being Himself Life, He said this: "I lay it down of myself." And He who gives life bountifully to all, has His side pierced with a spear. And He who raises the dead is wrapped in linen and laid in a sepulchre, and on the third day He is raised again by the Father, though Himself the Resurrection and the Life. For all these things has He finished for us, who for our sakes was made as we are.

17.5. Epiphanius, *Panarion*, 62.1.1-6; 62.2.1; 62.2.4-7. Salamis, Cyprus, A.D. 375–78.

Source: Epiphanius, *Panarion*, trans. P. R. Amidon, 209–10.

Epiphanius speaks here of the modalism of Sabellius. Sabellius' ideas, he claims, are the outcome of the ideas of Noetus. Sabellius' modalism is seen in the analogies that Epiphanius attributes to him, namely, the analogy to humans as composed of body, soul, and spirit, and to the sun as illuminating, warming, and having shape. All operations, or modes, reflect the same subject.

[1.1] Sabellius, from whom derive those called Sabellians, arose not long ago (he is a recent figure). [1.2] He [taught] doctrines like those of the Noetians, except for a few additional things which he taught. [1.3] There are many insane people in Mesopotamia and the region of Rome who hold to his doctrine.

[1.4] He and the Sabellians who derive from him teach that he who is the Father is the same one who is the Son and the same one who is the Holy Spirit, so that there are three names in one hypostasis; [1.5] or as in a human being there are body and soul and spirit, so the Father is, so to speak, the body, the Son is, so to speak, the soul, and as the spirit belongs to the human being, so also the Holy Spirit is in the godhead. [1.6] Or it is as in the sun, which is in one hypostasis, but has three actualities: the illuminative, the warming, and the round shape itself....

[2.1] They accept all the books of the Old and New Testaments, but with certain passages which they choose according to their own bogus nonsense and insanity.

[2.4] All of their error and the essence of their error they acquire from certain apocryphal works, especially from what is called the *Egyptian Gospel*, the name which some have given to this work. [2.5] In it are presented many such doctrines as though given out in secret and in the form of mysteries by the Savior, who explains to the disciples that he who is Father is the same one who is the Son and the same one who is the Holy Spirit. [2.6] Then when they meet simple, unsophisticated people who have no clear knowledge of the sacred scriptures, the first thing they do is alarm them by asking, "What shall we say, good people: do we have one God or three Gods?" [2.7] When some pious person hears this who has no perfect understanding of the truth, he is at once disturbed and assents to their error, and so comes to deny that the Son and Holy Spirit exist.

Quartodecimans

"Quartodecimans" (or "Fourteenthers") is a designation for a group of Christians, primarily in Asia Minor in the second century A.D., who celebrated a Christian Passover—including a commemoration of Jesus' death and resurrection—on the fourteenth day of the Jewish month called Nisan. In so doing, they followed the chronology of the Gospel of John regarding the day of Jesus' death (14 Nisan). Their fasting ended on that day and was followed by an Easter vigil in the evening. This practice resulted in the celebration of Easter on any day of the week (on whatever day 14 Nisan occurred). Meanwhile, the custom had emerged in Rome of always celebrating Easter on a Sunday in commemoration of Christ's resurrection on a Sunday. The discrepancy gave rise to what has been called the "Easter Controversy."

On the surface, this does not appear to be a theological debate of great consequence. It is, however, a significant debate in the history of the church in that it is the first recognizable illustration of the rise of the power of the Roman episcopate.

Attempts by Polycarp and Anicetus to settle the debate concerning the celebration of Easter were at first amicable, though inconclusive. The dual practice of the commemoration of Easter by those who followed the Asian or Roman model soon became divisive in Rome. Victor, Bishop of Rome (A.D. 189–98), convened various synods that backed the Roman model, and finally excommunicated those congregations who, following Polycrates, Bishop of Ephesus, refused to conform. In spite of continued divisive debate over the years that followed, the Roman model prevailed, and the power of the Roman Bishop over church life outside the confines of its own sphere began to be felt.

18.1. Hippolytus, *Refutation of All Heresies* 8.11. Rome, ca. A.D. 230.

Source: *The Ante-Nicene Fathers*, ed. A. Roberts and J. Donaldson, 5:123.

The argument of Hippolytus against the Quartodecimans takes the form of a complaint against quarrelsomeness and legalistic attitudes. It can be assumed from Hippolytus' argument that, by his time, this debate is regarded as a failure to accept the authority of the Roman bishop.

And certain other [heretics], contentious by nature, [and] wholly uninformed as regards knowledge, as well as in their manner more [than usually] quarrelsome, combine [in maintaining] that Easter should be kept on the fourteenth day of the first month [[= Nisan]], according to the commandment of the law, on whatever day [of the week] it should occur. [But in this] they only regard what has been written in the law, that he will be accursed who does not so keep [the commandment] as it is enjoined. They do not, however, attend to this [fact], that the legal enactment was made for Jews, who in times to come should kill the real Passover. And this [paschal sacrifice, in its efficacy,] has spread unto the Gentiles, and is discerned by faith, and not now observed in letter [merely]. They attend to this one commandment, and do not look unto what has been spoken by the apostle: "For I testify to every man that is circumcised, that he is a debtor to keep the whole law" [[Gal. 5:3]]. In other respects, however, these consent to all the traditions delivered to the Church by the Apostles.

18.2. Eusebius, *Ecclesiastical History* 5.23-25. Caesarea, ca. A.D. 325.

Source: Eusebius, *History of the Church*, trans. G. Williamson, 229–34.

Eusebius is concerned that the struggle over the commemoration of Easter be dealt with peaceably, without serious contention. He also points out that the debate was not only about the day of the commemoration, but about the character of the fast. Here, as with Hippolytus, there is a certain comfort surrounding the issue since the authority of the Roman bishop, and the synods that he called, is assumed.

23. It was at that stage [[i.e., late in the second century A.D.]] that a controversy of great significance took place, because all the Asian dioceses

thought that in accordance with ancient tradition they ought to observe the fourteenth day of the lunar month as the beginning of the Paschal festival—the day on which the Jews had been commanded to sacrifice the lamb: on that day, no matter which day of the week it might be, they must without fail bring the fast to an end. But nowhere else in the world was it customary to arrange their celebrations in that way: in accordance with apostolic tradition, they preserved the view which still prevails, that it was improper to end the fast on any day other than that of our Saviour's resurrection. So synods and conferences of bishops were convened, and without a dissentient voice, drew up a decree of the Church, in the form of letters addressed to Christians everywhere, that never on any day other than the Lord's Day should the mystery of the Lord's resurrection from the dead be celebrated, and that on that day alone we should observe the end of the Paschal fast. There is extant to this day a letter from those who attended a conference in Palestine presided over by Bishop Theophilus of Caesarea and Narcissus of Jerusalem; and from those at Rome a similar one, arising out of the same controversy, which names Victor as bishop. There are others from the Pontic bishops, presided over by Palmas as the senior; from the Gallic province, of which Irenaeus was archbishop, and from the bishops in Osrhoene and the cities of that region. There are also personal letters from Bishop Bacchyllus of Corinth and very many more, who voiced one and the same opinion and judgement and gave the same vote. All these laid down one single rule—the rule already stated.

24. The Asian bishops who insisted that they must observe the custom transmitted to them long ago were headed by Polycrates, who in the letter which he wrote to Victor and the Roman church sets out in the following terms the tradition that he had received:

We for our part keep the day scrupulously, without addition or subtraction. For in Asia great luminaries sleep who shall rise again on the day of the Lord's advent, when He is coming with glory from heaven and shall search out all His saints—such as Philip, one of the twelve apostles, who sleeps in Hierapolis with two of his daughters, who remained unmarried to the end of their days, while his other daughter lived in the Holy Spirit and rests in Ephesus. Again there is John, who leant back on the Lord's breast, and who became a sacrificing priest wearing the mitre, a martyr, and a teacher; he too sleeps in Ephesus. Then in Smyrna there is Polycarp, bishop and martyr; and Thraseas, the bishop and martyr from Eumenia, who also sleeps in Smyrna. Need I mention Sagaris, bishop and martyr, who sleeps in Laodicea, or blessed Papirius, or Melito the eunuch, who lived entirely in the Holy Spirit, and who lies in Sardis waiting for the visitation from heaven when he shall rise from the dead? All of these kept the fourteenth day of the month as the beginning of the Paschal festival, in accordance with the Gospel, not deviating in the least but following the rule of the Faith. Last of all I too, Polycrates, the least of you all, act according to the tradition of my family, some members of which I have actually followed; for seven of them were bishops and I am the eighth, and my family have always kept the day when the people put away the leaven. So I, my friends, after spending sixty-five years in the Lord's service and conversing with Christians from all parts of the world, and going carefully through all Holy Scripture, am not scared of threats. Better people than I have said: "We must obey God rather than men" [Acts 5:29].

Referring to the bishops who were with him when he wrote, and shared his opinion, he adds:

I could have mentioned the bishops who are with me and whom I summoned in response to your request. If I write their names, the list will be very long. But though they know what an insignificant person I am, they approve my letter, knowing that I have not frittered away my long life but have spent it in the service of Christ Jesus.

Thereupon Victor, head of the Roman church, attempted at one stroke to cut off from the common unity all the Asian dioceses, together with the neighbouring churches, on the ground of heterodoxy, and pilloried them in letters in which he announced the total excommunication of all his fellow-Christians there. But this was not to the taste of all the bishops: they replied with a request that he would turn his mind to the things that make for peace and for unity and love towards his neighbours. We still possess the words of these men, who very sternly rebuked Victor. Among them was Irenaeus, who wrote on behalf of the Christians for whom he was responsible in Gaul. While supporting the view that only on the Lord's Day might the mystery of the Lord's resurrection be celebrated, he gave Victor a great deal of excellent advice, in particular that he should not cut off entire churches of God because they observed the unbroken tradition of their predecessors. This is how he goes on:

The dispute is not only about the day, but also about the actual character of the fast. Some think that they ought to fast for one day, some for two, others for still more; some make their "day" last forty hours on end. Such variation in the observance did not originate in our own day, but very much earlier, in the time of our forefathers, who—apparently disregarding strict accuracy—in their naïve simplicity kept up a practice which they fixed for the time to come. In spite of that, they all lived in peace with one another, and so do we: the divergency in the fast emphasizes the unanimity of our faith.

This argument he illustrates with two anecdotes which I may with advantage quote:

Among these were the presbyters before Soter, who were in charge of the church of which you are the present leader—I mean Anicetus, Pius, Hyginus, Telesphorus, and Xystus. They did not keep it themselves or allow those under their wing to do so. But in spite of their not keeping it, they lived in peace with those who came to them from the dioceses in which it was kept, though to keep it was more objectionable to those who did not. Never was this made a ground for repulsing anyone, but the presbyters before you, even though they did not keep it, used to send the Eucharist to Christians from dioceses which did. And when Blessed Polycarp paid a visit to Rome in Anicetus's time, though they had minor differences on other matters too, they at once made peace, having no desire to quarrel on this point. Anicetus could not persuade Polycarp not to keep the day, since he had always kept it with John the disciple of our Lord and the other apostles with whom he had been familiar; nor did Polycarp persuade Anicetus to keep it: Anicetus said that he must stick to the practice of the presbyters before him. Though the position was such, they remained in communion with each other, and in church Anicetus made way for Polycarp to celebrate the Eucharist—out of respect, obviously. They parted company in peace, and the whole Church was at peace, both those who kept the day and those who did not.

Irenaeus, whose name means "peaceable" and who by temperament was a peacemaker, pleaded and negotiated thus for the peace of the churches. He corresponded by letter not only with Victor but with very many other heads of churches, setting out both sides of the question under discussion.

25. The Palestinian bishops of whom I spoke a little while ago, Narcissus and Theophilus, with Bishop Cassius of Tyre, Clarus of Ptolemais, and the others assembled with them, composed a lengthy review of the tradition about the Easter festival which had come down to them without a break from the apostles, at the end of which they add this appeal:

Try to send a copy of our letter to every diocese, so that we may not fail in our duty to those who readily deceive their own souls. We may point out to you that in Alexandria they keep the feast on the same day as we do, for we send letters to them and they to us, to ensure that we keep the holy day in harmony and at the same time.

18.3. Epiphanius, *Panarion* 50.1.1-8; 50.3.2-4. Salamis, Cyprus,
A.D. 375–78.

Source: Epiphanius, *Panarion*, trans. P. R. Amidon, 175–76.

Epiphanius points out that the source of the quartodeciman dating of Easter is a legalistic interpretation of a scriptural curse. The curse (cited at 1.4 below) does not actually exist in the Old Testament; it can be arrived at only by combining the content of a series of texts (Lev. 23:5; Num. 9:4-5; and Deut. 27:26). Even this legalism, however, did not prevent them from having disputes among themselves. Epiphanius praises the church's wisdom because it chose the date of Easter at least in part on the basis of the sequence of Jesus' deeds and by securing its yearly celebration.

The reading below (at 1.5) refers to the apocryphal Acts of Pilate. *Apparently some Quartodecimans inferred from the prologue of that document that Jesus' death fell on 25 March. Epiphanius claims (at 1.8) that Jesus actually died on 29 March, which is no less speculative than the views of his opponents.*

[1.2] [The Quartodecimans] hold everything that the church does, but fall away from everyone else through not keeping to the discipline and doctrine of what is lawful, but keeping still to Jewish fables.… [1.3] For they have one day a year on which they obstinately keep the Paschal festival, although their doctrine concerning the Father and Son and Holy Spirit is correct and the same [as ours], and they accept the prophets, apostles, and evangelists, and confess likewise the resurrection of the flesh, the future judgment, and eternal life. [1.4] But their great failure is that they hold to the statement in the law: "Cursed is he who does not keep the Passover on the fourteenth day of the month." [1.5] But others of them in observing one and the same day, fasting one and the same day, and performing the rites, boast that they have found the correct observance in the *Acts of Pilate*, where it says that the Savior suffered on the 25th of March. [1.6] That is the day on which they prefer to keep the Paschal festival, no matter when the fourteenth day of the [lunar] month falls. But those in Cappadocia observe one and the same day: the 25th of March. [1.7] So there is quite a disagreement among them, some of them upholding the fourteenth of the [lunar] month and others the 25th of March. [1.8] What is more, we have found copies of the *Acts of Pilate* which indicate that the Passion took place on the 18th of March. The truth is, though, as we can say with great certitude, that the Savior suffered on the 29th of March. But some say that it was on the 23rd of March....

[3.2] ...But God's holy church observes not only the fourteenth day, but also the seventh day which recurs cyclically [in the] order of the seven days of the week, so that the feast of the Resurrection may occur [as] it did originally, according to the things accomplished by the Lord. [3.3] And it observes not only the fourteenth day of the [lunar] month, but also the sun's course, lest we celebrate two Easters in one year and not even one Easter in another. [3.4] While therefore we take account of the fourteenth day, we pass over the equinox and bring the observance to its completion on the holy Day of the Lord.

Heresiologists and
Sources Cited

The Acts of the Apostles

The Acts of the Apostles was written by Luke, the author of the Gospel according to Luke. The two volumes offer a continuous narrative of the ministry of Jesus and the first three decades of the infant Christian church. They are usually thought to have been composed around A.D. 80–90. Acts is our primary source for early Christianity, and much of it can be considered reliable. Modern scholarship has shown, however, that some of its accounts reflect the interests of Luke and still others are based on traditions that he has used uncritically. What the heresiologists draw from Acts in particular are its account of Simon Magus in 8:9-24 and its reference to Nicolaus the proselyte from Antioch in 6:5.

Clement of Alexandria, *Stromateis*

Clement of Alexandria (ca. A.D. 150–215) is thought to have been born in Athens of pagan parents. He searched for truth and meaning far and wide for several years until he came under the influence of Pantaenus at Alexandria. After his conversion he was ordained, and around 190 he succeeded his mentor in providing instruction in the Christian faith. He left Alexandria in 202 when persecution broke out and probably settled in Cappadocia, where, it is believed, he died.

Clement was a major Christian scholar and author whose theology had a gnostic coloring. His *Stromateis* (sometimes designated *Stromata* and also known as his *Miscellanies*) contains a collection of his thoughts about theology. Written near the end of the second century, it provides information on theological currents of the day. In it he argues, among other things, for the superiority of Christianity as he knows it (the religion of the "true Gnostic") to the teachings of the Gnostics. He discusses the system of Carpocrates, an Alexandrian Gnostic, in particular.

Clementine Homilies

Along with the *Clementine Recognitions*, the *Clementine Homilies* are attributed to Clement of Rome (first century A.D.) and together make up the so-called "Pseudo-Clementines." The *Clementine Homilies* contain twenty homilies (or sermons), plus two introductory letters. Although attributed to Clement, they are anonymous (therefore pseudepigraphal) in terms of actual authorship. They are generally judged to have been produced in Syria early in the third century A.D., although they are based on earlier sources.

Epiphanius, *Panarion*

The *Panarion* of Epiphanius was written around A.D. 375–78. Epiphanius was born at Besanduc in Palestine around A.D. 310–20, was raised as a Christian, and received his education in Palestine and Egypt. He founded a monastery at Eleutheropolis in Palestine and became Bishop of Salamis, Cyprus, in 367. He died around 403.

A strict exponent of Nicene orthodoxy, Epiphanius sought to refute all the heresies known to him in his *Panarion*, which means "Medicine Chest." He describes eighty sects from the time of Adam to his own, of which sixty can be considered Christian heresies or at least related to Christianity. In writing the *Panarion* Epiphanius clearly made use of the works of other heresiologists before him, sometimes quoting from them extensively; these include Irenaeus, Hippolytus, and Clement of Alexandria, and the historian Eusebius. Generally his work is considered reliable when he describes heretics and movements close to his own time, but less reliable when he deals with persons and movements of earlier times. He makes inferences that are unfounded, and he attributes to early figures the views held by their followers many years later.

Eusebius, *Ecclesiastical History*

Eusebius was born in approximately A.D. 260 in Palestine, probably at Caesarea, where he also died around 340. He was educated in Alexandria,

Egypt, and was elected Bishop of Caesarea around 315. He played a major role at the Council of Nicea in A.D. 325.

Eusebius wrote his ten-volume *Ecclesiastical History* in stages, finishing about A.D. 325. The final edition records events up to the year 323. This work is the main source of the history of Christianity from the apostolic age to the early part of the fourth century. One of its features is that it contains materials that he copied from earlier writers which have otherwise perished.

The work of Eusebius is invaluable for the information it contains. If Eusebius has a fault, it is primarily that he does not use as much critical judgment as the modern interpreter would wish from him.

Hippolytus, *Refutation of All Heresies*

Hippolytus (ca. A.D. 170–236) wrote his *Refutation of All Heresies* about A.D. 230 in Rome. The thirty-three heresies he discusses and seeks to refute in this book are mostly gnostic sects known to him at the time. Generally he accuses them of taking their doctrines from pagan sources. Hippolytus is one of the early heresiologists, and his work is a valuable source book on the sects that existed at his time.

Irenaeus, *Against Heresies*

Irenaeus (ca. A.D. 130–200) wrote his *Against Heresies* in five books over several years, perhaps during the last two decades of the second century (although some scholars have claimed that parts may have been written even earlier). Although Irenaeus wrote his work in Greek, only extracts of it exist in that language; the entire work is in Latin alone. The work is one of the earliest concerning heretical teachers and movements and is therefore of great importance as an early witness. Generally Irenaeus is considered one of the most important Christian theologians of the second century; he is sensitive to the nuances between various theological positions.

Justin, *Apology* and *Dialogue with Trypho*

Justin (ca. 100–165), known also as Justin Martyr and sometimes as Justin the Philosopher, was born in Samaria of pagan parents. During his early years he examined various philosophies, and he was converted to

Christianity about A.D. 130. He taught at Ephesus, and it is probably there (about 135) that he had his disputation with Trypho, a Jewish critic of Christianity. Later he moved to Rome, where he founded a school and produced his writings. He wrote his *First Apology* and his *Dialogue with Trypho* about 155. He also wrote a *Second Apology* about 161. He was martyred in Rome around 165.

Justin has been regarded as one of the most important apologists ("defenders") of Christianity against its critics. Moreover, his writings provide some of the earliest materials available on various leaders and movements in early Christianity, including some of the early Gnostics, Marcion (a contemporary in Rome), and the Ebionites.

Origen, *Against Celsus*

Origen (ca. A.D. 185–254) wrote his *Against Celsus* (*Contra Celsum*) around A.D. 250 at Alexandria. It consisted of eight volumes written in response to Celsus, a pagan philosopher who had written a work called *True Discourse* (ca. 178), the first known literary attack on Christianity. Some ninety percent of the book by Celsus, which otherwise is lost, is thought to be presented in *Against Celsus*.

Tertullian, *Adversus Marcionem*

Tertullian (ca. A.D. 160–225), often called the first Latin church father, wrote his five-volume *Adversus Marcionem* (*Against Marcion*) at Carthage, North Africa, in three stages between about A.D. 198 and 208. It is the earliest large-scale treatment of Marcion and Marcionite Christianity available, as well as the most valuable.

The Revelation to John

The book of Revelation is a Christian apocalyptic book written by a man named John (1:1, 4, 9; 22:8), known variously as John the Seer or John of Patmos—the place of his vision (1:9) and perhaps the place where he wrote the book. The book is usually thought to have been written near the end of the reign of Emperor Domitian (reigned A.D. 81–96). The book gives evidence of the existence, near the end of the first century, of a sect called the Nicolaitans (Rev. 2:1-7, 12-17).

Bibliography

Part 1: Surveys and Sources

General Works

Caird, G. B. *The Apostolic Age*. London: G. Duckworth, 1955.

Campenhausen, Hans von. *Ecclesiastical Authority and Spiritual Power in the Church of the First Three Centuries*. Stanford, Calif.: Stanford University Press, 1969.

———. *The Fathers of the Greek Church*. London: A. & C. Black, 1963.

Carrington, Philip. *The Early Christian Church*. 2 vols. Cambridge: Cambridge University Press, 1957.

Chadwick, Henry. *The Early Church*. Baltimore: Penguin Books, 1967.

Cross, F. L. *The Early Christian Fathers*. London: G. Duckworth, 1960.

Di Berardino, Angelo, ed. *Encyclopedia of the Early Church*. 2 vols. Translated by Adrian Walford. New York: Oxford University Press, 1992.

Ferguson, Everett, ed. *Encyclopedia of Early Christianity*. New York: Garland Publishing, Inc., 1990.

Frend, W. H. C. *The Early Church*. London: Hodder & Stoughton, 1965.

———. *The Rise of Christianity*. Philadelphia: Fortress Press, 1984.

Goppelt, Leonhard. *Apostolic and Post-Apostolic Times*. Grand Rapids: Baker Book House, 1970.

Grant, Robert M. *After the New Testament*. Philadelphia: Fortress Press, 1967.

———. *Heresy and Criticism: The Search for Authenticity in Early Christian Literature*. Louisville, Ky: Westminster/John Knox Press, 1993.

———. *Second Century Christianity: A Collection of Fragments*. London: S.P.C.K., 1957.

Hamell, Patrick J. *Handbook of Patrology*. Staten Island, N.Y.: Alba House, 1968.

Kelly, J. N. D. *Early Christian Doctrines*. 2nd ed. New York: Harper & Row, 1960.

Moule, C. F. D. "The New Testament and the Doctrine of the Trinity: A Short Report on an Old Theme." *Expository Times* 88 (1976): 16–20.

Neiswender, Don. "Scripture and Culture in the Early Church." *Christianity Today* 12 (1967): 111–12.

Pelikan, Jaroslav J. *The Emergence of the Catholic Tradition (100–600)*. Chicago: University of Chicago Press, 1971.

Quasten, Johannes. *Patrology*. 4 vols. Westminster, Md.: Christian Classics, 1983–86.

Sell, Alan P. F. "Theology and the Philosophical Climate: Case-Studies from the Second Century AD." *Vox Evangelica* 13 (1983): 41–66.

Wagner, Walter H. *After the Apostles: Christianity in the Second Century*. Minneapolis: Fortress Press, 1994.

Wilken, Robert L. "Toward a Social Interpretation of Early Christian Apologetics." *Church History* 39 (1970): 437–58.

Primary Sources of Early Christian Texts

Epiphanius. *The Panarion of Epiphanius of Salamis*. Translated by Frank Williams. 2 vols. Nag Hammadi Studies 35 & 36. New York: E. J. Brill, 1987–94.

———. *The Panarion of St. Epiphanius, Bishop of Salamis: Selected Passages*. Translated by Philip R. Amidon. New York: Oxford University Press, 1990.

Eusebius. *The History of the Church from Christ to Constantine*. Translated by G. A. Williamson. Minneapolis: Augsburg Publishing House, 1975.

Klijn, A. F. J., and G. J. Reinink, eds. *Patristic Evidence for Jewish-Christian Sects*. Supplements to Novum Testamentum 36. Leiden: E. J. Brill, 1973.

Lake, Kirsopp, ed. *The Apostolic Fathers*. 2 vols. Loeb Classical Library. New York: G. P. Putnam's Sons, 1912–13.

Oulton, John E. L., and Henry Chadwick, eds. *Alexandrian Christianity*. Library of Christian Classics 2. Philadelphia: Westminster Press, 1954.

Richardson, Cyril C., ed. *Early Christian Fathers*. Library of Christian Classics 1. Philadelphia: Westminster Press, 1953.

Roberts, Alexander, and James Donaldson, eds. *The Ante-Nicene Fathers*. 10 vols. Buffalo, N.Y.: The Christian Literature Publishing Company, 1885–96; reprinted, Peabody, Mass.: Hendrickson Publishers, 1994.

Schneemelcher, Wilhelm, ed. *New Testament Apocrypha*. 2 vols. Rev. ed. Louisville: Westminster/John Knox Press, 1991–92.

Williams, Lukyn A., ed. *Justin Martyr: Dialogue with Trypho*. Translations of Christian Literature, Series 1: Greek Texts. New York: Macmillan, 1931.

Orthodoxy and Heresy

Adler, William. "The Origins of the Proto-Heresies: Fragments from a Chronicle in the First Book of Epiphanius' Panarion." *Journal of Theological Studies* 41 (1990): 472–501.

Allison, C. FitzSimons. *The Cruelty of Heresy: An Affirmation of Christian Orthodoxy*. Harrisburg, Pa.: Morehouse Publishing Company, 1994.

Bauer, Walter. *Orthodoxy and Heresy in Earliest Christianity*. Philadelphia: Fortress Press, 1971.

Brown, H. O. J. *Heresies: The Image of Christ in the Mirror of Heresy and Orthodoxy from the Apostles to the Present*. Garden City, N.Y.: Doubleday, 1984.

Christie-Murray, David. *A History of Heresy*. New York: Oxford University Press, 1989.

Davies, J. G. "The Origins of Docetism." *Studia Patristica* 6 (1962): 13–35.

Frend, W. H. C. *Saints and Sinners in the Early Church: Differing and Conflicting Traditions in the First Six Centuries*. Wilmington: Michael Glazier, 1985.

Grossi, V. "Heresy–Heretic." In *Encyclopedia of the Early Church*, vol. 1, 376–77. 2 vols. Edited by Angelo Di Berardino. New York: Oxford University Press, 1992.

Hultgren, Arland J. *The Rise of Normative Christianity*. Minneapolis: Fortress Press, 1994.

Koester, Helmut. "GNOMAI DIAPHOROI: The Origin and Nature of Diversification in the History of Early Christianity." *Harvard Theological Review* 58 (1965): 279–318.

La Piana, George. "The Roman Church at the End of the Second Century." *Harvard Theological Review* 18 (1925): 201–77.

Logan, Alistair H. B. *Gnostic Truth and Christian Heresy.* Edinburgh: T. & T. Clark, 1995.

McCue, James F. "Orthodoxy and Heresy: Walter Bauer and the Valentinians." *Vigiliae Christianae* 33 (1979): 118–30.

McGucklin, J. A. "The Concept of Orthodoxy in Ancient Christianity." *Patristic and Byzantine Review* 8 (1989): 5–23.

Mitros, Joseph F. "The Norm of Faith in the Patristic Age." *Theological Studies* 29 (1968): 444–71.

Outler, Albert C. "Method and Aims in the Study of the Development of Catholic Christianity." *The Second Century* 1 (1981): 7–17.

Parrott, Douglas M. "Gnostic and Orthodox Disciples in the Second and Third Centuries." In *Nag Hammadi, Gnosticism, and Early Christianity,* 193–219. Edited by Charles W. Hedrick and Robert Hodgson, Jr. Peabody, Mass.: Hendrickson Publishers, 1986.

Rahner, Karl. *On Heresy.* Quaestiones Disputatae 11. New York: Herder & Herder, 1964.

Robinson, James M., and Helmut Koester. *Trajectories through Early Christianity.* Philadelphia: Fortress Press, 1971.

Robinson, Thomas A. *The Bauer Thesis Examined: The Geography of Heresy in the Early Christian Church.* Lewiston, N.Y.: Edwin Mellen Press, 1988.

Turner, H. E. W. *The Pattern of Christian Truth: A Study in the Relations between Orthodoxy and Heresy in the Early Church.* London: A. R. Mowbray, 1954.

Wilken, Robert L. "Diversity and Unity in Early Christianity." *The Second Century* 1 (1981): 101–10.

Part 2: Figures and Movements

Gnosticism

Aland, Barbara, ed. *Gnosis: Festschrift für Hans Jonas.* Göttingen: Vandenhoeck & Ruprecht, 1978.

Armstrong, A. H. "Gnosis and Greek Philosophy." In *Gnosis: Festschrift für Hans Jonas,* 87–124. Ed. Barbara Aland. Göttingen: Vandenhoeck & Ruprecht, 1978.

Attridge, Harold W. "Gnosticism." In *Harper's Bible Dictionary,* 349–50. Edited by Paul J. Achtemeier. San Francisco: Harper & Row, 1985.

Bianchi, Ugo, ed. *The Origins of Gnosticism: Colloquium of Messina 13–18 April 1966.* Studies in the History of Religions 12. Supplements to Numen 12. Leiden: E. J. Brill, 1967.

———. *Selected Essays on Gnosticism, Dualism and Mysteriosophy.* Supplements to Numen 38. Leiden: E. J. Brill, 1978.

Bultmann, Rudolf. "*Gnosis* [and Related Words]." In *Theological Dictionary of the New Testament,* vol. 1, 689–719. 10 vols. Edited by Gerhard Kittel and Gerhard Friedrich. Grand Rapids: Wm. B. Eerdmans, 1964–76.

———. "Gnosticism." In *Primitive Christianity in Its Contemporary Setting,* 162–71. Cleveland: World Publishing Company, 1956.

Casey, R. P. "The Study of Gnosticism." *Journal of Theological Studies* 36 (1935): 45–60.

Colpe, Carsten. "New Testament and Gnostic Christology." In *Religions in Antiquity: Essays in Memory of Erwin Ramsdell Goodenough,* 227–43. Edited by Jacob Neusner. Supplements to Numen 14. Leiden: E. J. Brill, 1968.

Couliano, Ioan P. *The Tree of Gnosis: Gnostic Mythology from Early Christianity to Modern Nihilism.* San Francisco: HarperCollins, 1992.

Cross, F. L., and E. A. Livingstone, eds. "Gnosticism." In *The Oxford Dictionary of the Christian Church,* 573–74. 2nd ed. London: Oxford University Press, 1974.

Filoramo, Giovanni. "Gnosis–Gnosticism." In *Encyclopedia of the Early Church,* vol. 1, 352–54. 2 vols. Edited by Angelo Di Berardino. New York: Oxford University Press, 1992.

———. *A History of Gnosticism.* Translated by Anthony Alcock. Cambridge, Mass.: Basil Blackwell, 1990.

Foerster, Werner. *Gnosis: A Selection of Gnostic Texts.* 2 vols. New York: Oxford University Press, 1972–74.

Frend, W. H. C. "The Gnostic Sects and the Roman Empire." *Journal of Ecclesiastical History* 5 (1954): 25–37.

Goetz, Philip W., ed. "Gnosticism." In *The New Encyclopaedia Britannica,* vol. 5, 315. 31 vols. 15th ed. Chicago: Encyclopaedia Britannica, 1987.

Grant, Robert M. "Gnostic and Christian Worship." In *After the New Testament,* 173–82. Philadelphia: Fortress Press, 1967.

———. "Gnosticism." In *The Encyclopedia Americana,* vol. 12, 824–26. 30 vols. Edited by David T. Holland. Danbury, Conn.: Grolier, Inc., 1989.

————. *Gnosticism: A Sourcebook of Heretical Writings from the Early Christian Period*. New York: Harper & Brothers, 1961.

————. *Gnosticism and Early Christianity*. Rev. ed. New York: Harper & Row, 1966.

Green, Henry A. *The Economic and Social Origins of Gnosticism*. Society of Biblical Literature Dissertation Series 77. Atlanta: Scholars Press, 1985.

————. "Gnosis and Gnosticism: A Study in Methodology." *Numen* 24 (1977): 95–134.

Groningen, Gerard van. *First Century Gnosticism: Its Origins and Motifs*. Leiden: E. J. Brill, 1967.

Haardt, Robert. "Gnosis." In *Sacramentum Mundi*, vol. 2, 379–81. 6 vols. Edited by Karl Rahner. New York: Herder & Herder, 1968.

————. *Gnosis: Character and Testimony*. Leiden: E. J. Brill, 1971.

Jonas, Hans. *The Gnostic Religion: The Message of the Alien God and the Beginnings of Christianity*. 3rd ed. Boston: Beacon Press, 1970.

————. "Gnosticism." In *The Encyclopedia of Philosophy*, vol. 3, 336–42. 8 vols. Edited by Paul Edwards. New York: Macmillan, 1967.

Krause, Martin, ed. *Gnosis and Gnosticism: Papers Read at the Seventh International Conference on Patristic Studies, Oxford, September 8th–13th, 1975*. Nag Hammadi Studies 8. Leiden: E. J. Brill, 1977.

————, ed. *Gnosis and Gnosticism: Papers Read at the Eighth International Conference on Patristic Studies, Oxford, September 3rd–8th, 1979*. Nag Hammadi Studies 17. Leiden: E. J. Brill, 1981.

Layton, Bentley, ed. *The Rediscovery of Gnosticism*. 2 vols. Studies in the History of Religions 41. Leiden: E. J. Brill, 1980–81.

Logan, A. H. B., and A. J. M. Wedderburn, eds. *The New Testament and Gnosis: Essays in Honour of R. McL. Wilson*. Edinburgh: T. & T. Clark, 1983.

MacRae, George W. "Apocalyptic Eschatology in Gnosticism." In *Apocalypticism in the Mediterranean World and the Near East*, 317–25. Edited by David Hellholm. Tübingen: J.C.B. Mohr (Paul Siebeck), 1983.

————. "Gnosticism." In *New Catholic Encyclopedia*, vol 6, 523–28. 15 vols. Edited by William J. McDonald. New York: McGraw-Hill Book Company, 1967.

————. "Why the Church Rejected Gnosticism." In *Jewish and Christian Self-Definition*, vol. 1, 126–33. 3 vols. Edited by E. P. Sanders. Philadelphia: Fortress Press, 1980–82.

Ménard, Jacques E. "Normative Self-Definition in Gnosticism." In *Jewish and Christian Self-Definition*, vol. 1, 134–50. 3 vols. Edited by E. P. Sanders. Philadelphia: Fortress Press, 1980–82.

Munck, Johannes. "The New Testament and Gnosticism." In *Current Issues in New Testament Interpretation: Essays in Honor of Otto A. Piper*, 224–38. Edited by W. Klassen and G. F. Snyder. New York: Harper & Row, 1962.

Pagels, Elaine. *The Gnostic Gospels*. New York: Random House, 1979.

———. *The Gnostic Paul*. Philadelphia: Fortress Press, 1975.

Pearson, Birger A. "Early Christianity and Gnosticism: A Review Essay." *Religious Studies Review* 13 (1987): 1–8.

———. "Jewish Elements in Gnosticism and the Development of Gnostic Self-Definition." In *Jewish and Christian Self-Definition*, vol. 1, 151–60. 3 vols. Edited by E. P. Sanders. Philadelphia: Fortress Press, 1980–82.

Perkins, Pheme. "Gnosticism." In *Encyclopedia of Early Christianity*, 371–76. Edited by Everett Ferguson. New York: Garland Publishing, Inc., 1990.

———. *Gnosticism and the New Testament*. Minneapolis: Fortress Press, 1993.

———. "Gnosticism as a Christian Heresy." In *The Encyclopedia of Religion*, vol. 5, 578–80. 16 vols. Edited by Mircea Eliade. New York: Macmillan, 1987.

———. *The Gnostic Dialogue: The Early Church and the Crisis of Gnosticism*. New York: Paulist Press, 1980.

Pétrement, Simone. *A Separate God: The Christian Origins of Gnosticism*. San Francisco: Harper & Row, 1990.

Puech, Henri-Charles. "Other Gnostic Gospels and Related Literature," revised by Beate Blatz. In *New Testament Apocrypha*, vol. 1, 354–413. 2 vols. Edited by Wilhelm Schneemelcher. Rev. ed. Louisville: Westminster/John Knox Press, 1991–92.

Quispel, Gilles. "Gnosticism and the New Testament." In *The Bible in Modern Scholarship*, 252–71. Edited by J. P. Hyatt. Nashville: Abingdon Press, 1965.

———. "Gnosticism from Its Origins to the Middle Ages." In *The Encyclopedia of Religion*, vol. 5, 566–74. 16 vols. Edited by Mircea Eliade. New York: Macmillan, 1987.

Reicke, Bo. "Traces of Gnosticism in the Dead Sea Scrolls?" *New Testament Studies* 1 (1954/55): 137–41.

Renwick, A. M. "Gnosticism." In *The International Standard Bible Encyclopedia*, vol. 2, 484–90. 4 vols. Edited by Geoffrey W. Bromiley. Grand Rapids: Wm. B. Eerdmans, 1979–88.

Rudolph, Kurt. *Gnosis: The Nature and History of Gnosticism*. San Francisco: Harper & Row, 1983.

———. "Gnosticism." In *The Anchor Bible Dictionary*, vol. 2, 1033–44. 6 vols. Edited by David N. Freedman. New York: Doubleday, 1992.

Schenke, Hans-Martin. "The Problem of Gnosis." *The Second Century* 3 (1983): 73–87.

Schlier, H. "Man in Gnosticism." In *The Relevance of the New Testament*, 94–112. New York: Herder & Herder, 1968.

Schmithals, Walter. "The Apostle in Gnosticism." In *The Office of Apostle in the Early Church*, 114–92. Nashville: Abingdon Press, 1969.

———. *Gnosticism in Corinth: An Investigation of the Letters to the Corinthians*. Nashville: Abingdon Press, 1971.

———. *Paul and the Gnostics*. Nashville: Abingdon Press, 1972.

Schoedel, William R. "The Rediscovery of Gnosis: A Study of the Background to the New Testament." *Interpretation* 16 (1962): 387–401.

Scholem, Gershom G. *Jewish Gnosticism, Merkabah Mysticism, and Talmudic Tradition*. 2nd ed. New York: Jewish Theological Seminary, 1965.

Scholer, David M. "Bibliographica Gnostica." *Novum Testamentum* 13 (1971): 322–36. Bibliography appears annually in subsequent volumes.

Segal, Alan F. *Two Powers in Heaven: Early Rabbinic Reports about Christianity and Gnosticism*. Studies in Judaism in Late Antiquity 25. Leiden: E. J. Brill, 1977.

Stead, G. C. "In Search of Valentinus." In *The Rediscovery of Gnosticism: Proceedings of the International Conference on Gnosticism at Yale, New Haven, Connecticut, March 28–31, 1978*, 1:75–95. 2 vols. Edited by Bentley Layton. Studies in the History of Religions. Supplements to Numen 41. Leiden: E. J. Brill, 1980–81.

Stroumsa, Gedaliahu A. G. *Another Seed: Studies in Gnostic Mythology*. Nag Hammadi Studies 24. Leiden: E. J. Brill, 1984.

Talbert, Charles H. "An Anti-Gnostic Tendency in Lucan Christology." *New Testament Studies* 14 (1967/68): 259–71.

———. *Luke and the Gnostics: An Examination of the Lucan Purpose*. Nashville: Abingdon Press, 1966.

Widengren, Geo. *The Gnostic Attitude*. Santa Barbara, Calif.: University of California Institute of Religious Studies, 1973.

Wilson, Robert McL. "Ethics and the Gnostics." In *Studien zum Text und zur Ethik des Neuen Testaments: Festschrift zum 80. Geburtstag von Heinrich Greeven*, 440–49. Ed. Wolfgang Schrage. Berlin: Walter de Gruyter, 1986.

———. "Gnosis/Gnostizismus: II. Neues Testament, Judentum, Alte Kirche." In *Theologische Realenzyklopädie*, vol. 13, 535–50. Edited by Gerhard Krause and Gerhard Müller. Berlin: Walter de Gruyter, 1977—.

———. *Gnosis and the New Testament*. Philadelphia: Fortress Press, 1968.

———. *The Gnostic Problem: A Study of the Relations between Hellenistic Judaism and the Gnostic Heresy*. London: A. R. Mowbray, 1958.

———. "Gnostics—in Galatia?" In *Studia Evangelica IV*, 358–67. Edited by F. L. Cross. Berlin: Akademie Verlag, 1968.

———. "Some Recent Studies in Gnosticism." *New Testament Studies* 6 (1959/60): 32–44.

Wink, Walter. "Appreciating Gnosticism." *dialog* 33 (1994): 99–105.

Yamauchi, Edwin M. *Pre-Christian Gnosticism: A Survey of the Proposed Evidences*. 2nd ed. Grand Rapids: Baker Book House, 1983.

Gospel of Thomas

Best, E. "The Gospel of Thomas." *Biblical Theology* 10 (1960): 1–10.

Blatz, Beate. "The Coptic Gospel of Thomas." In *New Testament Apocrypha*, vol. 1, 110–33. Edited by Wilhelm Schneemelcher. 2 vols. Rev. ed. Louisville: Westminster/John Knox Press, 1991–92.

Brown, Raymond E. "The Gospel of Thomas and St John's Gospel." *New Testament Studies* 9 (1962/63): 155–77.

Cameron, Ron. "Thomas, Gospel of." In *The Anchor Bible Commentary*, vol. 6, 535–40. 6 vols. Edited by David N. Freedman. New York: Doubleday, 1992.

Cullmann, Oscar. "The Gospel according to St. Thomas and Its Significance for Research into the Canonical Gospels." *Hibbert Journal* 60 (1962): 116–24.

———. "The Gospel of Thomas and the Problem of the Age of the Tradition Contained Therein: A Survey." *Interpretation* 16 (1962): 116–24.

Desjardins, Michael. "When Was the Gospel of Thomas Written?" *Toronto Journal of Theology* 8 (1992): 121–33.

Frend, W. H. C. "The Gospel of Thomas: Is Rehabilitation Possible?" *Journal of Theological Studies* 18 (1967): 13–26.

Gärtner, Bertil E. *The Theology of the Gospel according to Thomas.* New York: Harper & Brothers, 1961.

Grant, Robert M., and David N. Freedman. *The Secret Sayings of Jesus.* Garden City, N.Y.: Doubleday, 1960.

Grobel, Kendrick. "How Gnostic is the Gospel of Thomas?" *New Testament Studies* 8 (1962/62): 367–73.

MacRae, George W. "The Gospel of Thomas—*Logia Iesou?*" *The Catholic Biblical Quarterly* 22 (1960): 56–71.

Montefiore, H. W. "A Comparison of the Parables of the Gospel according to Thomas and of the Synoptic Gospels." *New Testament Studies* 7 (1961): 220–49.

Quispel, Gilles. "The Gospel of Thomas and the New Testament." *Vigiliae Christianae* 11 (1957): 189–207.

———. "Some Remarks on the Gospel of Thomas." *New Testament Studies* 5 (1958/59): 276–90.

Turner, H. E. W., and Hugh Montefiore. *Thomas and the Evangelists.* Studies in Biblical Theology 35. Naperville, Il.: Alec R. Allenson, 1962.

Walls, A. F. "The References to Apostles in the Gospel of Thomas." *New Testament Studies* 7 (1960/61): 266–70.

Wilson, Robert McL. "The Coptic 'Gospel of Thomas.'" *New Testament Studies* 5 (1958/59): 273–76.

———. *Studies in the Gospel of Thomas.* London: A. R. Mowbray, 1960.

Wisse, Frederik. "The Nag Hammadi Library and the Heresiologists." *Vigiliae Christianae* 25 (1971): 205–23.

Nag Hammadi

Flory, Wayne S. *The Gnostic Concept of Authority and the Nag Hammadi Documents.* Lewiston, N.Y.: Mellen Press, 1995.

Gold, Victor R. "The Gnostic Library of Chenoboskion." In *The Biblical Archaeologist Reader,* 299–329. Edited by David N. Freedman and G. Ernest Wright. New York: Doubleday, 1961.

Hedrick, Charles W., and Robert Hodgson, eds. *Nag Hammadi, Gnosticism, and Early Christianity.* Peabody, Mass.: Hendrickson Publishers, 1986.

Helmbold, Andrew K. "Nag Hammadi Literature." In *The International*

Standard Bible Encyclopedia, vol. 3, 472–76. 4 vols. Edited by Geoffrey W. Bromiley. Grand Rapids: Wm. B. Eerdmans, 1979–88.

Layton, Bentley, trans. *The Gnostic Scriptures: A New Translation*. Garden City, N.Y.: Doubleday, 1987.

Nock, A. D. "A Coptic Library of Gnostic Writings." *Journal of Theological Studies* 9 (1958): 314–24.

Pearson, Birger A. "Nag Hammadi." In *The Anchor Bible Dictionary*, vol. 4, 982–93. 6 vols. Edited by David N. Freedman. New York: Doubleday, 1992.

Piper, Otto A. "Change of Perspective: Gnostic and Canonical Gospels." *Interpretation* 16 (1962): 402–17.

Puech, Henri-Charles. "Other Gnostic Gospels and Related Literature," revised by Beate Blatz. In *New Testament Apocrypha*, vol. 1, 354–413. 2 vols. Edited by Wilhelm Schneemelcher. Rev. ed. Louisville: Westminster/John Knox Press, 1991–92.

Robinson, James M. "Introduction." In *The Nag Hammadi Library in English*, 1–26. 3rd ed. Edited by James M. Robinson. San Francisco: Harper, 1988.

———, ed. *The Nag Hammadi Library in English*. 3rd ed. San Francisco: Harper, 1988.

Scholer, David M. *Nag Hammadi Bibliography 1948–1969*. Nag Hammadi Studies 1. Leiden: E. J. Brill, 1971.

Unnik, W. C. van. *Newly Discovered Gnostic Writings: A Preliminary Survey of the Nag Hammadi Find*. Studies in Biblical Theology 30. Naperville, Il.: Alec R. Allenson, 1960.

Wilson, Robert McL. "The Gnostic 'Library' of Nag-Hammadi." *The Scottish Journal of Theology* 12 (1959): 161–70.

———. "Nag Hammadi and the New Testament." *New Testament Studies* 28 (1982): 289–302.

———. "Second Thoughts: XI. The Gnostic Gospels from Nag Hammadi." *Expository Times* 78 (1966/67): 36–41.

Wisse, Frederik. "The Nag Hammadi Library and the Heresiologists." *Vigiliae Christianae* 25 (1971): 205–23.

Apelles

Foerster, Werner, ed. "Associates of Marcion." In *Gnosis: A Selection of Gnostic Texts*, vol. 1, 44–47. 2 vols. Oxford: Clarendon Press, 1972–74.

Grant, Robert M. "The Syllogistic Exegesis of Apelles." In *Heresy and Criticism: The Search for Authenticity in Early Christian Literature*, 75–88. Louisville, Ky.: Westminster/John Knox Press, 1993.

Quasten, Johannes. "Apelles." In *Patrology*, vol. 1, 272–74. 4 vols. Westminster, Md.: Christian Classics, 1983–86.

Rudolph, Kurt. "Apelles." In *Gnosis: The Nature and History of Gnosticism*, 294–98. San Francisco: Harper & Row, 1983.

Basilides

Cross, F. L., and E. A. Livingstone, eds. "Basilides." In *The Oxford Dictionary of the Christian Church*, 141–42. 2nd ed. London: Oxford University Press, 1974.

Foerster, Werner, ed. "Basilides." In *Gnosis: A Selection of Gnostic Texts*, vol. 1, 59–83. 2 vols. Oxford: Clarendon Press, 1972–74.

———. "Das System des Basilides." *New Testament Studies* 9 (1963): 233–55.

Grant, Robert M. "Gnostic Origins and the Basilidians of Irenaeus." *Vigiliae Christianae* 13 (1959): 121–25.

MacRae, George W. "Basilides." In *New Catholic Encyclopedia*, vol. 2, 160. Edited by William J. McDonald. 15 vols. New York: McGraw-Hill Book Company, 1967.

Quasten, Johannes. "Basilides." In *Patrology*, vol. 1, 257–59. 4 vols. Westminster, Md.: Christian Classics, 1983–86.

Quispel, Gilles. "Gnostic Man: The Doctrine of Basilides." In *The Mystic Vision: Papers from the Eranos Yearbooks*, 210–46. Bollingen Series, 30, vol. 6. Princeton: Princeton University Press, 1968.

Rudolph, Kurt. "Basilides." In *Gnosis: The Nature and History of Gnosticism*, 309–17. San Francisco: Harper & Row, 1983.

Wolfson, H. A. "Negative Attitudes in the Church Fathers and the Gnostic Basilides." *Harvard Theological Review* 50 (1957): 145–56.

Carpocrates

Cross, F. L., and E. A. Livingstone, eds. "Carpocrates." In *The Oxford Dictionary of the Christian Church*, 243. 2nd ed. London: Oxford University Press, 1974.

Foerster, Werner, ed. "The First Christian Gnostics." In *Gnosis: A Selection of Gnostic Texts*, vol. 1, 34–43. 2 vols. Oxford: Clarendon Press, 1972–74.

MacCrae, George W. "Carpocrates." In *New Catholic Encyclopedia*, vol. 3, 145. 15 vols. Edited by William J. McDonald. New York: McGraw-Hill Book Company, 1967.

Rudolph, Kurt. "Carpocrates." In *Gnosis: The Nature and History of Gnosticism*, 299. San Francisco: Harper & Row, 1983.

Smith, Morton. "Carpocrates." In *Clement of Alexandria and a Secret Gospel of Mark*, 266–78. Cambridge, Mass.: Harvard University Press, 1973.

Cerinthus

Cross, F. L., and E. A. Livingstone, eds. "Cerinthus." *The Oxford Dictionary of the Christian Church*, 261. 2nd ed. London: Oxford University Press, 1974.

Enslin, M. S. "Cerinthus." In *The Interpreter's Dictionary of the Bible*, vol. 1, 549. 4 vols. Edited by George A. Buttrick. Nashville: Abingdon Press, 1962.

Foerster, Werner, ed. "The First Christian Gnostics." In *Gnosis: A Selection of Gnostic Texts*, 34–43. 2 vols. Oxford: Clarendon Press, 1972–74.

Klijn, A. F. J. "Cerinthus." In *Encyclopedia of the Early Church*, vol. 1, 158–59. 2 vols. Edited by Angelo Di Berardino. New York: Oxford University Press, 1992.

Rudolph, Kurt. *Gnosis: The Nature and History of Gnosticism*, 298–99. San Francisco: Harper & Row, 1983.

Clement of Alexandria

Clemens, Titus Flavius, of Alexandria. *The Writings of Clement of Alexandria*. Translated by William Wilson. Edinburgh: T. & T. Clark, 1872–80.

Davies, J. G. "Clement of Alexandria (A.D. 155–215)." *Expository Times* 80 (1968): 18–20.

Ferguson, John. *Clement of Alexandria*. New York: Twayne Publishing, 1974.

Kovacs, Judith Lee. "Clement of Alexandria and the Valentinian Gnostics." Ph.D. diss., Columbia University, 1978.

Lilla, Salvatore R. C. *Clement of Alexandria: A Study in Christian Platonism and Gnosticism.* London: Oxford University Press, 1971.

Steely, John E. *Gnosis: The Doctrine of Christian Perfection in the Writings of Clement of Alexandria.* Madison, Wis.: Microcard Foundation for the ATLA, 1959.

Timothy, Hamilton Baird. *The Early Christian Apologists and Greek Philosophy: Exemplified by Irenaeus, Tertullian and Clement of Alexandria.* Assen: Van Gorcum, 1973.

Van Eijk, A.H.C. "The Gospel of Philip and Clement of Alexandria." *Vigiliae Christianae* 25 (1971): 94–120.

Wagner, Walter. "Another Look at the Literary Problem in Clement of Alexandria's Major Writings." *Church History* 37 (1968): 251–60.

Ebionites

Burtchaell, James T. "Ebionites." In *The Encyclopedia Americana*, vol. 9, 570. 30 vols. Edited by David T. Holland. Danbury, Conn.: Grolier, Inc., 1989.

Daniélou, Jean. *The Theology of Jewish Christianity.* Chicago: Henry Regnery Company, 1964.

Fitzmyer, Joseph A. "The Qumran Scrolls, the Ebionites and Their Literature." In *Essays on the Semitic Background of the New Testament*, 435–80. Society of Biblical Literature Sources for Biblical Study 5. Missoula, Mont.: Scholars Press, 1974.

Goetz, Philip, ed. "Ebionite." In *The New Encyclopaedia Britannica*, vol. 4, 344. 31 vols. 15th ed. Edited by Philip Goetz. Chicago: Encyclopaedia Britannica, 1987.

Goranson, Stephen. "Ebionites." In *The Anchor Bible Dictionary*, vol. 2, 260–61. 6 vols. Edited by David N. Freedman. New York: Doubleday, 1992.

Keck, Leander E. "The Poor among the Saints in the New Testament." *Zeitschrift für die neutestamentliche Wissenschaft* 56 (1965): 100–129.

Klijn, A. F. J. "The Study of Jewish Christianity." *New Testament Studies* 20 (1974): 419–31.

Murphy, Francis X. "Ebionites." In *New Catholic Encyclopedia*, vol. 5, 29. 15 vols. Edited by William J. McDonald. New York: McGraw-Hill Book Company, 1967.

Schoeps, Hans-Joachim. "Ebionite Christianity." *Journal of Theological Studies* 4 (1953): 219–24.

——. *Jewish Christianity: Factional Disputes in the Early Church.* Philadelphia: Fortress Press, 1969.

Simon, Marcel. "The Fate of Jewish Christianity." In *Verus Israel: A Study of the Relations between Christians and Jews in the Roman Empire, 135–425*, 237–70. New York: Oxford University Press, 1986.

Strecker, Georg. "On the Problem of Jewish Christianity." In *Orthodoxy and Heresy in Earliest Christianity*, 241–85. Edited by Walter Bauer. Philadelphia: Fortress Press, 1971.

Taylor, R. E. "Attitudes of the Fathers towards Practices of Jewish Christians." *Studia Patristica* 4 (1961): 504–11.

Vielhauer, Philipp, and Georg Strecker. "Jewish-Christian Gospels." In *New Testament Apocrypha*, vol. 1, 134–78. 2 vols. Edited by Wilhelm Schneemelcher. Rev. ed. Louisville: Westminster/John Knox Press, 1991–92.

Wessel, Walter W. "Ebionites; Ebionism." In *The International Standard Bible Encyclopedia*, vol. 2, 9–10. 4 vols. Edited by Geoffrey W. Bromiley. Grand Rapids: Wm. B. Eerdmans, 1979–88.

Wilken, Robert L. "Ebionites." In *Encyclopedia of Religion*, vol. 4, 576–77. 16 vols. Edited by Mircea Eliade. New York: Macmillan, 1987.

Encratites

Desprez, Vincent. "Christian Asceticism Between the New Testament and the Beginning of Monasticism: The Second Century." *The American Benedictine Review* 42 (1991): 163–78.

Grobel, Kendrick. "How Gnostic is the Gospel of Thomas?" *New Testament Studies* 8 (1962): 367–73.

Eusebius

Chestnut, Glenn F., Jr. "Fate, Fortune, Free Will and Nature in Eusebius of Caesarea." *Church History* 42 (1973): 165–82.

——. *The First Christian Histories: Eusebius, Socrates, Sozomen, Theodoret and Evagrius.* Paris: Éditions Beauchesne, 1977.

Eusebius of Caesarea. *The Essential Eusebius.* Edited and translated by Colm Luibheid. New York: The New American Library, 1966.

Grant, Robert M. *Eusebius as Church Historian.* Oxford: Clarendon Press, 1980.

Hollerich, Michael J. "Religion and Politics in the Writings of Eusebius:

Reassessing the First 'Court Theologian.'" *Church History* 59 (1990): 309–25.

Lawlor, Hugh Jackson. *Eusebiana: Essays on the Ecclesiastical History of Eusebius Pamphili, ca. 264–329 A.D. Bishop of Caesarea. Preceded by Essays on the Hypomnenata of Hegesippus, ca. 120–180 A.D. With Publication of the Remaining Fragments of the Memorials, and On the Heresy of the Phrygians; With Critical and Historical Notes, an Index of Passages Referred to and a General Index.* Amsterdam: Philo Press, 1973.

Pritz, Ray A. "Jewish Christianity According to Eusebius." *Mishkan* 13 (1990): 43–53.

Stevenson, James. *Studies in Eusebius.* Cambridge: Cambridge University Press, 1929.

Wallace-Hadrill, D. S. *Eusebius of Caesarea.* Westminster, Md.: Canterbury, 1961.

Irenaeus

Ammundsen, Vlademar. "The Rule of Truth in Irenaeus." *Journal of Theological Studies* 13 (1912): 574–80.

Farkasfalvy, Denis. "The Theology of Scripture in St. Irenaeus." *Revue Benedictine* 78 (1968): 319–33.

Ford, John. "Irenaeus." In *The Encyclopedia Americana*, vol. 15, 437. 30 vols. Edited by David T. Holland. Danbury, Conn.: Grolier, Inc., 1989.

Goetz, Philip, ed. "Irenaeus." In *The New Encyclopaedia Britannica*, vol. 6, 380–81. 31 vols. 15th ed. Chicago: Encyclopaedia Britannica, 1987.

Hinson, E. Glenn. "Irenaeus." In *Encyclopedia of Religion*, vol. 7, 280–83. 16 vols. Edited by Mircea Eliade. New York: Macmillan, 1987.

Hitchcock, Francis R. M. *Irenaeus of Lugdunum: A Study of His Teaching.* Cambridge: Cambridge University Press, 1914.

Jenkins, D. E. "The Make-up of Man according to St. Irenaeus." *Studia Patristica* 6 (1962): 91–95.

Lawson, J. *The Biblical Theology of St. Irenaeus.* London: Epworth Press, 1949.

Quasten, Johannes. "Irenaeus." In *Patrology*, vol. 1, 287–313. 4 vols. Westminster, Md.: Christian Classics, 1983–86.

Reist, Irwin W. "The Christology of Irenaeus." *Journal of the Evangelical Theological Society* 13 (1970): 241–49.

Schoedel, William R. "Theological Method in Irenaeus." *Journal of Theological Studies* 35 (1984): 31–49.

Wingren, Gustav. *Man and the Incarnation: A Study of the Biblical Theology of Irenaeus.* Philadelphia: Muhlenberg Press, 1959.

Justin

Chadwick, Henry. "Justin Martyr's Defence of Christianity." *Bulletin of the John Rylands Library* 47 (1964–65): 275–97.

Droge, Arthur. "Justin Martyr and the Restoration of Philosophy." *Church History* 56 (1987): 303–19.

Kline, Leslie L. "Harmonized Sayings of Jesus in the Pseudo-Clementine Homilies and Justin Martyr." *Zeitschrift für die neutestamentliche Wissenschaft* 66 (1975): 223–41.

Morgan-Wynne, J.E. "The Holy Spirit and Christian Experience in Justin Martyr." *Vigiliae Christianae* 38 (1984): 172–77.

Williams, George H. "Justin Glimpsed as Martyr among His Roman Contemporaries." In *The Context of Contemporary Theology: Essays in Honor of Paul Lehmann*, 99–126. Ed. Alexander J. McKelvey. Atlanta: John Knox Press, 1974.

Wright, David F. "Christian Faith in the Greek World: Justin Martyr's Testimony." *Evangelical Quarterly* 54 (1982): 77–87.

Marcion

Aland, Barbara. "Marcion–Marcionites–Marcionism." In *Encyclopedia of the Early Church*, vol. 1, 523–24. 2 vols. Edited by Angelo Di Berardino. New York: Oxford University Press, 1992.

Balas, D. "Marcion Revisited: A 'Post-Harnack' Perspective." In *Texts and Testament: Critical Essays on the Bible and Early Church Fathers*, 95–108. Edited by W. E. March. San Antonio: Trinity University Press, 1980.

Blackman, Edwin C. *Marcion and His Influence.* London: S.P.C.K., 1948.

Clabeaux, John J. "Marcion." In *The Anchor Bible Dictionary*, vol. 4, 514–16. 6 vols. Edited by David N. Freedman. New York: Doubleday, 1992.

Drijvers, H. J. W. "Marcionism in Syria: Principles, Problems, Polemics." *The Second Century* 6 (1987–88): 153–72.

Evans, Ernest, ed. *Tertullian adversus Marcionem*. 2 vols. Oxford: Clarendon Press, 1972.

Frend, W. H. C. "Marcion." *Expository Times* 80 (1969): 328–32.

Goetz, Philip W., ed. "Marcionite." In *The New Encyclopaedia Britannica*,
vol. 7, 825–26. 31 vols. 15th ed. Chicago: Encyclopaedia Britannica,
1987.

Grant, Robert M. "Marcion, Gospel of." In *The Anchor Bible Dictionary*,
vol. 4, 516–20. 6 vols. Edited by David N. Freedman. New York:
Doubleday, 1992.

———. "Marcion's Criticism of Gospel and Apostle." In *History and Criticism: The Search for Authenticity in Early Christian Literature*, 33–47.
Louisville, Ky.: Westminster/John Knox Press, 1993.

Harnack, Adolf von. *Marcion: The Gospel of the Alien God*. Durham, NC:
Labyrinth Press, 1990.

Hoffmann, R. Joseph. "How Then Know This Troublous Teacher? Further Reflections on Marcion and His Church." *The Second Century* 6
(1987–88): 173–91.

———. *Marcion: On the Restitution of Christianity: An Essay on the Devel-
opment of Radical Paulinist Theology in the Second Century*. American
Academy of Religion Academy Series 46. Chico, Calif.: Scholars
Press, 1984.

Knox, John. "Marcion." In *The Encyclopedia Americana*, vol. 18, 303. 30
vols. Edited by David T. Holland. Danbury, Conn.: Grolier, Inc.,
1989.

———. *Marcion and the New Testament: An Essay in the Early History of the
Canon*. Chicago: University of Chicago Press, 1942.

May, Gerhard. "Marcion in Contemporary Views: Results and Open
Questions." *The Second Century* 6 (1987–88): 129–51.

Quasten, Johannes. "Marcion." In *Patrology*, vol. 1, 268–72. 4 vols. Westminster, Md.: Christian Classics, 1983–86.

Rudolph, Kurt. "Marcion." In *Gnosis: The Nature and History of Gnosticism*, 313–16. San Francisco: Harper & Row, 1983.

Stephenson, Anthony A. "Marcion." In *New Catholic Encyclopedia*, vol. 9,
193–94. 15 vols. Edited by William J. McDonald. New York:
McGraw-Hill Book Company, 1967.

Wilken, Robert L. "Marcion." In *Encyclopedia of Religion*, vol. 9, 194–96.
16 vols. Edited by Mircea Eliade. New York: Macmillan, 1987.

———. "Marcionism." In *Encyclopedia of Religion*, vol. 9, 196. 16 vols.
Edited by Mircea Eliade. New York: Macmillan, 1987.

Williams, David S. "Reconsidering Marcion's Gospel." *Journal of Biblical Literature* 108 (1989): 477–96.
Wilson, Robert S. *Marcion: A Study of a Second-Century Heretic.* London: J. Clarke, 1933.

Menander

Foerster, Werner, ed. "Simon and Menander." In *Gnosis: A Selection of Gnostic Texts*, vol. 1, 27–33. 2 vols. Oxford: Clarendon Press, 1972–74.
Rudolph, Kurt. "Menander and Satornilos." In *Gnosis: The Nature and History of Gnosticism*, 298. San Francisco: Harper & Row, 1983.

Monarchianism

Hübner, Reinhard M. "Die Hauptquelle des Epiphanius (Panarion, Haer. 65) über Paulus von Samosata: Ps.-Athanasius, Contra Sabellianos." *Zeitschrift für Kirchengeschichte* 90 (1979): 55–74.
Neville, R.C. "Creation and the Trinity." *Theological Studies* 30 (1969): 3–26.
Norris, Frederick W. "Paul of Samosata: Procurator Ducenarius." *Journal of Theological Studies* 35 (1984): 50–70.
Sample, Robert L. "The Christology of the Council of Antioch (268 C.E.) Reconsidered." *Church History* 48 (1979): 18–26.

Monophysites

Vööbus, Arthur. "The Origin of the Monophysite Church in Syria and Mesopotamia." *Church History* 42 (1973): 17–26.

Montanus/Montanism

Aland, Kurt. "Montanism." In *Encyclopedia of Religion*, vol. 10, 81–82. 16 vols. Edited by Mircea Eliade. New York: Macmillan, 1987.
———. "Montanus." In *Encyclopedia of Religion*, vol. 10, 82–83. 16 vols. Edited by Mircea Eliade. New York: Macmillan, 1987.
Barnes, Timothy D. "The Chronology of Montanism." *Journal of Theological Studies* 20 (1970): 403–8.
Bonwetsch, Gottlieb N., ed. *Texte zur Geschichte des Montanismus.* Kleine Texte 129. Bonn: A. Marcus, 1914.

Calder, W. M. "Philadelphia and Montanism." *Bulletin of the John Rylands Library* 7 (1923): 309–54.

Ford, J. Massyngberde. "Was Montanism a Jewish-Christian Heresy?" *Journal of Ecclesiastical History* 17 (1966): 145–58.

Gero, Stephen. "Montanus and Montanism according to a Medieval Syriac Source." *Journal of Theological Studies* 28 (1977): 520–24.

Goetz, Philip, ed. "Montanism." In *The New Encyclopaedia Britannica*, vol. 8, 277–78. 31 vols. 15th ed. Chicago: Encyclopaedia Britannica, 1987.

———, ed. "Montanus." In *The New Encyclopaedia Britannica*, vol. 8, 278. 31 vols. 15th ed. Chicago: Encyclopaedia Britannica, 1987.

Heine, Ronald E., ed. *The Montanist Oracles and Testimonia*. Patristic Monograph Series 14. Macon, Ga.: Mercer University Press, 1989.

———. "Montanus, Montanism." In *The Anchor Bible Dictionary*, vol. 4, 898–902. 6 vols. Edited by David N. Freedman. New York: Doubleday, 1992.

Labriolle, Pierre C. de. *La crise montaniste: Les sources de l'histoire du Montanisme: Textes grecs, latins, syriaques*. Paris: E. Leroux, 1913.

Lawlor, H. J. "The Heresy of the Phrygians." *Journal of Theological Studies* 9 (1978): 481–99.

Powell, Douglas. "Tertullianists and Cataphrygians." *Vigiliae Christianae* 29 (1975): 33–54.

Schlepelern, W. *Der Montanismus und die phrygischen Kulte: Eine religionsgeschichtliche Untersuchung*. Tübingen: J.C.B. Mohr (Paul Siebeck), 1929.

Tabbernee, W. "Early Montanism and Voluntary Martyrdom." *Colloquium* 17 (1985): 33–43.

Wright, David F. "Why Were the Montanists Condemned?" *Themelios* 2 (1976): 15–22.

Nicolaitans

Beck, D. M. "Nicolaitans." In *The Interpreter's Dictionary of the Bible*, vol. 3, 547–48. 4 vols. Edited by George A. Buttrick. Nashville: Abingdon Press, 1962.

Cross, F. L., and E. A. Livingstone, eds. "Nicolaitans." In *The Oxford Dictionary of the Christian Church*, 973–74. 2nd ed. London: Oxford University Press, 1974.

Donaldson, Terence L. "Nicolaitans." In *The International Standard Bible*

Encyclopedia, vol. 3, 533–34. 4 vols. Edited by Geoffrey W. Bromiley. Grand Rapids: Wm. B. Eerdmans, 1979–88.

Harnack, Adolf von. "The Sect of the Nicolaitans and Nicolaus, the Deacon in Jerusalem." *Journal of Religion* 3 (1923): 413–22.

Hemer, Colin J. *The Letters to the Seven Churches of Asia in Their Local Setting.* Journal for the Study of the New Testament Supplement Series 11. Sheffield: JSOT Press, 1986.

Mackay, W. M. "Another Look at the Nicolaitans." *Evangelical Quarterly* 45 (1973): 111–15.

Watson, Duane F. "Nicolaitans." In *The Anchor Bible Dictionary*, vol. 4, 1106–7. 6 vols. Edited by David N. Freedman. New York: Doubleday, 1992.

Origen

Chadwick, Henry. "The Evidence of Christianity in the Apologetic of Origen." *Studia Patristica* 2 (1957): 331–39.

———. "Origen, Celsus, and the Resurrection of the Body." *Harvard Theological Review* 41 (1948): 83–102.

Crouzel, Henri. *Origen.* San Francisco: Harper & Row, 1989.

Hanson, R.P.C. "Origen's Doctrine of Tradition." *Journal of Theological Studies* 49 (1948): 17–27.

Norris, Richard A. *God and World in Early Christian Theology: A Study in Justin Martyr, Irenaeus, Tertullian and Origen.* New York: Seabury Press, 1965.

Patterson, Lloyd G. "Origen's Place in Early Greek Christian Theology." *Studia Patristica* 17 (1982): 924–43.

Smith, John Clark. *The Ancient Wisdom of Origen.* Lewisburg: Bucknell University Press, 1992.

Pseudo-Clementines

Jones, F. Stanley. "The Pseudo-Clementines: A History of Research, Part I and Part II." *The Second Century* 2 (1982): 63–96.

Irmscher, Johannes, and Georg Strecker. "The Pseudo-Clementines." In *New Testament Apocrypha*, vol. 2, 483–541. Edited by Wilhelm Schneemelcher. 2 vols. Rev. ed. Louisville: Westminster/John Knox Press, 1991–92.

Quartodecimans

Brox, Norbert. "Tendenzen und Parteilichkeiten im Osterfeststreit des zweiten Jahrhunderts." *Zeitschrift für Kirchengeschichte* 83 (1972): 291–324.

Kilmartin, Edward J. "Liturgical Influence on John 6." *Catholic Biblical Quarterly* 20 (1960): 183–91.

Richardson, Cyril C. "A New Solution to the Quartodeciman Riddle." *Journal of Theological Studies* 24 (1973): 74–84.

Strand, Kenneth A. "John as Quartodeciman: A Reappraisal." *Journal of Biblical Literature* 84 (1965): 251–58.

———. "Sunday-Easter and Quartodecimanism in the Early Christian Church." *Andrews University Seminary Studies* 28 (1990): 127–36.

Saturninus

Castagno, A. Monaci. "Satornilus (or Saturninus)." In *Encyclopedia of the Early Church*, vol. 2, 758. 2 vols. Edited by Angelo Di Berardino. New York: Oxford University Press, 1992.

Cross, F. L., and E. A. Livingstone, eds. "Saturninus." In *The Oxford Dictionary of the Christian Church*, 1238. 2nd ed. London: Oxford University Press, 1974.

Foerster, Werner, ed. "The First Christian Gnostics." In *Gnosis: A Selection of Gnostic Texts*, vol. 1, 34–43. 2 vols. Oxford: Clarendon Press, 1972–74.

Grant, Robert M. "Saturninus' System." In *Gnosticism and Early Christianity*, 100–119. Rev. ed. New York: Harper & Row, 1966.

Rudolph, Kurt. "Satornilos." In *Gnosis: The Nature and History of Gnosticism*, 298. San Francisco: Harper & Row, 1983.

Simon

Aune, David E. "Simon Magus." In *The International Standard Bible Encyclopedia*, vol. 4, 516–18. 4 vols. Edited by Geoffrey W. Bromiley. Grand Rapids: Wm. B. Eerdmans, 1979–88.

Barrett, C. K. "Light on the Holy Spirit from Simon Magus (Acts 8:4–25)." In *Les Actes des Apôtres*, 281–95. Edited by J. Kremer. Bibliotheca Ephemeridum Theologicarum Lovaniensium 48. Louvain: Leuven University Press, 1979.

Beyschlag, Karlmann. *Simon Magus und die christliche Gnosis.* Wissenschaftliche Untersuchungen zum Neuen Testament 16. Tübingen: J.C.B. Mohr (Paul Siebeck), 1974.

Cross, F. L., and E. A. Livingstone, eds. "Simon Magus." In *The Oxford Dictionary of the Christian Church*, 1277. 2nd ed. London: Oxford University Press, 1974.

Filoramo, Giovanni. "Simon Magus and the Origins of Gnosticism." In *A History of Gnosticism*, 142–52. Translated by Anthony Alcock. Cambridge, Mass.: Basil Blackwell, 1990.

Foerster, Werner, ed. "Simon and Menander." In *Gnosis: A Selection of Gnostic Texts*, vol. 1, 27–33. 2 vols. Oxford: Clarendon Press, 1972–74.

Fossum, Jarl. "Sects and Movements: Simon Magus." In *The Samaritans*, 357–89. Edited by Alan D. Crown. Tübingen: J.C.B. Mohr (Paul Siebeck), 1989.

Grant, Robert M. "Simon Magus and Helen, His Thought." In *Gnosticism and Early Christianity*, 70–96. Rev. ed. New York: Harper & Row, 1966.

Grassi, Joseph A. "Simon Magus." In *New Catholic Encyclopedia*, vol. 13, 223. 15 vols. Edited by William J. McDonald. New York: McGraw-Hill Book Company, 1967.

Lüdemann, Gerd. "The Acts of the Apostles and the Beginnings of Simonian Gnosticism." *New Testament Studies* 33 (1987): 420–26.

———. *Untersuchungen zur simonianischen Gnosis.* Göttinger theologische Arbeiten 1. Göttingen: Vandenhoeck & Ruprecht, 1975.

McCasland, S. V. "Simon Magus." In *The Interpreter's Dictionary of the Bible*, vol. 4, 358–60. 4 vols. Edited by George A. Buttrick. Nashville: Abingdon Press, 1962.

Meeks, Wayne A. "Simon Magus in Recent Research." *Religious Studies Review* 3 (1977): 137–42.

Rudolph, Kurt. "Simon Magus." In *Gnosis: The Nature and History of Gnosticism*, 294–98. San Francisco: Harper & Row, 1983.

Stoops, Robert F., Jr. "Simon Magus." In *The Anchor Bible Dictionary*, vol. 6, 29–31. 6 vols. Ed. David N. Freedman. New York: Doubleday, 1992.

Wilson, Robert McL. "Simon and Gnostic Origins." In *Les Actes des Apôtres*, 485–91. Edited by J. Kremer. Bibliotheca Ephemeridum Theologicarum Lovaniensium 48. Louvain: Leuven University Press, 1979.

Yamauchi, Edwin M. "Simon Magus." In *Pre-Christian Gnosticism: A Survey of the Proposed Evidences*, 58–65. 2nd ed. Grand Rapids: Baker Book House, 1983.

Tatian

Barnard, L. W. "The Heresy of Tatian—Once Again." *Journal of Ecclesiastical History* 19 (1968): 1–10.

Edwards, O. C., Jr. "Tatian." In *The Anchor Bible Dictionary*, vol. 6, 335–36. 6 vols. Edited by David N. Freedman. New York: Doubleday, 1992.

Elze, M. *Tatian und seine Theologie*. Göttingen: Vandenhoeck & Ruprecht, 1960.

Goetz, Philip W., ed. "Tatian." In *The New Encyclopaedia Britannica*, vol. 11, 576–77. 31 vols. 15th ed. Chicago: Encyclopaedia Britannica, 1987.

Grant, Robert M. "The Heresy of Tatian." *Journal of Theological Studies* 5 (1956): 62–68.

Hawthorne, Gerald F. "Tatian and His Discourse to the Greeks." *Harvard Theological Review* 57 (1964): 161–88.

Tatian. *The Earliest Life of Christ Ever Compiled from the Four Gospels, Being the Diatessaron of Tatian*. Translated by J. Hamlyn Hill. Edinburgh: T. & T. Clark, 1894.

———. *Oratio ad Graecos: English Oratio ad Graecos and Fragments*. Edited by Molly Whittaker. Oxford Early Christian Texts. New York: Clarendon Press, 1982.

Tertullian

Church, F. Forrester. "Sex and Salvation in Tertullian." *Harvard Theological Review* 68 (1975): 83–101.

Cross, F. L., and E. A. Livingstone, eds. "Tertullian." In *The Oxford Dictionary of the Christian Church*, 1352–53. 2nd ed. London: Oxford University Press, 1974.

Evans, Ernest, ed. *Tertullian Adversus Marcionem*. 2 vols. Oxford Early Christian Texts. Oxford: Clarendon Press, 1972.

Gonzalez, Justo L. "Athens and Jerusalem Revisited: Reason and Authority in Tertullian." *Church History* 43 (1974): 17–25.

Guerra, Anthony J. "Polemical Christianity: Tertullian's Search for Certitude." *Second Century* 8 (1991): 109–23.

Jansen, John. "Tertullian and the New Testament." *Second Century* 2
(1982): 191–207.

Kaufman, Peter Iver. "Tertullian on Heresy, History, and the Reappropria-
tion of Revelation." *Church History* 60 (1991): 167–79.

O'Malley, Thomas P. *Tertullian and the Bible: Language, Imagery, Exegesis.*
Utrecht: Dekker & Van de Vegt, 1967.

Powell, Douglas. "Tertullianists and Cataphrygians." *Vigiliae Christianae*
29 (1975): 33–54.

Sider, Robert D. *Ancient Rhetoric and the Art of Tertullian.* London:
Oxford University Press, 1971.

———. "Approaches to Tertullian: A Survey of Recent Scholarship."
Second Century 2 (1982): 228–60.

Stead, G. C. "Divine Substance in Tertullian." *Journal of Theological
Studies* 14 (1963): 46–66.

Waszink, J. H. "Tertullian's Principles and Methods of Exegesis." In *Early
Christian Literature and the Classical Intellectual Tradition: Essays in
Honor of Robert M. Grant,* 17–31. Edited by William R. Schoedel
and Robert L. Wilken. Paris: Éditions Beauchesne, 1979.

Wilken, Robert L. "Tertullian and the Early Christian View of Tradition."
Concordia Theological Monthly 38 (1967): 221–33.

Valentinus

Brooke, Alan, ed. *The Fragments of Heracleon.* Cambridge: Cambridge
University Press, 1891.

Casey, Robert P., ed. *The Excerpta ex Theodoto of Clement of Alexandria.*
Studies and Documents 1. London: Christophers, 1934.

Cross, F. L., and E. A. Livingstone, eds. "Valentinus." In *The Oxford Dictionary of the Christian Church,* 1423. 2nd ed. London: Oxford University Press, 1974.

Edwards, M. J. "Gnostics and Valentinians in the Church Fathers." *Journal of Theological Studies* 40 (1989): 26–47.

Foerster, Werner, ed. "Valentinianism." In *Gnosis: A Selection of Gnostic
Texts,* vol. 1, 121–243. 2 vols. Oxford: Clarendon Press, 1972–74.

Goetz, Philip W., ed. "Valentinus." In *The New Encyclopaedia Britannica,*
vol. 12, 243. 31 vols. 15th ed. Chicago: Encyclopaedia Britannica,
1987.

Jonas, Hans. *The Gnostic Religion: The Message of the Alien God and the Beginnings of Christianity*. 3rd ed. Boston: Beacon Press, 1970.

Layton, Bentley, ed. *The School of Valentinus*. Vol. 1, *The Rediscovery of Gnosticism*. 2 vols. Studies in the History of Religion 41. Leiden: E. J. Brill, 1980.

MacRae, George W. "Valentinus." In *New Catholic Encyclopedia*, vol. 14, 518–19. 15 vols. Edited by William J. McDonald. New York: McGraw-Hill Book Company, 1967.

Mirecki, Paul A. "Valentinus." In *The Anchor Bible Dictionary*, vol. 6, 783–84. 6 vols. Edited by David N. Freedman. New York: Doubleday, 1992.

Quasten, Johannes. "Valentinus." In *Patrology*, vol. 1, 260–61. 4 vols. Westminster, Md.: Christian Classics, 1983–86.

Quispel, Gilles. "The Original Doctrine of Valentine." *Vigiliae Christianae* 1 (1947): 43–73.

Reimherr, Otto. "Irenaeus and the Valentinians." *The Lutheran Quarterly* 12 (1960): 55–59.

Rudolph, Kurt. "Valentinus." In *Gnosis: The Nature and History of Gnosticism*, 317–25. San Francisco: Harper & Row, 1983.

Stead, G. C. "The Valentinian Myth of Sophia." *Journal of Theological Studies* 20 (1969): 75–104.

Wilson, Robert McL. "Valentinus and Valentinianism." In *The Encyclopedia of Philosophy*, vol. 8, 226–27. 8 vols. Edited by Paul Edwards. New York: Macmillan, 1967.

Index of Ancient Sources

Index of Subjects

CPSIA information can be obtained at www.ICGtesting.com
Printed in the USA
LVOW050812070812

293175LV00003B/70/P